TEXAS
Takes Wing

A CENTURY OF FLIGHT
IN THE LONE STAR STATE

by Barbara Ganson

University of Texas Press
Austin

Requests for permission to reproduce material from this work
should be sent to:
 Permissions
 University of Texas Press
 P.O. Box 7819
 Austin, TX 78713-7819
 http://utpress.utexas.edu/index.php/rp-form

♾ The paper used in this book meets the minimum
requirements of ANSI/NISO Z39.48-1992 (R1997)
(Permanence of Paper).

LIBRARY OF CONGRESS
CATALOGING-IN-PUBLICATION DATA
Ganson, Barbara Anne, 1953–
 Texas takes wing : a century of flight in the Lone Star State /
by Barbara Ganson. — First edition.
  pages   cm. — (Bridwell Texas history series)
 Includes bibliographical references and index.
 ISBN 978-0-292-75408-9 (cloth : alkaline paper)
 1. Aeronautics—Texas—History. 2. Air pilots—Texas—
Biography. 3. Air power—Texas—History. 4. Aerospace
industries—Texas—History. I. Title.
 TL522.T4G36 2014
 387.709764—dc23
                                              2013016687

doi:10.7560/754089

To the memory of my parents,
Elaine and Richard Ganson,
for allowing me the freedom for my dreams to take wing.

Contents

Preface

*T*HE YEAR 2010 REPRESENTED THE ONE HUN-
dredth anniversary since the beginning of powered
flight in Texas. Over the past century, Texas has grown
to become a major world leader in the aerospace industry. The history
of aviation in Texas is the story of industry innovation, record-setting
achievements, gravity-defying feats, and the soaring human spirit.
Texas has been and continues to be a leader in aerospace manufacturing, commercial aviation, space exploration, and scholarship—driving
the global economy year after year with new research and billions of
dollars in revenue. A comprehensive study by the Texas Department of
Transportation in 2005 showed that the state's general aviation (flying performed by civilians other than regularly scheduled commercial airlines) accounted for $8 billion in output, sixty thousand jobs,
and $2.5 billion in payroll. In honor of the men and women who made
Texas aviation what it is today, this book celebrates Texas's aeronautical achievements.

Texas Takes Wing tells the story of powered flight as it evolved
in Texas since 1910. This work seeks to show how Texas fits into the
wider scope of the development of aviation in the nation and the
world. Aviators not only from Texas and other parts of the United
States but Europe, Canada, Latin America, and other parts of the
world have been attracted by Texas's favorable flying weather, flat terrain, and wide-open spaces. Texas has more airports than any of the
other contiguous forty-seven states and is considered one of Amer-

ica's most aviation-friendly states. This work highlights the major accomplishments of Texas aviators, many of whom set U.S. national and world aviation records, including notable world firsts. Early Texas aviators overcame great obstacles to achieve their dreams of flight. The first licensed Texas woman pilot, Elizabeth "Bessie" Coleman, learned French and traveled to France for flying lessons in 1921 because no one in the States would teach a black woman. Katherine and Marjorie Stinson and the Women Airforce Service Pilots also fought the obstacles of gender prejudice. Tuskegee airmen such as Walter McCreary, Percy Sutton, and John Miles of San Antonio faced the challenges of segregation; Douglas Corrigan and Jeana Yeager (who bears no relationship to test pilot Chuck Yeager) struggled with financial difficulties, and Wiley Post became the first person to fly solo around the world despite physical limitations, having lost an eye in an oil drilling accident in Texas. Such courage, confidence, perseverance, innovation, and competitive spirit enabled the technology and culture of flight to grow and reach even greater heights.

Texas was the place where many individuals pioneered new aerospace technologies and revolutionized air travel. Texans established several of the country's major airports and airlines, manufactured and designed extraordinary aircraft, raced across America, circumnavigated the globe, traveled in space, and even walked on the moon. This book shows how pivotal Texas has been in military training, wartime aircraft manufacture, and defending national interests in peacetime as well as in providing services for the agricultural, commercial, military, and general aviation industries. Helicopters in particular are utilized in search and rescue work, in border control, in military operations, in the offshore petroleum industry, in emergency medical transport services, and in humanitarian efforts. Finally, *Texas Takes Wing* seeks to inspire some nostalgia for the golden age of aviation and bring credit not only to those Texas pioneers but also to the companies and contributors that are heavily involved in the aerospace industry today and those who will have an impact on aviation tomorrow.

Texas Takes Wing is unique and goes beyond previous studies (such as *Aviation in Texas*, the fine work of Roger Bilstein and Jay Miller). It is the only book that provides an appraisal of the first century of powered flight in Texas. It looks back on and takes note of a century of rapid technological change from regional, national, and international perspectives. Besides highlighting individual stories of Texas aviators, designers, manufacturers, and those who work in aviation-related services, this book includes a valuable timeline of landmark moments in Texas aviation history, from the first flight and the first U.S. military logbook to the end of the space shuttle program. This work also tells individual stories of aviation personalities—some famous, others lesser known—providing a richer understanding of Texas's valuable aeronautical contributions.

The research is based on oral interviews and the aeronautical collections at the History of Aviation Collection, McDermott Library, the University of Texas at Dallas; Texas Woman's University; the University of Texas at Austin; Texas A&M University; the University of Texas at Arlington; public libraries in Austin, Dallas, Fort Worth, and Houston; Houston Metropolitan Research Center; San Jacinto Museum of History; Austin History Center; Fort Sam Houston Museum; No. 1 British Flying Training School Museum in Terrell; International Women's Air and Space Museum, Cleveland, Ohio; Ninety-Nines Museum of Women Pilots, Oklahoma City; Howard Hughes Collections at the Florida Air Museum in Lakeland and the University of Nevada Las Vegas; the Pan American Airlines Collection at the University of Miami; the Edward H. White II Memorial Museum, Brooks Air Force Base; the National Air and Space Museum; the American Airlines C. R. Smith Museum; the Vintage Flying Museum, Meacham Municipal Airport, Fort Worth; the Texas Air Museum, San Antonio; Frontiers of Flight Museum, Dallas; the Stanzel Brothers Model Airplane Museum, Schulenburg; the Lone Star Flying Museum, Galveston; Commemorative Air Force, Midland; the Katherine Stinson Otero Collection, Center for Southwest Research, University of New Mexico, Albuquerque; the American Heritage Center at the University of Wyoming; Musée de l'Air et de l'Espace, Paris; the Imperial War Museum, London; the General Benjamin Foulois Collection at the College Park Aviation Museum in Maryland; U.S. National Archives, NASA History Office; and special collections in the Manuscript Division and Print and Photographs Reading Room of the Library of Congress.

My goal is to impart new knowledge about the dynamic role Texas has played and continues to play in the history of aviation and the aeronautical industry. An educational guide, *Tango Alpha Charlie: Texas Aviation Celebration, Educator Guide*, is available to enhance the learning experiences of students by engaging their interest in the subject and providing them with some of the basic skills necessary to become aviators or at least aviation enthusiasts. This publication is available through the Bob Bullock Texas State History Museum.

Photographs of aviators, astronauts, and those who work in aerospace services are often readily available online. Hopefully, readers young and old will realize the importance of developing a real passion in life, whether it be challenging oneself to embark on a new career or hobby or even learning to fly an airplane.

Acknowledgments

THE WORK OF A HISTORIAN IS USUALLY SOLI-
tary, sitting long hours in libraries and archives and
later writing a scholarly book or articles. I have had the
great pleasure of retooling my investigative skills through extensive
work on the special exhibit *Tango Alpha Charlie: Texas Aviation Celebration* for the Bob Bullock Texas State History Museum in Austin.
Honoring the Texas Centennial of Powered Flight, 1910–2010, this exhibit opened on September 10, 2010, and ran through January 9, 2011.
The experience greatly enhanced my professional development in the
fields of public history and aviation history.

It was a great pleasure to work with a team of highly professional
museum experts on the content and design of the exhibit, as well as
with personnel who work in administration, the development office,
educational outreach, and strategic initiatives department at the Bob
Bullock Texas State History Museum. I especially would like to ac-
knowledge Joan Marshall, Kathryn Siefker, David Denney, Toni Bed-
lock, Catherine Kenyon, Denise Bradley, Jennifer Lewis, and Tom
Wancho. I also benefited from the expertise of the exhibit's advisory
board, especially B. Keith Graff, Maureen Kerr, Robert Crawford,
Troy Kimmel, Larry Gregory, Cynthia Buchanan, and Jay Miller.

I also wish to express my sincere gratitude to Florida Atlantic University for providing a one-semester sabbatical in fall 2009. Teaching fellowships in 2011 and 2012 allowed me to offer my course on the
birth of aviation and its impact on the twentieth century in the honors

program at the university and provided additional travel and department funding.

This book would not have been possible without the willingness
of numerous interviewees to share their personal memories, photographs, insights, and expertise; aviators, designers, and manufacturers and their relatives provided me with a better understanding
of the aerospace history of Texas. At Southwest Airlines, cofounder
Herb Kelleher and corporate historian Brian Lusk were especially
generous with their time, support, and ideas. Theodore Windecker
kindly shared his manuscript about his father, Dr. Leo Windecker.
Cindy Gilmer showed me the extensive collection of Flying Tigers
memorabilia that had belonged to her father, Charles Bond. Stephanie A. Lynch arranged for me to interview her father, retired lieutenant colonel and Tuskegee Airman Walter McCreary, in Burke, Virginia. Likewise, Kristin Edwards, vice president of sales at Air Tractor
Inc., arranged the interview with her father, aeronautical engineer Leland Snow.

As researchers know, directors and staff of special collections at libraries and archives provide assistance vital to the success of any book
project. At the Eugene McDermott Library of the University of Texas
at Dallas, head of special collections Paul Oelkrug and curator of the
aviation collection Thomas J. Allen identified valuable archival collections and provided photographic images. Don Carleton, executive director of the Dolph Briscoe Center for American History at the University of Texas at Austin, also facilitated the research. My special
thanks to collections manager Chris Takacs and space historian and
museum trustee Marcy Frumker of the International Women's Air
and Space Museum in Cleveland, Ohio. I also appreciate the articles
provided by William Gallagher, curator of the National Soaring Museum in Elmira, New York. In Paris, historian Guillaume Candela and
archivist Sylvie Lallement assisted with photographic images from
the Musée de l'Air et de l'Espace.

The following individuals and institutions were also of assistance
with research or photographs: Joel D. Draut of the Houston Metropolitan Research Center; Mark Callahan and John Manguso of the Fort
Sam Houston Museum; Tom Gaylord and Roger Freeman of the Pioneer Flight Museum in Kingsbury, Texas; Mary Clark of Continental (United) Airlines; Jay Luippold, Jeffrey D. Johns, and Bob Ko-
pitzke of American Airlines C. R. Smith Museum; Ronald Whitney
of Bell Helicopter Textron Inc.; Brenda Reuland and Len Jennings of

American Eurocopter; Scott Glover of Mount Pleasant, Texas; Norman Huneycut, Clifford N. Taylor, Mair Cawston, and Freda Freeman of No. 1 British Flying Training School Museum in Terrell, Texas; Thomas Norris, photographer and private aviation history collector; Andrea M. Weddell and Robin Price of Texas A&M University at Commerce; Mark Fairchild, general manager at Syberjet in San Antonio, Texas; Alfred L. Wolf and Constance Wolf Aviation Fund; Dick Atkins and Joseph Angelone of Vought Heritage Center in Grand Prairie, Texas; Susan Harrison, Bill Wheat, Stanley Feller, and Barry Hodkin of Mooney Aircraft Company in Kerrville, Texas; International Mooney Society, San Antonio; Rudolph J. Purificato, Civ USAF, of Edward White II Memorial Museum, Brooks Air Force Base, Texas; Jay Pascke, chief pilot and director of the Fort Worth Police Air Support; historian Jennifer M. Ross-Nazzal and librarian Mike Gentry of NASA's Johnson Space Center; Colin A. Fries of NASA History Center, Washington, DC; Linda Hieger, independent scholar; Norman B. Robbins of Lockheed Martin, Fort Worth, Texas; Brian Dunaway, president of Epic Helicopters, Fort Worth; Laura Cappell of Richter Library's Pan American Airlines Collection at the University of Miami; Kathryn Black Morrow of the University of Houston at Clear Lake, Texas; Ernie Sanborn, director of the Florida Air Museum in Lakeland, Florida; and John Tosh of the Texas Air Museum at Stinson Municipal Airport, San Antonio. These individuals, among many others, made this book possible.

By visiting places firsthand and talking with a variety of people, I obtained great appreciation for the rich history of air and space in Texas since 1910. Aviation adventurer Gustavus "Gus" McLeod made me better aware of the many hardships and dangers of the early fliers and commented on several initial chapters. McLeod's enthusiasm for aviation was so contagious that I earned my private pilot's license in 2008. I was also inspired to fly by my mother's love of flight. Women Airforce Service Pilots (WASPs) Ruth Shafer Fleisher and Helen Wyatt Snapp shared their memories of flight training at Avenger Field in Sweetwater, Texas. On March 10, 2010, I witnessed the ceremony awarding the Congressional Gold Medal to more than 200 WASPs at the U.S. Capitol. My tour of Randolph Air Force Base near San Antonio, with its Spanish mission revival architecture, was most memorable. There, I conducted interviews with several original Tuskegee airmen and visited the top of Taj Mahal, the enclosed water tower in the administration building, and the original air traffic control tower.

Retired Lieutenant Colonel Leo Gray and Dianne Bays provided additional details about Tuskegee airmen from Texas. Richard Garriott sparked my interest in space tourism. At NASA, Louis A. Parker arranged my tour of the Johnson Space Center and viewing of the launch of the space shuttle *Atlantis* mission STS-129 at Kennedy Space Center in November 2009. I also visited several aircraft factories in Texas, including Mooney, Air Tractor, Bell Helicopter Textron, American Eurocopter, Vought Aircraft Heritage Restoration Hangar, and Lockheed Martin.

Professors William Saric, Dimitris Lagoudas, Helen Reed, Walter Haisler, and Paul Cizmas—as well as several graduate research assistants, especially Jerrod Hofferth, PhD—provided details about the Department of Aeronautical Engineering at Texas A&M University and arranged a tour of research facilities. My appreciation to Professor Armand Chaput for providing information about the Department of Aerospace Engineering at the University of Texas at Austin. Specifics about the aerospace engineering program at the University of Texas at Arlington were generously given by Professor Frank K. Lu of the Department of Mechanical and Aerospace Engineering; many thanks also to Dean Jean-Pierre Bardet of the College of Engineering, Professor and Chair of Mechanical and Aerospace Engineering Erian Armanios, and other faculty members.

Hillary Walsh, former reservations manager at the Holiday Inn in northern Washington, DC, extended outstanding service, which facilitated the archival and library research. Texas author Debra Winegarten was very kind to invite me into her home in Austin, as were my aunt and uncle, Betty and Jack Barno, in Richmond Heights, Ohio. My former college roommate from the University of Texas at Austin, Dr. Barbara Raudonis Ford, and her husband, Tony, were perfect hosts in Arlington, Texas. I occasionally shared moments of joy, good humor, and discovery with my brother Michael and sister Ricarda.

It is wonderful to have my second book come out with University of Texas Press. I am extremely grateful to Allison Faust, sponsoring editor and assistant to the director, manuscript editor Lynne Chapman, editorial fellow Sandra Spicher, director Dave Hamrick, and other members of the staff as well as the outside readers of the manuscript. I will gladly share any credit that I may receive from publishing this book with all those named or unnamed. Of course, I take sole responsibility for any of its shortcomings.

Texas Takes Wing

Chapter 1

Flying Takes Off in Texas

O N FEBRUARY 18, 1910, THIRTY-FIVE HUNDRED aviation enthusiasts gathered at Aviation Camp in South Houston to observe French aviator Louis Paulhan fly his Farman biplane. The crowd patiently waited as the Frenchman carefully inspected the aircraft prior to takeoff. His curvy moustache and small stature on display, Paulhan examined every wire and the entire length of the wooden frame, checked the engine, and made sure all the levers were in their proper position before his departure. The twenty-six-year-old then started the motor and manipulated levers before ascending several hundred feet above the ground. Paulhan accomplished what so many individuals had dreamed of, flying in the wide-open Texas sky. His performance did not disappoint. The large crowd cheered as he flew the Farman biplane overhead. This event marked the first public exhibition of controllable, powered flight in the state of Texas.[1] In the absence of documentation such as photographs of other aviators flying airplanes, without a doubt Paulhan performed the first heavier-than-air powered flight in Texas.[2]

The French aviator was on a coast-to-coast flying exhibition. He demonstrated flying skills that he had acquired in France and previously performed at Rheims, France, in August 1909 and Dominguez Hills near Los Angeles in January 1910, respectively the first aerial exhibitions in the world and in the United States. In 1907 Paulhan had begun his aviation career as a mechanic for dirigibles in Paris. He won an aircraft through entering a newspaper contest and then taught himself to fly. During the earliest days of aviation, aviators' first flights were often their first solo flights, following several minutes of ground instruction.

Along with American aviator and New York aircraft designer Glenn Curtiss, Paulhan had been the star at the country's first international air meet at Dominguez Field on January 10–20, 1910. There on January 12, Paulhan set a world altitude record of 4,165 feet.[3] He proceeded to set endurance and cross-country records, earning a total of $19,000, then a considerable sum, in prize money.[4] Paulhan was by no means a fair-weather flyer. Before arriving in Houston, he flew through a snowstorm in Denver in nearly whiteout conditions before crashing without injury to himself. Paulhan was passing through south Texas on his journey back to France when he demonstrated his aircraft in Houston. Fifteen French mechanics assisted in maintaining his four airplanes, two Farmans and two Bleriots, even though he was a skilled mechanic.

Paulhan made four flights on that winter day in Houston. All were ten to twelve minutes in length. He performed no special stunts and did not attempt to exceed the altitude record of over four thousand feet—a record he himself had set the month before—due to strong winds. *Houston Chronicle* reporter B. H. Carroll, Jr., enthusiastically described Paulhan's performance that day:

> Paulhan himself is but an operator of a machine, a dexterous chauffeur of the air, a sky pilot, a jockey of aerial race horses, an aeronaut because he was first an athlete of master dexterity and amazing skill, who has dared to try out the mettle of the Pegasus that was created by the genius of other men, and to soar to heights that eagles do not dare.[5]

So enthralled were the crowds with the sight of an airplane in the sky that six thousand spectators showed up for another performance by Paulhan on the following day.[6]

Even before 1910, powered flight gripped the public's imagination in Texas. Yet Texans only began to share in the marvels of flight several years after Orville and Wilbur Wright first solved the problem of creating and flying a powered, controllable heavier-than-air flying machine in 1903. The Wright brothers had kept their invention closely veiled until 1908, when they publically demonstrated their airplane at Fort Myer (near Washington, DC) and in France. The world

French aviator Louis Paulhan performed the first recorded flight in Texas using a Farman biplane on the outskirts of Houston, February 18, 1910. Photograph no. 52. Courtesy of the Musée de l'Air et de l'Espace, Paris.

suddenly took notice of the creative abilities of the two bicycle makers from Dayton, Ohio.

Paulhan soared in the Texas sky in spite of the Wright brothers' legal maneuvers attempting to keep him and others from benefiting financially from use of their patented invention of the airplane. Judges lifted a temporary injunction against Paulhan and designer Glenn Curtiss until the courts could rule on whether Paulhan's flying machines had actually violated the Wright brothers' patent rights.

The actions of the Wright brothers and their lawyers in New York left a poor impression on the French aviator, especially after the Wrights had been so well treated by Parisians when they demonstrated their flyer to a disbelieving public for the first time in 1908. Paulhan considered the Wrights' decision to protect their patent using the courts a sign of poor sportsmanship. The Frenchman transferred ownership of his two biplanes and two monoplanes to his wife, who accompanied him and sometimes flew as his passenger. He quietly sailed back to Europe, where he would win the 136-mile London-to-Manchester race in what proved to be an exciting finish in gusty winds, earning ten thousand English pounds.[7]

Houston crowd observing Paulhan fly his Farman biplane, February 18, 1910. Courtesy of the Houston Metropolitan Research Center, Houston Public Library (MSS-0253-0075), and the San Jacinto Museum of History.

The Rise of General Aviation in Texas

Among the crowd in Houston who witnessed Paulhan's display were Guy Hahnt, L. F. "Creary" Smith, and Leslie L. "Shorty" Walker. Hahnt's father financed the building of a Curtiss pusher airplane. Smith, a machinist, worked on it and attempted to fly but ground-looped on takeoff—meaning that the airplane weathervaned, whipping around 180 degrees without ever leaving the ground. In a separate effort, Walker built an aircraft based on the Bleriot, a French design. These were the first powered aircraft built and flown in the state by residents of Texas in early 1910.

In the early days of aviation, prior to the Air and Commerce Act of 1926, any individual who had the courage could fly an airplane without a license. Walker was born in Willow Springs, Missouri, on October 2, 1888. He attended Oklahoma A&M University but left to work on the construction of the Panama Canal. He then came to Houston where he raised a family and owned an automobile business in the Houston area.[8]

On April 10, 1910, Walker flew his Bleriot monoplane for the first time. His plane had a forty-horsepower, four-cylinder concentric-valve Kemp engine. He also owned and flew a Curtiss biplane with a sixty-horsepower Hall-Scott V-8 engine. On November 12, 1911, Walker performed at the Houston Air Show.

One morning Walker crashed the Curtiss biplane on takeoff when a wheel strut broke. He sold the engine, gas tank, and radiator. Walker became a member of the Early Birds when this exclusive club of aviation pioneers was established in 1929. Membership required having flown an airplane prior to December 17, 1916.

Otto W. Brodie (1888–1913), First to Fly in North Texas

On March 3, 1910, twenty-three-year-old Otto W. Brodie, a Chicago flyer, flew a Herring-Curtiss biplane at the fairgrounds near Dallas. Brodie managed to get off the ground some fifteen to twenty feet, two-thirds across the field of a racetrack in what was ground effect,[9] not entirely to the satisfaction of all five hundred spectators. The plane soared only a few seconds, even though his mechanics had worked all night to assemble it. This, nonetheless, was the first recorded flight in North Texas. On March 5, Brodie tried again but the gusty winds tossed him out, with the plane landing on top of him. He suffered some mild scratches on his face.[10] A photograph of Otto Brodie shows him sitting in a Herring-Curtiss biplane with several ladies dressed in long white gowns from his public exhibition at the fairgrounds in Dallas on March 4 and 5, 1910.[11]

The Vin Fiz, *First Transcontinental Flight, Crosses through Texas, 1911*

A New York socialite and avid sportsman with an interest in racing motorcycles and automobiles, Calbraith "Cal" Rodgers was among the first aviators to introduce the airplane to many Texas communities. After learning to fly in June and July 1911, Rodgers was the top winner—of $11,285—at the Chicago International Air Meet in August 1911. The Armour Company sponsored his attempt to fly from the Atlantic to the Pacific coast, including a stop in Chicago, within thirty days—the first aviator to do so would win a prize of $50,000 offered by William Randolph Hearst. On September 17, Rodgers departed from Brooklyn's Sheepshead Bay in a Wright Flyer EX named *Vin Fiz* for the Armour Company's grape-flavored soft drink. His support team was comprised of three mechanics, including Charles Taylor, who had worked for the Wright brothers in building the engine for the first airplane in 1903. In return for advertising, the Armour Company agreed to pay Rodgers between four and five dollars for every mile he flew. The company also arranged for a three-car train to cover the route: a Palmer-Singer touring coach for Rodgers's wife, mother, mechanics, and other assistants; a baggage car outfitted as a repair shop; and a car carrying $4,000 in spare parts, fuel, and oil. A truck trailed behind in case Rodgers injured himself and needed to be rushed for medical care. Slightly smaller than the Wright B flyer biplane, the *Vin Fiz* was entirely rebuilt multiple times before it reached the Pacific coast.

Rodgers primarily followed the railroad tracks from Jersey City to Pasadena, California. He had no special affinity with Texas or Texans, but the route through El Paso was the easiest way to avoid crossing the Rocky Mountains. Rodgers took the southern route and crossed Texas, stopping in at least twenty-five different sites. Some of these were planned legs; others were only intended to be for refueling; still others were the sites of unplanned emergency landings mainly due to engine problems. Crowds of Texans met Rodgers at each leg along his route.

On October 17, 1911, Rodgers crossed into Texas flying over the Red River, North Denison, and Denison at sixty miles per hour. He was supposed to refuel at Denison but flew on to Pottsboro, to the disappointment of Denison's residents. He finally refueled at Gainesville, an unplanned stop. There, local Texans wanted to touch and write their names on his plane and meet the pilot, but Rodgers treated the crowd as a nuisance. In the absence of his mechanics, he had no one to guard his airplane. At Fort Worth, with crowd control in place, Rodgers was in a less foul mood when he arrived that afternoon. Eight to ten thousand watched him arrive in the *Vin Fiz*. The next day Rodgers made a pass over Fort Worth before heading east to Dallas. Large crowds welcomed him at the Dallas State Fair on October 18, designated "East Texas Day." On October 19, Rodgers left to fly south toward Austin and San Antonio. Within an hour and forty minutes after his departure, Texans in Waco observed the *Vin Fiz* flying over the city. Rodgers landed and spent the night. He received plenty of Texas hospitality.

Calbraith Rodgers in Dallas, 1911. Courtesy of the *Fort Worth Star-Telegram* Collection, Special Collections, the University of Texas at Arlington Library, Arlington, Texas.

On October 20, Rodgers landed at Ridgetop in North Austin, a scheduled stop where three thousand people greeted him, after flying at a thousand feet so that they could observe his plane from some eight to ten miles away. Crowds came out to greet him and inspect the first airplane to reach the capital of Texas. The stop at Austin gave Rodgers the opportunity to have lunch and refuel the plane, as interested viewers milled around the aircraft and its pilot, who wore a sports jacket, slacks, shirt and a bow tie.[12] It was an unforgettable day for those who were present. Rodgers took off and then circled the dome around the capital three times at about eight hundred feet before again turning south. Shortly after four that afternoon, Rodgers landed unexpectedly two miles north of Kyle, having experienced engine problems. He spent the night in Kyle while mechanics made repairs. On October 21, already the thirty-sixth day of the trip, Rodgers was only fifteen miles south of Austin. He came to realize the great vastness of Texas and the long way he still had to travel to reach the Pacific coast. The Hearst prize was beyond him. With a good quartering wind the next day,

Rodgers pushed on regardless, reaching San Marcos where he landed safely. After changing clothes and refueling the airplane, Rodgers resumed his flight.

Rodgers approached San Antonio at an altitude of about three thousand feet, which enabled the residents of San Antonio to observe his flight, before landing in the center of a polo field at 12:40 p.m. Rodgers had intended to leave San Antonio the next day, but when the mechanics checked the plane, its condition required further attention, an overhaul of the motor and additional wiring. Rodgers enjoyed a day of rest. He had hoped to entertain the crowds by flying a Wright flyer that was property of the U.S. Signal Corps and brought to Fort Sam Houston in 1911 by Lieutenant Benjamin Foulois and Wright aviator Phil Parmalee, but the U.S. Army objected to its use by a civilian. Rodgers anticipated reaching El Paso in four days, after gathering information about the best landing sites and the terrain west of San Antonio, but that proved to be impossible. With the thirty-five-horsepower, four-cylinder engine skipping, Rodgers made an emergency landing near Lacoste. The mechanics fixed the magneto (an electrical generator) and Rodgers again took off, only to make a series of other forced landings along the way. Rodgers gave short exhibitions at Sabinal and Uvalde. After flying to Spofford, he hit a stump and almost demolished his airplane.

Following repairs at Spofford and stops at other towns along the border, including Del Rio, Rodgers finally reached El Paso on October 28, where he landed in a field beyond the railroad station. Rodgers thanked the people of El Paso for the attentive hospitality he had received in Texas.[13]

On November 5, Rodgers completed his transcontinental journey, reaching Pasadena, California, in forty-nine days. Although he did not win the Hearst prize, the Armour Company paid him well for each mile completed. Sadly, Rodgers perished soon after reaching the California coast. On April 4, 1912, he flew into a flock of seagulls off the coast of Long Beach, crashing into the surf. A seagull had lodged in the controls of his plane, which prevented Rodgers from recovering his aircraft—one of the first fatal bird strikes in U.S. aviation history. Rodgers had flown cross-country a total of 3,208 miles from New York to California, according to the *New York Times*.[14] Rodgers's transcontinental flight did not demonstrate the reliability of the airplane, but he did introduce it to many communities across the country.

Matilde Moisant, First Woman Pilot to Fly in Texas, 1912

Matilde Moisant (1878–1964) was one of twelve children from a famous flying family and the second woman in the United States to receive a pilot's license on August 13, 1911. On March 23, 1912, she performed over Dallas, earning $5,000 for a twenty-five-minute flight in her Bleriot. She was the first woman pilot to fly in Mexico as well as the first woman to fly an airplane in Texas. Moisant and Harriet Quimby (1875–1912), America's first licensed woman pilot, flew in aerial exhibitions in the United States and then in Mexico City for President Francisco Madero's inauguration in December 1911.[15] Moisant had learned to fly after receiving only thirty-two minutes of ground instruction before her first solo.

During her last announced public performance on April 14 at Wichita Falls, Moisant flew for about ten minutes. As she dropped closer to the ground to land, she saw people running toward her intended landing place. Spectators were unaware that early aircraft had no brakes. Fearing that the public would run straight toward her propeller, she nosed the airplane down and let the wheels touch, but then bounced up and nosed over, hitting the propeller into the ground. Propeller fragments sliced into the fuel tanks, igniting her Bleriot, which burst into flames. Moisant was pulled from the wreckage with her clothes afire, but fortunately her heavy wool flying costume saved her from any injury beyond burning her leather gloves. A Dallas cowpuncher, R. E. Marlow, then rode up to the burning plane and lassoed the engine, which put an end to the fire.[16]

Moisant complied with her family's wishes following the fatal crash of her brother, airplane designer and performer John Moisant, by giving up the sport altogether. She initially had become interested in flying when her brother returned from France, bringing his monoplane. But following his death, she came to detest the word "aviation."[17] By then, Cal Rodgers had been killed. Moisant's friend Quimby, the first woman to fly solo across the English Channel on April 16, 1912, had also perished—she and a passenger plunged to their deaths, having fallen out of their plane while not wearing seat belts during an aerial exhibition near Boston. A gust of wind or possibly a pilot error may have caused Quimby to lose control of her Bleriot airplane on July 1, 1912. Airplane designer Glenn L. Martin thought Quimby had

Matilde Moisant, first woman to fly an airplane in Texas, 1912. Courtesy of the National Air and Space Museum, Smithsonian Institution (SI 73-3564).

descended at too high a speed and lowered the elevator too quickly, causing pressure on the upper side of the wings. In his view, this would be sufficient to unseat both pilot and passenger.[18] Moisant had good sense to quit flying at a time when fatalities were common and fragile aircraft, which were made only of wood, wires, and fabric, proved to be so unstable.

The Pliska Airplane, Midland, 1912

On July 4, 1912, residents from Odessa gathered to view the airplane built by John W. Pliska, a blacksmith in Midland. John Pliska was originally from Tyne, Austria. But he became a naturalized citizen, the first one in town. The Pliska airplane only rose a few feet off the ground in short hops, much to the dismay of the crowd. But it flew in ground effect, nevertheless, and was one of the first designs to be built in Texas. At the time of this writing, the Pliska airplane is on display at Midland/Odessa International Airport.

The Dawn of Military Aviation in Texas

On March 2, 1910, Lieutenant Benjamin D. Foulois became the first U.S. military aviator to fly in Texas. Originally from Connecticut, Foulois was an enlisted man who served in Puerto Rico and the Philippines during the Spanish American War in 1898. In 1908 he took his first flight on the first U.S. military-owned dirigible. The following year, now a first lieutenant, he was sent to Fort Myer, Virginia, to learn to pilot the U.S. Army's new Wright Flyer. He was one of three men initially taught to fly by Orville Wright. Another, Lieutenant Frank P. Lahm, would eventually command the Eighth Army Air Force in England during World War II. The third member was Frederic Humphreys. Lahm and Humphreys both soloed. On July 30, 1909, Foulois and Orville Wright made the first cross-country flight from Fort Myer to Alexandria, Virginia, during official tests, and the Wright Flyer was accepted by the military. When Fort Myer proved to be too small an area for safety reasons, Lahm selected a large level field at College Park, Maryland. On October 20, Foulois began flying with Wilbur Wright and logged fifty-four minutes of instruction.[19] But on November 5, Lahm and Humphreys damaged the airplane during a low turn before Foulois could complete his solo flight.[20] The Army then decided to transfer Foulois, the newly acquired Wright Flyer, and a group of mechanics to Fort Sam Houston in San Antonio, where the weather was more favorable for flying. "Your orders are simple, Lieutenant. You are to evaluate the airplane. Just take plenty of spare parts—and teach yourself to fly," General James Allen told Lieutenant Foulois. Foulois used a hands-on approach to learn to fly.

On March 2, 1910, Foulois completed his first solo flight in the Wright Flyer at Fort Sam Houston, completing the first military flight in the state of Texas. The *U.S. Signal Corps Aeroplane Number One* was a pusher-type biplane with two propellers. Lieutenant Foulois kept a logbook of his flights, noting his successes, failures, weather conditions, and any improvements he made on the aircraft, as he taught himself to fly. "Much of my time at San Antonio's storied Fort Sam Houston that spring was spent writing to Orville Wright, asking him how to execute basic maneuvers, how to avoid basic disasters—in short, how to fly an airplane. As far as I know, I am the only pilot in history who learned to fly by correspondence." Years later he described his initial solo on March 2 as his "first solo flight, first takeoff, first landing, and first crack up." He knocked the whole tail off the plane, he explained to newspaper reporters, but was uninjured. However, he did learn to keep the nose down and stay with the ship. A week later, he resumed learning to fly. From January 1910 to March 1911, he was the only army officer on flying duty. Foulois flew solo but had a ground crew of at least nine enlisted men, including one mechanic, during his flight operations.[21]

In 1911 Foulois was among the first to fly more than one hundred miles nonstop. He was also the first military aviator to conduct an operational reconnaissance flight and the first to test the use of a radio in flight. On March 3, 1911, Foulois and civilian pilot Philip O. Parmalee completed a 106-mile nonstop cross-country flight in a Collier Wright flyer from Laredo to Eagle Pass, Texas, where a ground exercise was in progress, in an attempt to prove to ground forces the usefulness of the airplane. The flight lasted two hours and ten minutes. Parmalee flew with Foulois as a passenger as they received and sent radio messages and dropped written messages to army units during their flight near the Mexico/Texas border, according to the *Aircraft Yearbook* (1950).

Over the next year, Congress continued to invest in the fledgling Army Air Corps, and other pilots trained by Glenn Curtiss joined Foulois at Fort Sam Houston. One of those new pilots, Lieutenant George

Kelly, flying a newly acquired Curtiss Type IV plane, crash landed and died. As a result, Foulois returned to Washington, DC, where he worked to improve wireless radio communications and the safety belt. He qualified for the new military pilot rating at College Park, Maryland, in 1912.

By the summer of 1914, Captain Foulois found himself in command of the First Aero Squadron. He was the first commander of a tactical air unit. After leading his men in reconnaissance missions in Mexico as part of the Punitive Expedition in 1916, Foulois, now a major, found himself back in San Antonio scouting out locations to build an army facility for training pilots. The Army Air Corps was in Texas to stay.

In March 1917 Foulois moved to the Aviation Section in the Office of the Chief Signal Officer in Washington, DC. He worked on a proposal for wartime expansion of the air services. His work resulted in a plan that met the needs of an army of more than a million men. Its $640 million cost was approved by Congress on July 24, 1917. In 1918 Foulois became the first Chief of the Air Service, Army Expeditionary Forces, First Army. Foulois considered this plan to be his most significant contribution to military aviation. The plan laid the foundation for the United States in the First World War and postwar military aviation. Foulois served another nineteen years in the army, eventually rising to chief of the Air Corps. When he retired on January 1, 1936, he had achieved an impressive number of aviation firsts.

The following are excerpts from Foulois's original flight logbook from the Army's first airplane, *Aeroplane No. 1*, at Fort Sam Houston. The logbook chronicles not only his first flight on March 2, 1910, but also the improvements he made to the Wright Flyer to make it safer and more practical.

In the months that followed, *Army Aeroplane No. 1* became a familiar, grotesque figure in the San Antonio sky. The light craft often bucked like a mustang in unpredictable South Texas thermal currents, so the saddle maker of a field artillery battery modified a trunk strap to hold me to my seat. It worked perfectly. We had devised a safety belt.[22]

Application of wheels to aircraft was another innovation for us. The biplane couldn't take off in a cross-wind on its ski-type skids; one effort to do so had put *No. 1* in the shop for a week. So we decided to experiment with wheels under the plane. A set from a farm cultivator worked splendidly, and thereafter wheels became standard equipment.[23]

So was the plight of the nation's air force budget: my $150 maintenance fund dwindled quickly. I was forced to dip into my own pocket to purchase material and parts for new wings, new rudders, a new elevator, a new propeller. All told, I spent $300 of my personal funds keeping the one-plane, one-pilot . . . flying.[24]

Then came a day in April, 1911, when tired old *No. 1* was replaced by a sleek new Wright Model B Aeroplane."[25]

By then, Foulois had flown sixty-four flights and logged nine hours and ten minutes of flying.

The Punitive Expedition, 1916, Mexico

The Punitive Expedition was the first time in U.S. history that an airplane was employed in a military operation on foreign soil. On the night of March 9, 1916, Francisco "Pancho" Villa crossed the border into Columbus, New Mexico, with a force of one thousand to fifteen hundred men. They killed seventeen Americans, including nine civilians and eight soldiers of the Thirteenth Cavalry under the command of Colonel Herbert J. Slocum. The Mexican peasants destroyed considerable property before units of the Thirteenth Cavalry arrived to drive the Mexicans off. The American cavalry unit killed some one hundred Villista troops. The following day, President Woodrow Wilson sent Brigadier General John J. Pershing with six thousand soldiers into Mexico to assist the Mexican government in finding Villa. Pershing was then in charge of the garrison at El Paso, fifty miles from Columbus. The basic plan was to trap Villa between two fast-moving cavalry columns, but they never found the Mexican bandit. Eight airplanes, the extent of U.S. air power at the time, were sent primarily to be used for reconnaissance. There is no doubt that the expedition to chase Villa was done in haste.

Captain Benjamin D. Foulois, commander of the First Aero Squadron, loaded eight disassembled airplanes on a train that left Fort Sam Houston in San Antonio on March 13, 1916, and arrived at Columbus

Major General Benjamin Delahauf Foulois, Chief of U.S. Army Air Corps, 1931–1935. Photographer: U.S. Army Air Corps. Courtesy of the Edward H. White II Memorial Museum, San Antonio, U.S. Air Force.

on March 15. On March 16, 1916, Captain Townsend F. Dodd, Foulois, and his deputy made a reconnaissance flight over foreign territory. Foulois found the eight aircraft taken to Mexico to be in poor condition and totally unsuitable for flying across the rugged terrain and high Sierra Madres. Several pilots had to make emergency landings, often in remote locations. The men were inadequately supplied with water and food, in the event of a forced landing. In Chihuahua on April 7, 1916, Mexican peasants who were supporters of Villa threw stones at Lieutenant Herbert A. Dargue's airplane. A brave photog-

Assembling a Curtiss JN-4 Jenny for reconnaissance by the First Aero Squadron, Mexico, 1916. Courtesy of the U.S. National Archives, College Park, Maryland.

rapher managed to distract the crowd from further violence by having Lieutenant Dargue pose for photographs. Foulois had the eight aircraft returned to Columbus, condemned, and destroyed. He purchased four new airplanes from the Curtiss Aeroplane Company. Between April 23 and April 29, the First Aero Squadron tested the new aircraft, but these too proved unsuitable for flying over mountainous areas at altitudes of ten thousand feet and above. On May 1, 1916, two new Curtiss R2–type airplanes with 160-horsepower engines arrived. By May 25, twelve more aircraft arrived, but then the pilots had trouble with defective propellers and constant problems with the equipment. Pilots did manage to fly back and forth between Camp El Valle, Mexico, and Columbus, New Mexico, almost every day.[26]

Foulois noted in his memoirs that "historians have concluded that President Woodrow Wilson's overall policy regarding Mexico was both ineffective and unsuccessful. His military policy must be considered likewise. His dispatching of the punitive expedition without adequate backing, while assigning to it a most difficult mission, was an improper application of military persuasive force."[27] Foulois, however, also contended that

> Although Pershing failed to capture Villa, the activities of the American troops in Mexico and along the border were not wasted effort. The dispersal of his band by the penetration of American forces deep into Villa's territory put an end to serious border incidents. But more important from a military point of view was the intensive training in the field received by the regular Army and the National Guard on the border and in Mexico. Many defects in the military establishment, especially in the National Guard, were uncovered.[28]

> From the point of view of the airman I consider the experience of our eight-plane air force to have been a vital milestone in the development of military aviation in the country. The machines were inadequate for the task assigned. Not only were they inadequate, they were downright dangerous to fly because of their age. Yet, we did get a great amount of scouting over country in which cavalry and infantry could not operate, and we began and maintained the first regular aerial mail route for the United States and delivered thousands of letters to and from Pershing's troops.[29]

During the Punitive Expedition, one Texan, Clarence P. Young of Texarkana, received a Distinguished Service Medal as a member of the First Aero Squadron. He displayed notable skill and experience in connection with the maintenance and repair of all the airplanes and engines used in the operations of the First Aero Squadron in Mexico.[30]

Despite problems with flying the underpowered Curtiss JN-3 aircraft over difficult terrain in Mexico, Foulois was reassigned to Washington, DC, to help organize the U.S. Army's aviation division. He returned to Texas on a priority assignment to locate a permanent site for organizing, training, and operating new air units. He chose San Antonio. His site became Kelly Field, now Kelly Air Force Base. On July 24, 1917, he was promoted from major to brigadier general.[31]

General Foulois and the U.S. Army Airmail Service

Given his early contributions to air safety and multiple roles and responsibilities in developing and demonstrating the usefulness of air power, it is perplexing why the name Benjamin Foulois is not more readily recognizable in Texas history and aviation history in general. Other record setters and air racers garnered the attention of newspaper reporters and had their names on the front pages of newspapers across the country; Foulois was dedicated to doing his job well and working quietly behind the scenes with whatever means and equipment that he had without drawing attention to himself. This attitude contrasts starkly with the headliners of his era and more controversial proponents of air power, like General Billy Mitchell. Surprisingly, an airport has yet to be named for General Benjamin Foulois.

One of his last assignments, however, may partly explain why Foulois's numerous contributions to aviation may have been largely forgotten by the American public. On February 19, 1934, President Franklin D. Roosevelt cancelled all existing mail contracts and handed the flying of the airmail over to Foulois to organize a new airmail service run by the military.[32] Foulois had inadvertently advised Roosevelt that the U.S. Army Air Corps could take over the flying of the U.S. airmail with only two weeks' notice. Foulois, then chief of the Army Air Corps, had never anticipated that the president would ask him to take charge of organizing what the *New York Times* later reportedly called the largest "peacetime job ever asked of a military unit."[33]

Foulois proceeded to quickly organize the mail flying service using twelve hundred flying officers, nearly four hundred active reservists, and thirteen thousand enlisted men. Many of the 499 aircraft flown were military combat aircraft, some training types, 66 cargo planes, 326 reconnaissance aircraft, and a few experimental planes or craft that had been used for aerial photography. Many were old and slow even for that time. It had been well known that U.S. civilian airmail pilots paid a high price to demonstrate the feasibility of flying the mail under Postmaster General Otto Praeger's management.[34] Foulois's plan to have military aviators fly the mail turned out to be a disaster. By March 10, twelve military pilots had perished, a low point in Foulois's career.

On February 26, 1934, Foulois responded to a U.S. Senate inquiry by preparing a report, "Army Airmail Operation Accidents and Fatalities." He pointed out to U.S. Senator Kenneth McKellar that between fiscal years 1929 and 1933, there were 182 fatalities among civilian pilots and 257 fatalities among military pilots. The number of accidents reported by the military was far greater, he observed, because the military kept better records than civilian aviators and included student flight-training operations. Foulois recognized that military pilots occasionally used poor judgment, having flown into adverse weather conditions in seeking to perform their duties. The commercial airline pilots, Foulois noted, were all experienced flyers, which could account for their lower number of fatalities. He wrote in his report that the military airmail pilots, nonetheless, had several hundred flying hours, having graduated from Kelly, the advanced school of military flight training in San Antonio.[35]

Foulois's career suffered as a result of the Senate inquiry and negative press coverage—particularly a newspaper article that appeared in the *Washington Star*[36]—about the loss of recent military graduates, including several who had trained at Kelly Field who flew the airmail. Although Foulois asserted that the newspaper article was inaccurate, his reputation was damaged and he lost some credibility. Foulois had stressed to his men that safety was of the utmost importance, but extreme weather proved to be a factor, besides pilot error. Army airmail flyers sought to perform the duties assigned to them in a rigorous manner. They often took unnecessary risks and encountered some of the worst flying weather, resulting in the loss of growing numbers of military airmail pilots. In April 1934, the Army finally relieved the young military flyers from airmail duty at Kelly Field after six more pilots had perished and at least four others were injured. Nevertheless, according to Postmaster James A. Farley, not a single pound of mail was lost during the years the Army flew the airmail.[37]

In 1936 Foulois ended his military career on a positive note by accepting the designs from the Boeing Company for what became the B-17 *Flying Fortress*, which played a fundamental role in the U.S. Army Air Corps's ability to win the Second World War.[38]

THE YEAR 1910 IS SIGNIFICANT IN THE HISTORY of powered flight in Texas. It marked the beginning of a decade that witnessed the development of general aviation and military aviation in the state. Since the first Farman biplane flown by French aviator Louis Paulhan in Houston, aviation entered a new era. While teaching himself to fly at Fort Sam Houston in San Antonio, then Lieutenant

Benjamin Foulois initiated fundamental advancements in military aviation and air safety. Pioneer aviators would soon become civilian flight instructors working for outfits like the Curtiss School of Aeronautics and the Stinson Flying School, training military cadets who would serve in the Great War. Texas aviation soared to new heights as a result of the growing public interest in aerial exhibitions and increased demand for military flight training with the outbreak of the Great War in Europe in 1914.

Chapter 2

The Stinson Flying Family of San Antonio and Texas Aviators in the Great War

IN DECEMBER 1910, EMMA STINSON, MOTHER OF FOUR children—Katherine, Edward, Marjorie, and Jack—wrote to the Wright brothers to inquire the cost of an airplane. They offered her a Wright flyer for $5,000 plus $100 per day if the aircraft were to be utilized in aerial exhibitions. However, this usage fee demanded by the Wrights never took hold. Emma was a good businesswoman who encouraged her four children to learn to fly. Katherine, Edward, and Marjorie not only learned, they excelled: performing aerobatic maneuvers, setting records, and providing flight instruction. The youngest brother, Jack, also became a pilot but occupied himself doing mechanical repairs. Emma was the impetus behind establishing the Stinson flying school. Together, the Stinson family established the Stinson Aviation Company in Hot Springs, Arkansas. Then in 1913, they moved their operations to San Antonio, which offered plenty of blue sky and relatively flat terrain as well as military cadets interested in flight training. Initially the Stinsons used the parade grounds at Fort Sam Houston for flight training. Then they leased at least five hundred acres from the city of San Antonio, where they established Stinson Field. In 1916 some twenty-four students lived in tents and a hangar as carpenters worked to complete other hangars and workshops. The Stinson family aviation business, dedicated to instructing Americans and Canadians, underscores Texas's role as a primary center for military flight training when war broke out in Europe. Emma Stinson's role was significant; it shows that women were an integral part of aviation since its early years, albeit in very small numbers.

However, when it came to military aviation at the time of the First World War, the United States was behind Europe in aircraft technology and production. Aviation historians have often attributed the delay to the patent wars of the Wright brothers, but as we have seen, aviators kept flying and designing airplanes, regardless of alleged patent infringements and pending lawsuits. The United States was behind primarily because there was no strong demand for airplanes in this country. The U.S. military was reluctant to invest in an unproven technology. Militaries in Europe, in contrast, saw the value of the airplane and more readily purchased this new technology. The general public in the United States also did not have money to purchase new airplanes, which initially the Wrights offered to the U.S. military for $30,000 in 1908. By 1910, Wright biplanes cost $5,000, still a sizeable sum; moreover, not enough were sold by designers and manufacturers in these early years to foster research and innovation. The U.S. military kept some airplanes for reconnaissance purposes, but that was the extent of U.S. military interest in aviation prior to U.S. entry into the Great War.

Although not native to Texas, the Stinson family became closely associated with aviation and military flight instruction in San Antonio. As a military instructor, Eddie taught cadets and became a record setter and designer/manufacturer of Stinson aircraft. Katherine and Marjorie were among the daring, highly competent women flyers who demonstrated to a disbelieving public that women could fly. Marjorie excelled in the training of future cadets, while Katherine thrilled crowds as a professional aerial performer, earning a national and international reputation. Their contributions, along with those of their brother Eddie, stand out in aviation history.

Katherine Stinson (1891?–1977), Aerial Exhibition Flyer

Born in Fort Payne, Alabama, probably on February 14, 1893, Katherine Stinson became the fourth woman in the United States to receive a pilot's license on July 24, 1912: number 148 from the Aero Club of America, the governing agency for the Fédération Aéronautique Internationale. She learned to fly from Max Lillie in Chicago. Along with her rival Ruth Bancroft Law, Katherine performed death-defying stunts to the delight of thousands of spectators in the United States, Canada, Japan, and China.

Katherine Stinson on the cover of a Japanese aeronautical journal. Courtesy of the Katherine Stinson Otero Collection, Center for Southwest Research, the University of New Mexico at Albuquerque.

In 1915 Katherine Stinson became the first woman to fly in Asia. She went on an aerial exhibition tour of Japan and China, as arranged by her contract manager, Bill Pickens.[1] On December 15, 1916, nearly twenty-five thousand people gathered at the Aoyama Parade Grounds to witness Katherine's night flight. Using fireworks on her wings, she lit up the sky over Tokyo. She also flew for fascinated Chinese spectators in Peking. Katherine received several letters of appreciation from fans following her Asian trip. T. Furuya at Tung Wen College, Shang-

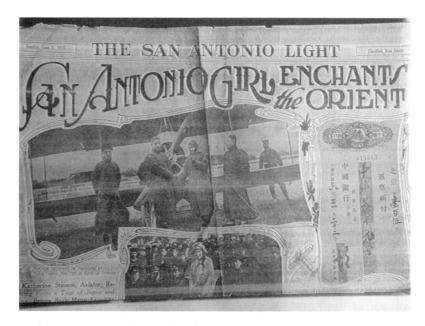

Katherine Stinson as depicted on the front page of a San Antonio newspaper. Courtesy of the Katherine Stinson Otero Collection, Center for Southwest Research, the University of New Mexico at Albuquerque.

hai, wrote two letters to her dated February 17, 1917. He expressed his appreciation for her spectacular flights, which amazed the Chinese people. She also received a lovely silver trophy, which is engraved "Miss Katherine Stinson as a token of appreciation from His Excellency Yangcheng, Special Envoy for Foreign Affairs, Shanghai, China, 24th February 1917."

On her return to the United States, Katherine continued to set records. She had already accumulated several aviation firsts to her credit: she was the first female night skywriter, the first U.S. woman to perform an inside loop, the first person to carry airmail in Western Canada, and among the first women to fly at night. On December 11, 1917, she broke rival Law's distance record by flying from San Diego to San Francisco. Stinson improved her own record on May 23, 1918, by flying 783 miles nonstop carrying the U.S. mail from Chicago to Binghamton, New York. As she failed to reach her intended destination in New York, that flight did not receive much public attention. Stinson crashed on landing two miles north of Binghamton. Although she flipped her airplane, breaking its propeller and wing, she was uninjured.

Katherine Stinson and Ruth Bancroft Law carried the U.S. airmail on a limited basis with success.[2] As early as September 24, 1913, the U.S. postal service swore Katherine in to carry the mail by air during the Montana State Fair.[3] On July 9, 1918, Katherine flew the first airmail service in Western Canada.

Katherine volunteered to drive an ambulance in Europe during the Great War. She also distributed leaflets in support of the Red Cross. After contracting tuberculosis, she settled in Santa Fe, New Mexico, where she became a notable architect and designer of pueblo-style houses. She never flew again. She married Miguel Antonio Otero, Jr., a prominent lawyer and judge. The couple never had children but spent some time raising her youngest brother's offspring. She and her husband died in 1977.

Marjorie Stinson (1895–1975), "Flying Schoolmarm"

Although the Wright brothers had refused to teach Ruth Bancroft Law to fly in 1912, by 1914 Orville and Wilbur Wright reconsidered. They allowed Marjorie Stinson to enroll in their flight school at Dayton, Ohio, only after the teenager obtained written parental permission.[4] In 1910 the Wrights were charging $25 per lesson, with ten to fifteen lessons required to operate their flying machine. Marjorie's first solo flight took place on August 4, 1914. The San Antonio teenager was alleged to be the "youngest flyer in America," according to the aeronautical journal *Aerial Age Weekly*.[5] Marjorie earned her license after four and a half hours of instruction from Howard Rinehart in a Wright B biplane with a thirty-horsepower motor. The Aero Club of America awarded her certificate No. 303 on August 12, 1914, after she performed a set of figure eights at a specified altitude.

Beginning on October 8 and 9, 1914, at Brownwood, Texas, Marjorie performed exhibition flights and carried many air passengers. She then began instructing at the Stinson School of Flying and at Fort Sam Houston in San Antonio in 1915. Marjorie taught American and Canadian cadets trying to earn their wings in order to enter the Royal Flying Corps before the First World War came to an end. She trained as many as sixteen cadets, including one from Mexico who learned to fly with the help of an interpreter. She flew a Wright B Flyer that had been modified by adding ailerons.

In addition to her teaching, Marjorie was formally sworn in by Postmaster George Armistead to carry the airmail from San Antonio to Seguin, a distance of about thirty-five miles, during the period of May 19 to May 31, 1915. High winds interfered with her flight, though, so she did not perform that service.[6]

In 1916 and 1917, while Katherine was performing stunts at state fairs and other aerial events, Emma, Eddie, and Marjorie Stinson operated the Stinson School of Flying at Stinson Field and Fort Sam Houston. Edward was president, Marjorie chief instructor. She also did some aerial photography. Marjorie noted that her sister Katherine was never connected with the school. Katherine, she explained, never taught anyone to fly.[7] The Stinson family organized a group of civilians interested in aviation known as the Texas Escadrille. Marjorie was extremely proud of her pupils, many of whom went overseas during the Great War.[8]

After the war, Marjorie moved to Washington, DC, where she worked for the Navy and its engineering department as a drafter until retiring in 1936.

Marjorie proved to be highly protective of her family's accomplishments, especially those of her sister Katherine. In January 1929, for example, Marjorie took issue with Amelia Earhart's proposal to the National Aeronautic Association to establish separate aviation records for women. Marjorie thought the idea of separate competitions would be harmful to the future well-being of women pilots in the United States. With twenty-seven hundred flight hours, Marjorie recognized that holding separate competitions would reinforce the generally accepted belief that women were incapable of competing against men. She strongly opposed the idea of separate sets of records and pointed out that many pioneering women who flew early on sacrificed their lives in the name of aviation and women's rights to fly powered aircraft. Marjorie claimed that competition only among women was a sign of being "ungrateful to our deceased heroines," like the late Harriet Quimby, the first licensed U.S. woman pilot, and the French Baroness Raymonde de Laroche, the first woman in the world to fly: "Both of them knew nothing of the superiority of men in flying competitions."[9]

During the Second World War, Marjorie served as a volunteer in the American Red Cross in Arlington, Virginia, until 1945. She then dedicated her time to the study of aviation history, still residing in Washington, DC, until she passed away at age seventy-nine in 1975.

Eddie Stinson (1894–1932): Flight Instructor, Record Setter, Designer, and Test Pilot

On December 29, 1915, Eddie Stinson obtained license no. 373, having taken some lessons at Dayton. He notably perfected a technique to recover from a spin during rotation, according to aviator Matty Laird. Captain Benjamin Foulois was so impressed with his spin recovery technique that he had Eddie teach it to the military pilots of the First Aero Squadron. While Eddie may not have been the first person to discover how to break a spin, he was definitely the first aviator to instruct military pilots on spin recovery. Air Force historians credit Eddie with reducing the fatality rate by training pilots how to get out of a spin.[10] Eddie went on to set a number of aviation records before becoming a partner in the design and manufacturing of Stinson aircraft in Detroit, Michigan.

On May 2, 1926, he formed the Stinson Aircraft Company. He flew as a test pilot on original Stinson designs. In March 1928, he set a new world endurance record with George Haldeman at Jacksonville, Florida, remaining in the air fifty-three hours, thirty-six minutes, and thirty seconds. They received a check for $5,000.[11] Sadly, in 1932, he perished as the result of an airplane accident after hitting a flagpole when he ran out of fuel. Eddie was an experienced pilot with approximately fifteen thousand flying hours. In the absence of his flight logbooks, it is difficult to know how many flying hours he had accumulated at the time of his death.

Texas Aviators in the Great War: Clyde Balsley Flies the Lone Star of Texas *in France*

Several aviators from Texas distinguished themselves during the First World War. Horace Clyde Balsley of San Antonio, one of the American volunteers who flew for the French prior to U.S. entry into the European war, became a member of the Escadrille Lafayette. Edgar Tobin and William Erwin were also among Texas's flying aces. Numerous other cadets trained at airfields like Brooks and

Kelly Fields in San Antonio, Love Field in Dallas, Call Field in Wichita Falls, Rich Field in Waco, several fields near Fort Worth, and Ellington Field near Houston, among other training sites. Future aircraft manufacturer Walter Beech, for example, learned to fly at Rich Field in Waco. There was a radio school and an air service school for radio officers at Penn Field in Austin, aviation supply depots near Houston and San Antonio, and an aviation repair depot at Dallas.[12]

Balsley earned his brevet to fly a Bleriot as a fighter pilot on January 2, 1916, after enlisting with the French on September 16, 1915. Previously he had volunteered to serve as an ambulance driver in the American Field Service in 1915. He served in the Escadrille from February 16 to April 1, 1916, then, as a member of the Réserve Général de l'Aéronautique from April 1, 1916, to May 26, 1916, and the Escadrille Lafayette from May 29, 1916, to June 18, 1916. He showed great courage by chasing enemy planes behind their lines on June 18, 1916. The son of a baker, Balsley stood out from other fighter pilots in that he flew a French Nieuport painted with a white lone star, the symbol of Texas. He achieved the rank of sergeant under the French and then was commissioned as a captain in the pursuit division of the U.S. military. He was decorated by the French with a Médaille Militaire and the Croix de Guerre with Palm.

On June 26, 1916, Balsley was seriously wounded in air combat when his gun jammed; he was attacked from behind and shot in the thigh. An exploding bullet shattered his hip and perforated his intestines in a dozen places. The first American aviator to be shot in combat, Balsley could no longer fly or serve at the front.[13] For days, his physician would not even allow him to drink water. He would have died without the care of an American nurse, a Miss Wolf (first name unknown), who helped pull him through until he was well enough to return to America the following autumn in 1917.

Balsley later retold how a figure appeared at his bedside. In dire need, he did not recognize the man with heavy black hair and dark eyes as his friend and fellow American aviator Victor Chapman. Chapman found Balsley delirious, sucking feverishly on a piece of wet muslin in the French hospital. Chapman asked a passing surgeon if he could bring Balsley some oranges, which the doctor allowed. Chapman declared that he would travel as far as Paris for the oranges, but the grateful Balsley would never see him again. Chapman was shot down after five Germans in two-seaters and three in Fokkers caught up with his Nieuport more than three miles into German territory.[14]

Two million Americans served in France; of those, as many as one hundred sixteen thousand perished.[15] Approximately eight to nine million people died in all. According to General Benjamin Foulois, between March and November 1918, 87 American pilots were killed, 62 were wounded, and 167 went missing. Among the observers that often accompanied pilots, 35 were killed, 62 were wounded, and 60 went missing.[16] Early military aviators carried observers who made reports on troop movements. We do not know how many Texans died, but the figures do shed some light on the limited use of the airplane under combat conditions. The U.S. Air Service only increased its inventory of aircraft from a few hundred at the beginning of the war to 6,200 by the end of the war; nearly 4,800 were manufactured in France. The U.S. produced 1,216 airplanes, almost all of foreign design.[17]

Although Balsley managed to land his plane, his serious wounds made it unmistakably clear that Americans were in Europe to help the French people.[18] Balsley continued to suffer from intestinal problems most of his life. He died in 1942 at age forty-eight in Los Angeles, California, due to complications of those wounds.[19]

Stuart McLeod Purcell (1890–1985), Photographic Journalist in Wartime France

Stuart McLeod Purcell of Austin documented what a soldier's life was like as a second lieutenant and adjutant of the 147th Aero Squadron, First Pursuit Group, of the American Expeditionary Forces, formed in San Antonio in 1917. Born in Austin on June 12, 1890, Purcell received a Bachelor of Arts degree from the University of Texas at Austin in 1916 before enrolling in law school that fall. When the United States entered World War I on April 6, 1917, Purcell left law school to enlist. He married Mabelle Agnes Umland of Waller and Edinburg, Texas, shortly before departing for France. Although he was not an aviator, he demonstrated his interest in aviation by documenting flyers' lives through the use of a camera lens. Beginning on January 26, 1918, Purcell served as his unit's adjutant (an administrative officer) at the rank of second lieutenant. He acted as supply and payroll officer for the 147th Aero Squadron, which was organized at Kelly Field.

Established in August 1917, Kelly Field was named for Second Lieutenant George E. M. Kelly, who became San Antonio's first air fatality on May 10, 1911, when he crashed a new-model Curtiss pusher by coming in too steep and hitting the nose gear, then bouncing up again before crashing. Kelly turned to avoid a line of tents. He perished a few hours later due to a skull fracture. An investigative board determined that his death was the result of pilot error.[20]

During World War I, flight training was divided into three stages: ground, primary, and advanced. Between May 1917 and February 1918, ground school was conducted at the School of Military Aeronautics at the University of Texas at Austin. It lasted six to eight weeks, and students learned the basics of aerodynamics and the mechanics of the airplane. Then primary flight training was held at eight sites, including Kelly and Brooks Fields in San Antonio. This stage lasted approximately three months. Students learned to fly the Curtiss JN-4D Jenny, a biplane. Successful cadets earned their wings as junior military aviators and a commission. In August 1917 Kelly Field officially opened in San Antonio. By December, there were more than thirty-two thousand troops, including eleven hundred officers and thirty-one thousand enlisted men. The first class graduated on November 23, 1917.[21] Advanced flight training started at Kelly in October 1917 at its School of Advanced Flying. Some 1,459 reserve military aviators and 298 flight instructors had graduated from the program by Armistice Day. Dangers, however, persisted. Flying accounted for twenty-three fatalities at Kelly during the war years.

An air mechanics school was also established at Kelly, along with a homing pigeon program. The mechanics school at Kelly and another at St. Paul, Minnesota, between them trained more than half of America's 14,176 mechanics during the First World War.

The pigeon department at Kelly trained homing pigeons, which accompanied pilots on cross-country flights. They could be released to notify of a pilot's whereabouts in the event of mechanical failure, if stranded. Several pigeons were actually decorated for outstanding service. In Europe, pigeons were even equipped with their own parachutes; pilots would release them from the airplane carrying messages home.[22]

One of Purcell's obligations was to issue boots to all the men. He also wrote a report on the efficiency of the SPAD airplane. He kept a journal, *World War I Diary of the 147th Aero Squadron*, which included photographic images of camp scenes and pilots talking to one another while in uniform. Edward "Eddie" Rickenbacker, America's highest achieving ace, commanded the Ninth Aero Squadron and appeared in Purcell's work.

The 147th Squadron served at Remember Port Aux Pots, France, in August 1918. After being discharged on February 3, 1919, Purcell returned to the United States, where he and his wife became farmers in Robtown, Texas, near Corpus Christi. They had three children. During the Great Depression, both worked as freelance journalists, and he became a schoolteacher. In 1938 Purcell and his wife with their three children moved to Austin, where the couple had met as students at the University of Texas. He worked in the Texas Department of Health and was employed by the U.S. Public Service. Purcell and his wife coauthored a book about Texas called *This is Texas* (1977).[23]

American military aviators such as Eddie Rickenbacker wore an equestrian type of uniform. To an extent, the U.S. Air Service was an outgrowth of the U.S. Cavalry, whose members served as scouts. Flying clothing of World War I pilots included riding breeches, a long leather flying jacket, tinted, shatterproof goggles, leather boots—some with thick linings—leather gloves, and a helmet with sheepskin lining. These were worn over woolen military uniforms, creating several layers. Some pilots wore leather face masks to help fight the bitterly cold temperatures, one of the major adverse conditions faced by all pilots who flew in open-cockpit airplanes at higher altitudes.

Eddie Rickenbacker often emulated General John Pershing's charismatic style.[24] Lieutenant George S. Patton, who served as an aide under Pershing in Mexico, also strove to copy Pershing's mannerisms and clothing style—even during World War II when he commanded U.S. forces in North Africa and Europe.[25] Some male pilots actually walked around carrying riding crops during the Great War because it looked stylish—not because they needed a riding crop to fly an airplane. Pilots followed the lead of their commander. Pershing expressed displeasure at pilots' refusal to wear spurs while flying during an inspection tour at Kelly Field in 1920.[26]

Like members of the cavalry who rode horses, World War I pilots lined up their Jennies at airfields at Brooks and Kelly Fields. Military aviators who flew during the Great War were not exactly safety conscious. None wore parachutes until the end of the war. Their usefulness was not demonstrated until German pilots adopted parachutes as a required safety measure. Even then, some pilots did not wish to carry them because their bulkiness took away from the manly image.

Stuart McLeod Purcell's photograph of American ace Eddie Rickenbacker in France during World War I (Eddie Rickenbacker with dog, di_08204). Courtesy of the Stuart McLeod Purcell Collection, Dolph Briscoe Center for American History, the University of Texas at Austin.

Brooks Field was named for the first cadet from San Antonio to die during World War I, Sidney Brooks (1895–1917). While on a return trip from Kelly Field, Brooks perished when he crashed his JN-4 Jenny biplane. Brooks and Kelly Fields each had thirty hangars for their JN-4 Jennies. Hangar 9, which still stands at Brooks, was built in early 1918. "Old 9" was also used for blind flying instruction, or instrument training, in the late 1920s. (See chapter 6.)

The Curtiss JN-4 Jenny, a slow but reliable biplane, was the mainstay of the U.S. Army Air Service training program during the war and the early 1920s. This primary trainer had a water-cooled engine with open valves, which had to be lubricated with castor oil before takeoff. This type of vegetable oil proved to be a good lubricant for early aircraft engines. Known to be a laxative, it also was a common household remedy. When flying in open-cockpit airplanes, pilots breathed in engine fumes; early aircraft engines leaked oil profusely—to the extent that when pilots removed their goggles, many looked like raccoons because drops of oil had splattered on their faces. The Jenny was not an easy aircraft to fly, as it was so underpowered that its nose tended to drop on turns. This basic trainer could be an unforgiving airplane, as shown by the number of crashes that took place at Texas airfields.

Canadian Cadets Trained near Fort Worth

Attracted by Texas's favorable flying weather, flat terrain, and wide-open spaces, in 1916 the Canadian Royal Flying Corps selected three fields south of Fort Worth for flight instruction. The United States, Britain, and Canada entered into a reciprocal agreement to train military pilots for combat. Canadian fliers trained at Hicks, Benbrook (Carruthers), and Barron Fields (known as Taliaferro Fields 1, 2, and 3, respectively). The Canadians named their fields after American flyer Walter Taliaferro, who perished in a crash. American and Canadian flight students trained in gunnery at Benbrook Field. Some Americans who enlisted in the Canadian military were assigned to Benbrook. The first Canadian trainees arrived in November 1917. Cadets flew two types of Jennies: the lighter Canadian Canuck and the Curtiss JN-4D. In 1918 numerous cadets died of influenza in an epidemic that affected millions of people worldwide; in April of that year the Canadian cadets returned to Canada. Among them were 1,960 pilots, 69 ground officers, and 4,150 men who were trained in various skills on the ground.[27]

World War I Texas Aces

Flying aces were the most celebrated of military aviators—those who shot down five or more enemy aircraft during combat. At least five Texans became aces: Howard E. Boyson of Dallas scored five victories, or kills, as a member of the RAF No. 66; Charles G. Catto of Dallas scored six as a member of the RFC No. 45; Henry R. Clay Jr. of Fort Worth earned eight as a member of the 148th Aero Squadron; William P. Erwin of Amarillo earned eight as a member of the First Aero Squadron, and Edgar G. Tobin of San Antonio scored six for the 103rd Squadron.[28]

Catto was born in Dallas on November 7, 1896. A medical student at Edinburgh University in Scotland when the European war broke out, he joined the Royal Flying Corps. He was assigned to Italy where he flew Sopwith Camels, claiming six victories and thereby becoming an ace in March 1918. Following the war, he resumed his medical studies and later returned to his native Texas, where he practiced medicine. He resided in Waco from 1958 until his death on June 24, 1972.[29]

Erwin was born in Ryan, Oklahoma, on October 18, 1898; his family moved to Texas when he was six months old. In 1912, Erwin graduated from high school in Amarillo. He then studied music in Chicago, Illinois. He volunteered for army pilot training upon America's entry into the war and was sent to France to fly Salmson 2A2s with the First Aero Squadron.

Flying with Lieutenant H. W. Dahringer, the first of a succession of observers, Erwin downed an unspecified German aircraft near Mamey on September 15, 1918. Two weeks later, this time with observer Lieutenant B. V. Baucom, he shot down a Rumpler over Fléville. With his third observer, Lieutenant A. E. Easterbrook, he claimed victory during a dawn patrol over St. Juvin. On October 6, Erwin became an ace when he and Easterbrook downed a pair of German airplanes during a late afternoon patrol in the Apremont, Sommerance, region. Teamed once again with Lieutenant Baucom, he shot down an unidentified German plane and a Fokker D.VII three days later. He finished the war with the destruction of another enemy airplane on

October 22 northwest of Ramonville. First Lieutenant Erwin was the recipient of the Distinguished Service Cross.[30]

After the war, Erwin tried wildcatting in the oil fields without success. He then earned a living giving rides to passengers, crop dusting, and air racing. Erwin's popularity soared in Dallas in 1927 when he entered the Pacific Air Race. James D. Dole, known as the Pineapple King, offered a $25,000 prize to the winner of an air race from California to Hawaii and $10,000 to the second-place finisher. Erwin entered the race from Oakland to Hawaii as part of a larger plan. He actually had intended to become the first person to fly from Dallas to Hong Kong and capture the Dallas-China Prize of $25,000 offered on May 27, 1927, by William Easterwood, Jr., a retired officer in the U.S. Marines and a pilot in Dallas.[31]

On August 6, 1927, ten thousand people showed up at Love Field for the unveiling of Erwin's *Dallas Spirit*, a green and white monoplane similar to a Swallow. On August 9, five thousand well-wishers, including his parents and his wife, went to Love Field to see Captain Erwin take off on the first leg of his flight to Oakland, California. The actual race began on August 16, with fifty thousand people waiting at the finish line on the North Shore of Oahu for the arrival of the eight competing airplanes. Only two of them would ever reach Hawaii. Two crashed on takeoff; another returned with a burned-out engine but landed safely. Erwin was forced to return to Oakland after only half an hour of flying. Against all advice, he and wireless operator Alvin Eichwoldt took off on August 19 in the *Dallas Spirit* to search for friends in the two missing planes. Erwin had considerable flying experience, but according to radio contact, the *Dallas Spirit* went into a spin from which Erwin could not recover.[32] The U.S. Navy zigzagged during its search, covering five hundred forty thousand square miles between Oakland and Honolulu at a cost of several million dollars, but the missing flyers were never found. Easterwood, the competition's sponsor, gave Erwin's widow Constance a cashier's check for $5,000. He expressed high regard for Erwin, who lost his life during an attempt to save others, and sympathy for her great loss.[33]

Another Texas ace, Edgar Gardner Tobin (1896–1954), was born in San Antonio on September 7, 1896.[34] He studied at the Texas Military Institute, Class of 1914. He joined the U.S. Army Signal Corps, Aviation Section, at Austin in May 1917. In July 1917 he completed ground school, which included the study of aerodynamics, weather, aircraft engines, and navigation at the University of Texas at Austin. He was

William P. Erwin and his wife Constance in front of the *Dallas Spirit*, 1927.
Courtesy of the Dallas Public Library.

promoted to first lieutenant on December 12, 1917. He joined the
Ninety-Fourth Aero Squadron on March 7, 1918, following gunnery
training, and transferred to 103rd Aero Squadron on April 2, 1918. He
was alleged to have become the youngest major in France at twenty-
two. He flew a SPAD XIII and had six confirmed kills. Tobin's first victory, a German two-seater brought down east of Thiaucourt on July 11,
1918, was shared with squadron mate Lieutenant E. B. Jones. Five
days later, leading a patrol of three SPADs near Viéville, he attacked
a formation of six Pfalz D.IIIs. Although a later Distinguished Service Cross citation credited him with destroying two during that en-
gagement, he was officially credited with a single victory. On August 1,
he brought down a reconnaissance airplane over Wurttemberg and a
Fokker D.VII on the tenth near Thiaucourt. The next day he became
an ace, sharing the victory over a Fokker D.VII with Lieutenants G. W.
Furlow and V. W. Todd. After the war, Tobin served as an assistant in
charge of Kelly Field. He then established Tobin Aerial Surveys, which
became the largest aerial mapping firm in the world. He did commer-

cial mapping for the Humble Oil and Refining Company, now Exxon, and other oil companies. During World War II, he mapped the entire United States for the federal government and served as a special advisor to General Henry "Hap" Arnold. He died on January 10, 1954, in an airplane crash as a passenger in a Grumman Mallard on Lake Wallace near Shreveport, Louisiana, following a duck hunting trip.[35]

BY THE END OF WORLD WAR I, MEMBERS OF THE U.S. military gradually came to accept the airplane as a useful technology; a few, like Foulois, became outstanding proponents of the importance of air power. Although not easily assessed, casualties as a result of the airplane probably numbered fewer than twenty thousand on all sides in the Great War. This is almost negligible in comparison to the number of men who died in the trenches.[36] With more than nine million people dead, ultimately the airplane did not contribute substantially to the slaughter of human beings in the First World War.

The use of air power in the Great War was essentially a duel among gentlemen from various countries. Most of the time pilots were shooting at one another in dogfights. No appreciable damage came from the small bombs dropped by any airplane or flechettes tossed by flyers. Airplanes were often used as balloon busters, destroying the enemy's observation balloons while protecting their own.

Although the airplane greatly improved reconnaissance, it still did not take all the surprise out of warfare; it provided the opportunity for new developments in a third dimension as aircraft technology advanced. Despite the appearance of monoplanes, larger engines, and bombers by the end of the war, the airplane did not determine the outcome of the war. The war did reveal some of what pilots could do with this new technology, but the airplane did not live up to its full potential as an instrument of war. Record-setting pilots and air racers would further demonstrate the reliability and practicality of the airplane during the interwar period.

Chapter 3

Between the World Wars
Barnstormers—Owners and Operators of Flying Services

A FEW AVIATORS FROM TEXAS, SUCH AS ONE-EYED Wiley Post and Elizabeth "Bessie" Coleman, came from extremely modest family backgrounds but managed to overcome major obstacles—whether financial, physical, race, or gender—to earn their wings. One avenue to becoming a pilot was to begin as a parachutist paid to perform jumps at aerial exhibitions in order to earn enough money for flying lessons. Another Texan, Douglas Corrigan, worked as an airplane mechanic and slept in a pup tent behind an airplane hangar until he could afford to buy his own airplane (see chapter 4). In contrast Howard Hughes came from a privileged family in Houston and leveraged his family fortune to become one of the wealthiest men in the world, a record setter, and aircraft designer. From parachutists to world record setters and air racers during the 1930s, Texans left an indelible mark on the development of the aviation industry between the world wars and even beyond.

The era immediately following the Great War, however, was the period of the barnstormer. These aerial performers gave rides to make a living. With no rules or regulations for pilots and their airplanes until the Air Commerce Act of 1926, barnstormers operated freely from any wide-open area. Aviators from Texas proved to be quite versatile in their ability to initiate tremendous interest in aviation through performing their various antics in the sky. Several set impressive aviation records or became aerial performers who did exhibition flights throughout the country, becoming recognizable national figures. A few left important legacies, although most have been largely forgotten.

After the end of the First World War and throughout the 1920s and into the 1930s, pilots stimulated interest in aviation by giving rides to common folk. Airplanes were such a novelty that pilots could make a living, albeit at times a meager one, by flying passengers. Barnstormers were pilots and aerial stunt performers who traveled from town to town and introduced aviation to a curious public in rural communities across North America, including parts of Canada and northern Mexico.

Barnstormers earned a living by giving rides or performing aerial stunts at fairgrounds and racetracks. They took passengers for short rides to give Americans the excitement of their first flight. Most people saw their first airplane when a barnstormer flew over their town or farm. These flyers landed their airplanes in open fields or on the beach, because few towns or cities had airports prior to U.S. entry into the Second World War.

Originally the term *barnstormers* referred to itinerant traveling actors who performed short skits in barns.[1] The name probably stuck because barnstormers traveled especially in rural areas, often storing their airplanes in barns. Barnstormers in Texas like Mississippian Floyd "Slats" Rodgers[2] knew they had to keep moving from one area of the country to the next, knowing that people would go up once or twice or even three times, but then that would be it.[3] Barnstormers played a crucial role in America by introducing the concept to the general public that airplanes could be quite pleasurable to ride in, a thrill, and potentially safe. Some made a living on the notion that flying was quite dangerous so as to excite crowds who came to expect that they might witness a fatality. This rather gruesome interest in seeing someone die was well depicted in the Hollywood motion picture *The Great Waldo Pepper* (1975), which was filmed east of San Antonio in Kingsbury, Texas, and featured actor Robert Redford. Some talented air circus performers actually managed to crash biplanes into a barn for a certain price in order to please the crowds. This was considered entertainment. Scantily clad women standing on the wings or next to aircraft also helped spark interest in aviation following the end of the Great War.

Pioneer flyers who owned and operated Houston Aerial Transport Company in Texas during the early 1920s appear to have been trendsetters in utilizing women's sexuality to promote airplane sales, rides, or the sale of aviation fuel and other flying services. Their use of staged promotional photographs of barely dressed women posing

In this publicity photo, women serve simply as props (not propellers). So many women on a wing might have caused the airplane to tip over under normal circumstances. Their shoes give them away as not being professional wing walkers, who were a rare commodity. The photograph was probably intended to be distributed to male potential customers, rather than female ones. Courtesy of the Houston Metropolitan Research Center, Houston Public Library, and the San Jacinto Museum of History.

as wing walkers shows how women's bodies were used to entice men. Such promotional images also serve to illustrate the gender stereotypes that serious women aviators had to overcome when entering a male-dominated field such as aviation. Generally the use of women pilots to promote aviation sales was more associated with the late 1920s and 1930s, as historian Joseph Corn notes.[4] These Texans were setting an early trend, perhaps even before U.S. women pilots had begun to demonstrate airplanes for major manufacturers and designers and before the airlines began to use women as flying hostesses or attendants in 1930.

A few barnstormers were lawless individuals. Slats Rodgers—who really was a Mississippian, not a Texan, born in Dark Hollow, Mississippi—whose family came to North Texas when he was fifteen, made

Promotional images of pioneer flyers and operators of a flying service in Houston, circa 1920. Courtesy of the Houston Metropolitan Research Center, Houston Public Library, and the San Jacinto Museum of History.

a living in aviation from a variety of ways. He not only offered rides but smuggled bootleg whiskey, illegal Chinese immigrants, watches, and perfume into Texas from Mexico and transported arms and ammunition into Mexico at the end of the Mexican Revolution after serving as a civilian flight instructor during World War I. Slats also earned a living as a pioneer crop duster. As could be expected, he only discussed crimes he could not be held accountable for in the description of his adventures in a classic work, *Old Soggy No. 1*, named for the aircraft he claimed to have built in 1912. Rodgers claimed to have built the first airplane in Texas. He did not. Embellishment was part of the trade of early barnstormers; pioneer flyers easily got away with making up lies and exaggerating their accomplishments in order to attract attention and assure getting an audience. It was far less dangerous for these colorful characters to make up stories and outright lie than to fly unstable aircraft before an audience, "knowing they [would] get a big kick out of seeing" him get "splattered on the ground."[5] Rodgers outright lies and contradicts himself 180 degrees in his lively account.

As a form of popular entertainment, barnstormers put on gravity-defying performances or simulated dogfights. Many formed flying circuses to attract large audiences and advertise upcoming performances. Barnstormers scattered thousands of handbills, alerting people in rural towns of an upcoming air circus. Texas's wide-open skies and favorable flying weather made it a popular stop for barnstormers and professional aerial performers in flying circuses who worked under contract. The cost of airplanes, maintenance, and aviation fuel and the need to keep the public's attention by improving upon solo acts encouraged barnstormers to form these air circuses, which usually comprised a few pilots and one or two wing walkers and parachutists.[6]

The vast majority of barnstormers were men. According to the 1920 census, of the 1,312 aeronauts, only 8 were women in the United States.[7] It is unclear how many were Texans, since there were aviators who never bothered to get certified. Young men and women were drawn to the risky business of barnstorming out of an addiction to fear or thrill-seeking or to achieve financial rewards and recognition.[8]

An overabundance of Curtiss Jennies, the first mass-produced aircraft, made barnstorming possible after the Great War. By Armistice Day, some six thousand Curtiss JN-4D Jennies had been produced for the United States and two thousand more for governments abroad at $5,000 per plane. An additional two thousand were built before Washington stopped their production. Prices fell dramatically, and the Jenny became America's principal general aviation aircraft. New ones could be purchased for anywhere between $500 and $2,000, and a used one might go for only $100.[9]

Being a barnstormer was a definite social marker, with a few exceptions for some young men like Charles Lindbergh, the son of a congressman who barnstormed in various states prior to entering the U.S. Army Air Corps and airmail service. Most barnstormers did not come from affluent backgrounds, particularly those who were wing walkers and parachutists. They included sons and daughters of farmers, ranch hands, day laborers, auto mechanics, carpenters, and former waitresses. Most were young men in their late teens, twenties, and early thirties. When they had money, they slept in hotels or stayed with a local farmer in exchange for an airplane ride. When funding was tight, they would camp in the open air under the wings. Barnstormers tended not to be particularly concerned about where they slept, the type of food they ate, their clothing, or their social standing. What they had in common was a passion for flying and for the freedom to feel the wind in their faces.

Carrying passengers and performing aerial stunts required favorable weather. If weather looked good toward the east, barnstormers would travel east. If it looked better out west, they traveled west. For every great day of barnstorming, they might face a week of poor weather conditions. Some pilots charged half price ($2.50) rather than $5.00 for carrying passengers, which discouraged other barnstormers from traveling to certain areas to give rides. Indeed, the barnstormers' lifestyle was characterized by periods of boom and bust. Being under contract, members of successful flying circuses did rather well financially. But they had less freedom of movement because performers had to be at a certain place at a specific time for a performance. To avoid their being treated as "carnival people," often a local organization in a town sponsored them and would be in charge of selling and collecting tickets at the gate and handling the money.[10]

Ormer Locklear (1891–1920), "King of the Air"

In the 1920s and 1930s, wing walking was the ultimate extreme sport, and Lieutenant Ormer Locklear initiated the craze and set the standard for the sport in America.[11] His aerial stunts appear to have come about by accident. According to the *Fort Worth Telegram*,

Ormer Locklear seated in an open-cockpit biplane, circa 1919. Courtesy of the Ormer Locklear Collection, History of Aviation Collection, Special Collections Department, McDermott Library, the University of Texas at Dallas.

"Lock's stunts may have originally been borne out of necessity. While in flight, the aviator climbed over the front cockpit to replace a dangling radiator cap."[12] According to author Art Ronnie in *Locklear: The Man Who Walked on Wings* (1973), it was a loosened spark plug wire he had to fix. On a previous occasion Locklear had climbed out of the cockpit while testing pilots' ability to read large words on panels on the ground for the military.[13]

Locklear was born in Greenville, Como Hopkins County, Texas, on October 28, 1891, and moved to Fort Worth in 1906. He attended elementary and high school in Fort Worth. He worked for his father's construction company until 1914, when he and his brother opened an auto repair shop. Between 1917 and 1918, Locklear enlisted in the U.S. Army Air Service at Fort Sam Houston in San Antonio. On January 5, 1918, Locklear entered the University of Texas at Austin School of Military Aeronautics. Then he transferred to Camp Dick in Dallas. He attended gunnery school at nearby Taliaferro Field and served as a flight instructor at Barron Field.[14] On November 8, 1918, according to *The Billboard*, Locklear became the first person to transfer from one plane to another in midair. Locklear was a daredevil from a young age, often performing stunts on his Indian motorcycle. He dazzled audiences and initiated a nationwide craze for wing walking and daredevilry. To prevent slippage, Locklear used resin on his shoes to walk on wings. He changed planes as low as fifty feet off the ground, but the height of his midair transfers depended on the weather.

In 1919 Locklear resigned his military commission to fly in the commercial air show circuit. Universal Film Company hired him as a stunt pilot in Hollywood, California; he proved to be absolutely fearless. Besides midair transfers, he landed an airplane on top of the Sir Francis Drake Hotel in San Francisco, California, in 1919, according to Viola Gentry—herself an endurance record setter and later cura-

Ormer Locklear performing a mid-air transfer, circa 1920. Courtesy of the Ormer Locklear Collection, History of Aviation Collection, Special Collections Department, McDermott Library, the University of Texas at Dallas.

tor of the aviation collection at the University of Texas at Austin. At the height of his career, Locklear regularly earned a thousand dollars a day. Sometimes he earned as much as three thousand dollars for one half-hour performance. His salary far exceeded those of barnstormers because he had no problem actually leaping from plane to plane, having been largely inspired by pioneer aerial stunt performers Lincoln Beachey, Ruth Bancroft Law, and Katherine and Marjorie Stinson.[15] He had also been inspired by Calbraith P. Rodgers, who came to Fort Worth on October 18, 1911, during his transcontinental flight.

However Locklear's wing walking career may have started, it brought him instant fame and success. In 1919 he received a call to star in a Hollywood film, *The Great Air Robbery*. On July 26, 1919, Locklear made a successful transfer from an automobile to an airplane. He anticipated signing a contract with Fox Film Corporation to earn $1,650 a week, a considerable sum at the time.[16]

Locklear's career as a wing walker and Hollywood stunt pilot was absolutely brilliant, but short. On August 2, 1920, while filming *The Skywayman*, Locklear and his pilot perished in an airplane crash when they could not recover from a dive in time. On August 7, he was buried at Greenwood Cemetery at Fort Worth. More than fifty thousand people attended; it was one of the largest funerals in the history of Texas.

Elizabeth "Bessie" Coleman (1892–1926), First Female Licensed Pilot from Texas

Another Texan stimulated interest in aviation by performing as a parachutist and pilot at aerial exhibitions around the country during the early 1920s. Texas's first licensed female flyer and the first licensed pilot of color in the world was born Elizabeth Coleman in Atlanta, Texas, in 1892. Nicknamed Bessie, she grew up in the cotton fields of northeast Texas and would become one of the more notable barnstormers in the country.

She was the sixth of thirteen children born to Susan and George Coleman, four of whom did not survive childhood. Coleman's heritage has been identified as African American, but three of George Coleman's grandparents were full-blooded Native American, probably Choctaw or Cherokee.[17] Coleman grew up in a small three-room house, picked cotton, and took in laundry. She helped her illiterate mother by keeping account books of how much cotton her family picked. In 1901 her father left the family to return to the Indian reservation in Oklahoma.[18] Coleman's mother chose to remain on the plot of land they owned in Waxahachie, thirty miles south of Dallas.[19]

In 1915 Coleman joined her brother in Chicago, attended beautician school, and became a manicurist at a beauty shop for people of color. Coleman also operated a chili parlor.[20] She finished at least the eighth grade (high school, according to her sister) and attended one semester at the Langston Industrial College in Oklahoma. She also learned to speak and read French and was an avid reader.[21]

On December 30, 1916, Coleman married Claude Glenn.[22] Circumstances surrounding the marriage are unclear, because Coleman kept it a secret.[23] Scholars can only speculate on the nature of the relationship. Exactly how Coleman came to her desire to fly is also unclear, but she displayed a toy airplane made by a black child in the window of the White Sox Barber Shop where she manicured.

With the financial support of Robert Abbott, publisher and editor of a black newspaper, the *Chicago Defender*, Coleman traveled to France and enrolled in the École d'Aviation des Frères Caudron at Le Crotoy in the Somme. At first, Coleman tried to enroll in a school in Paris but was turned away because two female students had already lost their lives. At Le Crotoy, Coleman assumed all responsibility and risk in learning to fly.[24]

Coleman did not fit the profile of a potential pilot; she was not athletic like some women pilots of the time. Being the quickest manicurist in Chicago was not a skill associated with aviation. Coleman did, however, possess one important pilot-worthy trait: the willingness to take bold risks.

She was also highly resourceful. On her U.S. passport application, Coleman denied having ever been married, which was a criminal offense, and listed her birthdate as 1896, not 1892. Coleman, like other women of her era, may have lied about her age to appear younger in an attempt to bolster her career. Her readiness to falsify federal government documents suggests that she was rather bold or aggressive—not necessarily negative traits for an aviator—in comparison to the average person.[25] Coleman also possessed other important traits: ambition, desire to learn, and acceptance of the risks involved in flying.

On June 15, 1921, at age twenty-nine, Coleman became the first American pilot of color to receive an international private pilot certificate directly issued by the Fédération Aéronautique Internatio-

Elizabeth "Bessie" Coleman, first licensed woman aviator from Texas, standing on the wheel of a Curtiss JN-4 Jenny, circa 1922. NASM Archives Reference No. 92-13721. Courtesy of the National Air and Space Museum, Smithsonian Institution (SI 92-13721).

nale. She earned the certificate two years before Amelia Earhart was licensed to fly.[26] Her flying certificate notes her birth date as January 20, 1896; the incorrect year was most likely copied from her U.S. passport.[27] Coleman managed to deal with the dilemmas of gender, race, and ethnicity in America by traveling to what was then the center of world aviation.[28]

Influenced by French military aviators, Coleman donned a tailored military officer's uniform, which consisted of a long leather jacket, leather helmet, goggles, scarf, riding boots and jodhpurs, and shirt and tie. She was elegant and stylish in her military dress.

In September 1921, Coleman left France and traveled by ship to New York City, then to Chicago.[29] A newspaper reporter noted that she had ordered a Nieuport, but it never was delivered. In February 1922, she returned to France and then traveled to Germany where she received advanced flight training from Robert Thelen at Adlershof, near Berlin. According to the *New York Times*, Coleman claimed to have piloted some of the largest aircraft ever flown by women while she was in Europe, including a Dornier flying boat. She also visited Amsterdam, where she flew planes designed by Anthony Fokker.[30] Although some of her aerial adventures may have been embellishments, typical of that era's pilots, she clearly demonstrated a keen desire to improve her flying skills.

In late 1922, Coleman made parachute jumps and exhibition flights as a barnstormer in several states, including New York, Massachusetts, Illinois, Tennessee, Montana, Texas, California, and Florida, where she earned the nickname "Brave Bessie." According to the *New York Times*, Coleman was the only aviator of color in the world who performed exhibition flights "among her own people," meaning that she sometimes flew under conditions of segregation.[31]

In California, Coleman had her first serious accident while flying for the Coast Tire and Rubber Company of Oakland. During an exhibition flight at the opening of a new fairground at Palomar Park in Los Angeles, she had a departure stall at three hundred feet. She suffered lacerations to her face, fractured three ribs, and sustained a double fracture to her left leg. She spent nearly three months in the hospital and took off nearly a year to recover from her injuries. Despite the accident, she got back into flying. Coleman explained that "I like flying and I am going into the business, I shall start a pilot's school in Chicago."[32] She also sought to make exhibition flights in the United States so that "people of her race," according to *Aerial Age Weekly*, would take up flying.[33]

On April 30, 1926, Coleman went for a maintenance test flight with her mechanic, twenty-four-year-old Texan William D. Willis, at Jacksonville, Florida. Suddenly the airplane nosedived. It flipped over and Coleman fell out. The airplane then crashed to the ground, killing the young mechanic. The normally safety-conscious Coleman was not wearing her parachute that day. Had she been, she probably would have survived. It was later determined that the controls jammed on the aircraft due to a misplaced wrench. After only a few seasons performing with an air show, both as a pilot and a parachutist, Bessie Coleman met death at age thirty-four. But she left a legacy of tremendous determination that continues to inspire aviators and astronauts to this day.

Grace McClelland, Barnstormer and Owner of a Flying Service in Austin

On October 15, 1928, Mrs. Grace M. McClelland earned her private pilot license in Austin. After four and a half hours of instruction from a local flyer, Matt Wilson, she made her solo flight. Being an expert marksman and aerial performer, she combined the two skills to make her specialty wing walking while shooting helium balloons as they were released from the ground. She performed in Germany, France, and Italy. After returning to Austin, she owned and operated Austin Air Service. A newsreel of the Texas Air Meet on September 8, 1927, demonstrates her outstanding ability to walk on wings as well as her expert marksmanship. The champion pistol shooter was not petite and slender like many women wing walkers of her era. She was tall, strong, and robust. Grace McClelland made a living by blurring the lines between the genders and seeking to be employed in what were then considered male pursuits. After her first husband passed away, she married Russell Riggs, an American Airways pilot who "thought one pilot in the family was enough." To please her second husband, she stopped flying. Ironically, Riggs perished in an airplane crash in 1934.

Jean LaRene (1901–1960) and the Lou Foote Flying Service, Love Field

Jean LaRene, born in Kansas City, Missouri, on December 31, 1901, was a flight instructor, co-owner (with her spouse, Lou Foote), and operator of the Lou Foote Flying Service in Dallas in the mid-1930s. In 1928 LaRene learned to fly at the Municipal Airport in Chicago. LaRene was then a private secretary to a Chicago businessman, who lent her money for lessons when she confided her desire to fly. She earned her transport license, aviation's highest rating, on October 1, 1929, while employed by the Command-Aire factory at Little Rock, Arkansas. She demonstrated airplanes for the American Eagle Aircraft Corporation in Kansas City, meaning she took potential buyers for rides and sold aircraft. In *The Fun of It* (1932), Amelia Earhart described LaRene as "one of the best known southern flyers, secretary of an aviation school," someone who gets in a considerable amount of flying just by being on hand.[34]

In 1930 LaRene became a secretary and flight instructor for the American Eagle Aircraft Corporation's flight school at Love Field, where she was in charge of all women students. While working for the Dallas Aviation School, LaRene took up passengers for cross-country flights—particularly on Sundays, when there were always large crowds

Lou and Jean LaRene Foote, Dallas, circa 1930. Courtesy of the Pioneer Flight Museum, Kingsbury, Texas.

at Love Field. She also placed third in the second women's air derby in 1930. During the 1932 women's derby, she made a forced landing north of Abilene and had to walk seven miles before she came upon a house. Abilene was still eleven miles away.

In June 1935 she began working for the Lou Foote Flying Service at Love Field. She did nothing but fly every day. She helped Foote, her future husband, run their flight school and fixed base operation, Lou Foote Flying Service. She became a competent airplane mechanic. LaRene distinguished herself from other pilots by wearing high heels with her white mechanic's overalls, which challenged gender norms. Her shoes served as a gentle reminder of her femininity. Together the

Jean LaRene Foote, pioneer woman pilot and airplane mechanic, Dallas, circa 1935. Courtesy of Thomas D. Gaylord, Pioneer Flight Museum, Kingsbury, Texas.

flying couple repaired and refueled aircraft, besides giving flight instruction and tours in the Dallas area.

A charter member of the Ninety-Nines, the first international organization of women pilots, LaRene served as the first governor of the South Central Section from 1931 to 1933. By 1938, she had 1,472 flying hours, more than most women aviators in the country, according to a feature in *Look* magazine. She and her husband trained Army and Navy cadets until a fire destroyed fourteen planes at their two hangars in September 1942. LaRene passed away in 1960.[35]

Browning Aerial Flying Service, Austin

Emma Carter Browning, Texas pioneer woman flyer and cofounder of Browning Aerial Flying Service in Austin, was born in Eastland, Texas, on October 26, 1910. She met her husband, pilot Robert Browning, Jr., in Abilene through a friend. There the couple established a flying service, or fixed base operation, which was one of the few ways other than barnstorming to make money in aviation. They provided general aviation services and sold flight training, aircraft, aircraft maintenance, aircraft parking, and fuel. In 1939 the couple came to Austin, where Robert taught Emma how to fly. She made her solo flight on a Taylorcraft biplane in the days of helmets and goggles. They trained pilots under the Civilian Pilot Training Program. In 1939 and 1940, Emma studied aviation and graduated in the second noncollege pilot training program sponsored by the Austin Chamber of Commerce.

In a favorite memory, Emma recalled how Amelia Earhart crashed a Pitcairn Autogiro at Abilene Airport in mid-June 1931 by running into three cars on takeoff during her national tour while traveling with a mechanic. Earhart was cited for being reckless but defended herself in *The Fun of It* (1932) by stating that she regretted any kind of accident, having done considerable damage to her ship. She thought

Graduates of the Second Noncollege Pilots Training School, Austin, 1939 and 1940. Emma Carter Browning is on the left, wearing a turban. Courtesy of the Austin History Center, Austin Public Library.

women pilots were penalized in that their accidents, even minor ones, were played up more in the newspapers than those of male pilots.[36] Emma's impression of Earhart was that she was friendly and outgoing but still somewhat reserved. Earhart had earned her transport license in Brownsville in 1929 but still needed more flight training, in Emma's view.

In 1946 the Brownings set up a fixed base operation at Robert Mueller Municipal Airport in Austin. Emma helped her spouse build Browning Aerial Flying Service from the ground up. When he passed in 1973, she took over its management. The operation occupied twenty-two acres with a one-hundred-thousand-square-foot hangar, thirteen airplanes, and forty employees. She oversaw Browning Aerial Services until August 1987 when she sold her interest. Seventy years earlier, equally important, she had helped found the National Air Transport Association, which represents the business interests of general aviation.

Emma left a legacy of independence, success, and an entrepreneurial spirit. She was an outstanding role model for women in business and aviation. Her love of, and dedication to, the aviation industry was recognized in 2005 when she was inducted into the Texas Aviation Hall of Fame at the Lone Star Flight Museum in Galveston.

BARNSTORMERS AND EARLY OPERATORS OF FLYing services helped to introduce the airplane to many Texans. Some entertained crowds across America and in foreign lands. Those aviators who began flying as barnstormers frequently went on to other aviation careers, becoming flight instructors, mechanics, and operators of flying services. A rare few went on to become prominent national figures as record setters, wing walkers, and Hollywood stunt pilots. Wing walkers and parachutists who performed in Texas noted that the federal government stepped in to try to run the flying circuses out of business in the mid-1920s and 1930s. The government wanted to promote air safety beginning with the Air Commerce Act of 1926; it did not want "daredevil pilots and aerial acrobats doing crazy stunts to thrill the crowds."[37] The days of barnstormers and flying circuses were numbered. As aviation, especially the airlines, grew as an industry, it required a reputation for safety. Crowds of people would flock instead to airports and airfields to see their aviation heroes, the record-setting pilots and air racers.

Chapter 4

Record Setters and Air Racers

*T*HE SETTING OF AVIATION RECORDS, INCLUDING world firsts, had definite promotional value that could lead to instant fame and fortune on a personal level and serve as a source of civic and national pride. Aviators occasionally named their aircraft after cities that sponsored their record-setting flights, such as Charles Lindbergh's *Spirit of St. Louis* and William Erwin's *Dallas Spirit*. There have been claims of scientific value associated with the setting of certain aviation records and exploring remote locations, but more often than not, there were none; if any experiments were performed, the general public quickly forgot them. For those rare individuals who persevered and took great risks to set aviation records, the rewards could be substantial. Yet record setters tended to be motivated more by their desire for fame, rather than pure financial gain. Record setters, more than anything else, appeared to enjoy the limelight—with some notable exceptions. Aviation generally was the preserve of the very rich, but some aviators from modest backgrounds managed to set prominent world records despite financial constraints or physical limitations.

Since the early days of powered flight, there have been official and unofficial aviation records. Established in 1905, the Fédération Aéronautique Internationale (FAI) was the international governing body for official aviation records; the Aero Club of America served as its affiliate in the United States until 1922 when the National Aeronautic Association (NAA) was founded. Aviation records depended on the type of aircraft in a specific category (engine type and size). There were records for altitude, maximum speed over a straight course, distance speed records between two points, and endurance flying—remaining aloft in a closed circuit. There were aerobatic records for consecutive inside and outside loops. Some were a measure of human endurance, courage, and pure daredevilry. Official records were monitored by members of the FAI and NAA.

Aviation records that represented world firsts were not officially sanctioned by the FAI and the NAA, but they still received attention. Some of these world firsts, such as the crossings of the Atlantic as a passenger and as a solo pilot, had far greater significance for the aviation community and the general public than did many records in the books created by the FAI. Pioneer fliers may have intended to go after aviation records set by other pilots, but more often than not they would quit as soon as they exceeded the record and got the public's attention. Often their equipment quit before they did.

After Lindbergh's transatlantic flight in 1927, aviation became so popular that there were even unofficial world firsts for passengers. Amelia Earhart gained overnight fame as a passenger on the *Friendship*, a trimotor Fokker seaplane with pilot Wilmer Stultz and mechanic Louis Gordon. After flying across the Atlantic twenty hours and forty minutes from Trepassey, Newfoundland, they landed safely at Burry Port, Wales on June 17, 1928. In 1928 Clara Adams became the first U.S. woman to fly across the Atlantic as a passenger in the lighter-than-air craft the *Graf Zeppelin* (LZ-127), from the United States to Germany in seventy-one hours.[1] The *Graf Zeppelin* passed over El Paso during its world flight in 1929, but Adams was not a passenger on this, the only world flight made in a dirigible.

Lindbergh's solo flight from New York to Paris in 1927 sparked tremendous interest in aviation, especially in setting new records across the oceans and across continents. On August 27, 1927, some seventy-five thousand people showed up at Dallas's Love Field to greet the world's most famous aviator during his nationwide tour.[2] Other aviators soon emulated Lindbergh by attempting transatlantic flight or other transoceanic records and races, such as that undertaken by Captain William Erwin (see chapter 2) in which he lost his life trying to save others. In the process of flying in air races and other events, many discovered their own niches—whether setting distance records, competing in closed-course pylon racing around tall towers or gates, or attempting altitude, speed, or endurance records. Those who became headliners in air racing and record setting recognized the constant need for publicity. Even those who were well connected and moderately affluent knew they needed to have their names in the public realm in order to get sponsorships and access to the fastest and best-equipped airplanes from the leading designers and manufacturers. Those without such financial means struggled to make a name for themselves.

Wiley Post (1898–1935) and His Many Firsts

Wiley Post allowed neither the loss of an eye nor financial constraints to stand in the way of his becoming a highly accomplished aviator and designer of the first pressurized flight suit. Post was born in Grand Saline in Van Zandt County, Texas, on November 22, 1898, the fourth son of farmers and proud of being part Cherokee. Post's youth was characterized by frequent relocations, little formal education, and no lasting friendships. Although born in Texas, Post considered himself more of an Oklahoman than a Texan. His accomplishments still inspired many Texas aviators, however, and he had relatives in the Lone Star State.

Post was fascinated by mechanical devices. He displayed his skill by repairing his father's farm machinery. At eleven, he decided that he had enough of grade schools. He saved enough money with his father's help to attend the Sweeney Automobile and Aviation School in Kansas City. Post took odd jobs and worked late into the night before going home to study for the next day's assignments. Often he went to bed hungry. He became an excellent student who never missed a lecture. His favorite subjects were physics, mathematics, and chemistry. When asked if he intended to work on machines in the future, Post responded that he intended to have machines work for him.

Post had a criminal past that few people knew about. At twenty-two in 1921, he was arrested for committing highway robbery outside Grady County, Oklahoma. Four eyewitnesses testified against him. Lack of employment or funds was no defense, since Post could have returned to work on his family's farm. With that crime, Post disgraced himself. He received a ten-year sentence but was paroled in 1922 after one year in prison. On December 27, 1934, Governor William Murray granted Post a full pardon. By then, he had become famous around the world and admired by many.

On being released from prison, Post went to work in the oil fields. While he was at work on a drilling job in eastern Oklahoma, an airplane passed by overhead. From then on, Post was determined to have a career in aviation. It began with a traveling flying circus. For his first parachute jump, he stepped off the plane as though taking his first step out of bed; he was a fearless, natural flyer. His only instruction was to pull the cord. Post made over one hundred jumps and only had one mishap, in which he was dragged by a mule that had gotten tangled in his parachute. He earned as much as $200 per jump, a considerable sum given that he often paid a pilot $25 for taking him up. Between parachuting for flying circuses, Post took flying lessons. In 1926 Post soloed after less than four hours of instruction.[3]

On October 1, 1926, Post began a new job for an oil-drilling company. On the first day, a metal chip flew off and struck his left eye. Infection set in; the eye had to be removed. He received nearly $1,700 in compensation. To continue to fly, Post learned to make up for his loss of depth perception by looking at trees, telephone poles, and other objects near landing fields. He purchased a damaged Canuck, the Curtiss JN-4 Canadian Jenny, for $240. Then he spent an additional $300 to have it rebuilt. He took some additional flying lessons. At age twenty-eight, he was all set to make a living in aviation when he visited family in Sweetwater, Texas, and ended up marrying his seventeen-year-old first cousin Mae.

On September 16, 1928, Post acquired enough flying hours to receive a transport license. Soon after, he began flying for a wealthy oilman, F. C. Hall, who shared his enthusiasm for aviation. Hall purchased a Lockheed Vega, the most advanced design at that time, and named the airplane after his daughter, *Winnie Mae*. Hall encouraged Post to use his airplane whenever Hall did not need it.

In 1929 Post piloted the official Lockheed Vega for the National Exchange Club, a service organization that sponsored the First Transcontinental Women's Air Derby from Santa Monica, California, to Cleveland, Ohio. The race crossed Texas on its fifth day, August 22. In 1930 Post entered the most prestigious cross-country air race, the Men's Air Derby from Los Angeles to Chicago. He earned $7,500 for winning first place.

Post attempted to set a new speed record for around-the-world flight in 1931 with navigator Harold Gatty of Tasmania. Post took off on June 23, 1931, completing his route near the top of the world in eight days, fifteen hours, and fifty-one minutes. Post then decided to make the first solo flight around the world and shorten the record even more to demonstrate convincingly that he was the pilot during the

Wiley Post and his Lockheed Vega 5C *Winnie Mae* following the first solo around-the-world flight, July 22, 1933. Courtesy of Women Airforce Service Pilots member Ruth Shafer Fleisher.

world flight and fully capable of flying around the world solo. Post was heavily bothered by Gatty's remark that Post was "just" the driver and that Gatty was the brains of the team and did all the work. On July 15, 1933, Post took off in the *Winnie Mae*, aided by two new instruments that needed flight testing: a Sperry autopilot he dubbed "Mechanical Mike" and a radio direction finder. He completed his solo round-the-world flight in seven days, eighteen hours, and forty-nine minutes, besting his earlier record by twenty-one hours. Post had demonstrated that long-distance flight was no longer a mere possibility but a reality. The Fédération Aéronautique Internationale awarded him a Gold Medal for completing the first solo world flight.

Post next sought to establish a new high-altitude record by attempting to fly higher than forty-seven thousand, three hundred feet, into the stratosphere. Post designed the first successful pressurized flight suit for the amount of $75 in April 1934, with the help of engineers from B. F. Goodrich in Los Angeles. The first tests of the pres-

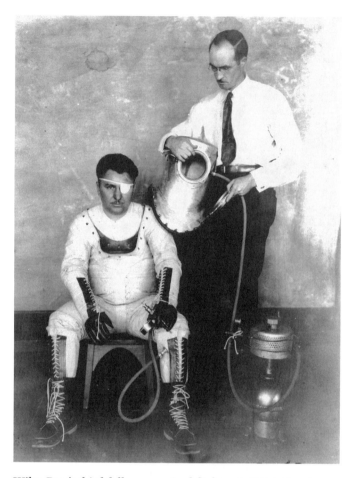

Wiley Post's third fully pressurized flight suit, 1934. Courtesy of the Edward H. White II Memorial Museum, San Antonio, U.S. Air Force.

sure suit showed not only major leakage of vaporized liquid oxygen but also an inability to hold pressure. Post could not take off in the second one. The third one had an inner suit made of rubber, which fit the contours of his body. Post had intended to enter and win the MacRobertson Race from England to Australia by traveling at high altitude in a pressure suit. Instead, Post tested his third space suit on September 5, 1934, attaining some forty thousand feet over Chicago. The suit worked well with some adjustments. He took off again on December 7, 1934, reaching his goal of some fifty thousand feet; unfortunately, his second barometer froze at thirty-five thousand feet, so the National Aeronautic Association could not certify his altitude record. But Post had designed and tested the first successful pressurized suit in the world. The ability to move is a key element in its design. Post had joints at the knees and elbows.

In 1935 Post and his friend, humorist and aviation enthusiast Will Rogers, flew to Alaska. Post added pontoons that were longer than the ones he had ordered to an airplane; the floats made its nose too heavy. Headed for Point Barrow, Post crashed on takeoff on August 15, 1935, killing both himself and Rogers. He was one of the great aviation pioneers of the early twentieth century; his development of the first successful space suit was a remarkable achievement.[4]

Dallas Features in More Historic Firsts

An estimated crowd of twenty to twenty-five thousand persons greeted French aviators Dieudonné Costes and Maurice Bellonte at Dallas's Love Field on September 4, 1930. Costes and Bellonte had departed Le Bourget Field in Paris on September 1. After thirty-seven hours and nineteen minutes, they arrived at Curtiss Field, Long Island, New York, on September 2, completing the first east-to-west crossing of the Atlantic Ocean from Paris to New York City. According to Costes, the success of the flight "was not due to heroism or courage, but radio, motor, and study."[5]

After enjoying a ticker-tape parade in New York City, the two Frenchmen headed for Texas to make a bid for the $25,000 Paris-New York-Dallas prize offered by Colonel William E. Easterwood, Jr., of Dallas. Easterwood inherited his vast wealth from his father, a banker who made a fortune from the sale of Orbit gum to Wrigley. While touring Europe with his wife, Easterwood met Costes and Bellonte and offered them $25,000 if they would continue their Paris-to-New York flight on to Dallas. His intention was to bring Dallas into the fold of the world of aviation, not unlike the businessmen from St. Louis who backed Lindbergh and the record-setting flight of the *Spirit of St. Louis*.

Costes and Bellonte flew a red Breguet XIX sesquiplane called *Point d'Interrogation* (*Question Mark*). It had a 650-horsepower

French aviators Dieudonné Costes and Maurice Bellonte, who flew the first nonstop flight from Paris to New York to Dallas, having flown across the Atlantic in a record-setting flight, 1930. Courtesy of the Musée de l'Air et de l'Espace, Paris.

Dallas crowds meeting the *Question Mark*, first airplane to fly from Paris to New York to Dallas, 1930. Courtesy of the Dallas Public Library.

Hispano-Suiza engine and a radio. After crossing the Atlantic, the uneventful flight to Dallas took eleven hours and twenty-seven minutes. The Easterwood prize brought Dallas into an aerial competition and incidental fame. Love Field received front-page coverage on nearly every major newspaper in the United States.

Douglas "Wrong Way" Corrigan (1907–1995), Transatlantic Flyer

Although crossing the Atlantic from New York to Ireland was not a record of any sort by 1938, Galveston native Douglas Corrigan gained national attention by defying federal authorities and doing so. Corrigan applied for government permission to fly his 1929 Curtiss Robin airplane across the Atlantic, but his request was denied; he was only permitted to fly across the United States from New York back to California. Corrigan lacked the financial backing of other long distance record-setting aviators such as Earhart, Lindbergh, and Howard Hughes, which endeared him to the common person even more. He also lacked connections in the Civil Aeronautics Authority of the time. Having had enough of the bureaucracy, Corrigan, an airplane mechanic, took matters into his own hands.

Born in Galveston on January 22, 1907, Corrigan worked as an airplane mechanic on Lindbergh's experimental *Spirit of St. Louis* in San Diego for airplane manufacturers T. C. Ryan and B. P. Mahoney in the spring of 1927. There, he was inspired by Lindbergh's example. In 1935 the Civil Aeronautics Authority (forerunner of the Federal Aviation Administration) issued him an airworthiness certificate equivalent to a ferry permit for a transcontinental record, because the authority agreed with reporters who described his 1929 Curtiss Robin as a "crate." Corrigan intentionally flew across the Atlantic in the opposite direction because he wanted to. "Wrong Way Corrigan" was the name he earned for defying federal authorities.

Corrigan "mistakenly" flew from New York to Ireland—when he was supposed to be flying from New York to California—because he claimed to have misread his compass. For Americans in the midst of the Great Depression, Corrigan's antic provided a great deal of humor and uplift. He became a national celebrity, a folk hero. In 1939 Hollywood even made a film about his life, *The Flying Irishman*, in which

Douglas Corrigan in a parade at the National Air Races, September 3, 1938.
Courtesy of the Western Reserve Historical Society, Cleveland, Ohio.

Corrigan starred as himself. Corrigan's nickname remained a stock colloquial phrase in popular culture for several decades.

As much fun as Corrigan's incident provides, many people do not understand all the complexities of his flight, nor do they appreciate the fact that he was a sound and accomplished pilot, besides being an experienced mechanic. Flying solo across the Atlantic was no simple feat. It took great courage, though Corrigan never admitted to having committed anything other than a navigational error.

Edna Gardner Whyte (1902–1992):
Air Racer, Flight Instructor, Airport Owner, and
Operator of Aero Valley Flying School Near Dallas

Edna Gardner was in the grandstands at the National Air Races in Cleveland, Ohio, enviously watching Florence Klingensmith, Mary Haizlip, Phoebe Omlie, and Gladys O'Donnell compete in the free-for-all women's pylon race (a closed-circuit competition flown around tall towers or gates), when she caught racing fever. She soloed in 1931 and then sought out her flight instructor's help to become a competitive racer.[6] While working as a registered nurse, having recently learned to fly, she read a poster about a pylon race with a $300 prize plus a trophy. She entered and won against a field of male pilots. Disappointed that a woman had won, the male pilots posted a notice the following year declaring their race to be for "men only." Edna Gardner went on to make her own mark in air racing. In 1933 she won the Kate Smith Trophy in the National Charity Air Pageant in New Orleans named in honor of the famous singer. Gardner competed in the 1934 local air meet on Long Island against twelve other women over a ten-mile closed course and won the $500 prize, following a two-hour dispute over the outcome of the race. No one had informed the contestants that only three laps were required to win, not the four laps that eleven of them flew. From then on, Gardner was a frequent victor at air meets. In 1934 she won the women's feature race at Dayton, Ohio, and earned $1,000.[7] She later won the women's handicap race at the All American Air Maneuvers of 1935 and 1939.[8]

Being such a competent pilot, Gardner applied for several airline

Edna Gardner, circa 1930. Courtesy of the *Fort Worth Star-Telegram* Collection, Special Collections, the University of Texas at Arlington Library, Arlington, Texas.

pilot jobs beginning in the mid-to-late 1930s. Central Airlines turned her down on one occasion for being too short, when she was the same height as one of her male flight students and a half-inch taller than another pilot whom they had just hired. In 1940, Braniff Airlines rejected her application on this basis: "Do you really think that people would climb aboard our airlines, if they saw a woman pilot in the cockpit?"[9] Gardner felt that women pilots, herself included, had a difficult time in aviation because of the "men-only attitude."[10] She observed that ". . . men resented her treading into a male domain . . . they felt she was stealing some of their glory."[11] As a flight instructor to numerous airline pilots, she resented not having the same opportunity to fly for the airlines. Gardner encountered the prejudice that dictated that men were the only legitimate breadwinners working for the airlines as pilots. Women's primary functions back then included "home and family, and cooking, dishes, and household chores,"[12] not flying commercially for the airlines.

With the outbreak of World War II, Gardner was chief instructor of her own flying school in New Orleans, the New Orleans Air College. She then joined the U.S. Navy War Training Service at the Southwest College of Aeronautics, Meacham Field, in Fort Worth, Texas, where she taught U.S. Army Air Corps personnel. She instructed some 225 graduates, some of whom flew for the Royal Air Force, Royal Canadian Air Force, U.S. Navy, and Army Air Corps.[13] Flight instructor Ernest Clark admired how Gardner taught pilots how to fly. She later served with the U.S. Army Nurse Corps in the Philippines. In August 1946 Edna Gardner married flight instructor and airplane mechanic George Murphy Whyte following a whirlwind courtship. Their first home was in Fort Worth. This was her second marriage; her first, to former U.S. marine Ray Kidd, had ended in divorce when Kidd got another woman pregnant.[14] By the mid-1950s, she had accumulated twelve thousand flying hours and earned twenty-six racing trophies.[15]

In 1970, she opened her own field, Aero Valley Airport, in Roanoke, Texas, close to Dallas.[16] It grew from a mobile home and former cotton field to more than one hundred businesses, numerous airplane hangars, a restaurant and office buildings, and many aircraft. She sold her interest in 1980. By 1978, she had taught more than four thousand students to fly. She kept teaching until she lost her medical certificate at age eighty-seven. Some of the students she taught were the grandchildren of her earlier students.

Vera Dawn Walker (1897–1978?), Air Racer in the First Transcontinental Women's Air Derby, 1929

Vera Dawn Walker had a West Texas cattle ranching up-bringing. She was of a modest background by comparison to some women aviators between the world wars. She earned her own way to pay for lessons by working as a stand-in and movie extra, mainly riding horses, for Hollywood pictures. Walker was born on February 3, 1897, in a small town named Robert Lee near Abilene.[17] In the early 1920s she traveled by automobile with one of her brothers to California, where the two worked as extras. During the making of *The Purple Sage*, she was introduced to aviation as a passenger on a one-dollar flight at Rogers Airport, a dirt strip in Los Angeles. She then learned to fly at the Standard Flying School in the fall of 1928. She would take twenty-minute lessons while working in real estate and making films. Walker soloed on December 28, 1928. She earned her private pilot's certificate on January 1, 1929. The nonprofit service organization National Exchange Club helped Walker find an experimental airplane, a Timm, to get enough hours and experience flying cross-country in order to qualify for the women's air derby. The club raised substantial prize money and hosted banquets along the derby route from Santa Monica, California, to Cleveland, Ohio. With the help of friends, she acquired a Curtiss Robin with a Challenger engine in time. Even so, her airplane developed a problem with its oil pump.[18] On August 22, 1925, day five of the women's derby, the contestants remaining in the race flew from El Paso to Pecos to Midland to Abilene and Fort Worth. A flock of Walker's relatives greeted her enthusiastically in her hometown, Abilene.[19] Walker explained that she came in tenth in the DW class (the class for heavier airplanes) because in Cincinnati she had no one to hand prop her Curtiss Robin.[20] After about an hour, she managed to start her own plane to get to Cleveland.[21] She was one of fourteen to reach Cleveland out of the original field of twenty aviatrixes.

Walker was among the few pioneering women pilots who flew on inaugural flights as copilots for the airlines for publicity purposes. She flew on the initial flight of Pickwick Airlines between San Francisco and Los Angeles on May 12, 1929, in a six-passenger Bach Trimotor christened *Glenn Curtiss*.[22]

She competed in the 1930 Women's Air Derby held in Chicago, but her plane developed engine trouble. She then flew cargo from Kansas

City to Guatemala in a Stinson cabin plane, always accompanied either by a young male copilot or a mechanic. In 1931 she contracted tuberculosis and gave up flying. She resided outside Phoenix until reaching age eighty-one, when she passed away after losing a battle with leukemia.

Frances Harrell Marsalis (1904–1934), Air Racer and Endurance Record Setter

One of the founders of the Ninety-Nines, an international organization of licensed women pilots, was Frances Harrell Marsalis. On October 9, 1929, she and fellow female pilots Neva Paris, Margery Brown, and Fay Gillis signed a joint letter of invitation to all 117 licensed women pilots at the time in the United States. Within a month, twenty-six women gathered at Curtiss Airport, Valley Stream, Long Island, New York, to form the first national organization of licensed women pilots. The group had to select a name. Suggestions ranged from Homing Pigeons, Gadflies, Climbing Vines, Noisy Birdwomen (to mock the male pilots' social club, the Quiet Birdmen), to the dignified National Association of Women Pilots. Amelia Earhart suggested that the organization be named for the sum total of charter members. The group adopted this idea unanimously.[23]

Marsalis was born in Del Rio, Texas, on December 26, 1904. Her father, William Harrell, was a rancher. Her mother, Ida Mae Cartier, was a homemaker. She attended elementary and high school all over Texas, graduating from El Paso High School. She attended Texas Christian College (now Texas Christian University) but did not finish. She worked for a short time as the credit manager of a furniture store in Houston. On her twenty-third birthday, she came into some money and used it to travel to New York. In November 1928 she began taking flying instruction at the Curtiss School at Minneola, New York. She made her first solo flight after eleven hours of instruction. On December 21, 1929, she married Lieutenant William Marsalis, her flight instructor at Curtiss Field, who later became an airline pilot.

In September 1929, Frances Harrell Marsalis set a new women's world record of twenty-two inside loops at Roosevelt Field in New York. In March 1930 she earned transport license number 7366, then aviation's highest rating. She joined the Curtiss-Wright exhibition team, traveled south to Miami, and performed in Cuba. She flew all types of Curtiss-Wright aircraft, including the Travel Air Mystery Ship.

She was considered an outstanding pilot by her peers, regardless of their gender. As a demonstration pilot, she flew some of the fastest aircraft in the world. She adored air racing. During the National Air Races at Cleveland, she explained that "You know whether I won anything or not, I had a good time flying that race."[24] Her in-depth knowledge of different types of aircraft served her well as an airplane demonstrator and salesperson. She worked in sales at Curtiss Wright Flying Service at Roosevelt Field from August 1929 to March 1930. She demonstrated and sold aircraft for Gypsy Moth, Cessna, Travel Air, Curtiss Fledgling, Thrushes and Birds, and Waco.[25] Between sales she instructed student pilots, ferried aircraft, and made two notable endurance record flights with Helen Richey and Louise Thaden, as well as racing in national and local meets.

Yet despite her training and experience, Frances Harrell Marsalis crashed her Waco aircraft at the finish line of the fifty-mile feature closed-circuit pylon race at the Women's National Air Derby at Vandalia on August 5, 1934. The exact cause of her accident is unclear, but the description of it by her friend Louise Thaden suggests that she died as a result of a piloting error. She was attempting to pass across and under another airplane while turning a pylon when her aircraft hit the propeller wash of the one ahead. It slipped into the ground without coming out of the turn at an estimated 130 miles per hour. Her airplane was a mass of splinters.[26] Marsalis liked to fly more than anything else and fulfilled her intention to fly all her life. She died at age thirty.

One of the leading factors that may have contributed to her death was her emotional state. She had been divorced only the week before. She may have been distracted as she was about to cross the finish line. Her friend Helen Richey, unaware of her accident, went on to win the race. Marsalis's death most likely reinforced the male pilots' and air racing officials' earlier decision that year to ban women from participating in the 1934 National Air Races.

Marsalis's death after a short but active career in aviation caused a great deal of sorrow among her fellow fliers, including women pilots Ruth Nichols, Elinor Smith, Amelia Earhart, Annette Gibson, Viola Gentry, Laura Ingalls, Margaret Cooper, and Louise Thaden, who all came to New York for her funeral.[27] Thaden recalled how her "coffin was not open at the funeral, so broken was she."[28] Thaden consoled herself and others by writing that "I know Frances never knew what happened. She must have gone painlessly, without having to face the realization that life on earth was no longer hers."[29] Thaden could not help but think about what Marsalis might have missed in life. Thaden recalled that Marsalis had repeated to her several times: "When my time comes, I hope it's in a plane where I can crack-up in one grand splurge, engine wide open. It's a sissy wish to want to die that way, but I don't want to lie on a bed for weeks or months suffering, knowing I would never be well."[30] Aviators, especially those who competed at the national level in air racing, frequently expressed fatalistic attitudes, knowing well that they could die as a result of an airplane crash. Emergency landings, accidents, and fatalities were common occurrences.

Howard Hughes (1905–1976):
Aviator, Airplane Designer, Filmmaker,
and Major Stockholder of Trans World Airlines

Howard Hughes was one of the most prominent and significant figures in the history of aviation from Texas during the twentieth century. His impact on aviation history went far beyond Texas's borders. Along with fellow Texan Wiley Post and several other aviators, Hughes set some of the most important records during the 1930s, as well as making notable contributions to technological developments during World War II and to the avionics industry in the postwar era. Hughes started out with wealth and could have lived a life of ease, but he put his ingenuity and money to work in diversified fields, including aviation, avionics, scientific invention, industrial development, and motion pictures.

Hughes's father, Howard Robard Hughes, was an inventor. The younger Hughes took his first airplane ride at age fourteen in 1920 while a student at Fessenden, an exclusive private school in Newton, Massachusetts. Hughes had also been educated at Thacher School in Ojai, California. After his father denied him a motorcycle, teenage Hughes showed his inventiveness by designing an electric bicycle. By the time he turned nineteen, both his parents had passed away. He took over the management—and later, sole ownership—of Hughes Tool Company in Houston. At nineteen, he also married a grade school acquaintance, Ella Rice, whose family had founded Rice University.

In 1925 Hughes took his first flight lessons from J. B. Alexander. He earned his pilot license on November 20, 1927. He then set out to make a film, *Hell's Angels*, based on the subject he was so passionate about: aviation. The film depicted the lives of Royal Air Force Pilots who defended London during the terrifying Zeppelin raids of World War I. Written, directed, and produced by the twenty-two-year-old aviator, *Hell's Angels* involved shooting three million feet of film (of which one percent was used) and spending nearly $4 million. In the end, the film reportedly brought in over $8 million.[31] In 1930 Hughes also acquired a large financial interest in Art Cinema Finance Corporation, a unit of United Artists; the percentage was not disclosed.[32]

A few months following the film's release, Hughes put in an order for his own Boeing 100A, a two-seat, open-cockpit airplane, the civilian equivalent of the U.S. Army Air Corps's P-12B and the Navy's F-4Bs. Hughes took his plane to Lockheed at Union Air Terminal in Burbank, California, for modification to increase its performance. He added a 450-horsepower Pratt and Whitney engine. Hughes spent much of his time making modifications to aircraft. Bored with being left alone in California, away from her friends and family, Ella Rice filed for divorce and returned to Houston.

In 1933 Hughes had his engineers design a number of notable aircraft, including the H-1 Racer. The H-1 would be the most meticulously built aircraft of the golden age of flight (1919–1939), with its flawlessly smooth surfaces and innovative streamlined design. The sleek airplane was ahead of its time; its notable innovations include flush riveting, power-driven retractable landing gear, jet-thrust exhaust, a bell-shaped cowling, air intakes on the leading edges of the wings, and drooping ailerons. The airplane convinced the U.S. military to consider the value of monoplanes as pursuit aircraft.

In 1935 Hughes set a landplane world speed record of 352 miles per hour in his H-1 Racer, breaking the established record by thirty-eight miles per hour. Hughes wanted to make one more pass but his engine died due to fuel starvation. He tried to switch to an auxiliary tank but it was too late to get the engine started. He successfully landed the racer, with landing gear up, in a beet field in Santa Ana. Hughes had intended to enter the 1936 Thompson race but decided in favor of another record attempt. In 1936 he set a new transcontinental speed record of nine hours, twenty-seven minutes, and ten seconds.[33] In 1937 he piloted the H-1 on yet another record-breaking transcontinental flight in seven hours and twenty-eight minutes, an average

Howard Hughes in his H-1 Racer, circa 1935. Courtesy of
Ernest Sanborn, Vice President, Florida Air Museum, Lakeland, Florida.

of 327.1 miles per hour. This record stood until 1946. Having flown it
some forty hours, Hughes retired his racer to a humidity-controlled
hangar at the Hughes Aircraft Company in California.

In 1937 Hughes came up with the specifications for the first mockup model of the Constellation, one of the fastest transport airplanes
to come into commercial use. To ensure that his design was well built,
Hughes contracted with Lockheed to build nine Constellations for
TWA (then Transcontinental & Western Air Inc., later Trans World
Airlines) in 1939 and later amended the contract to order forty at a cost
of approximately $20 million. He gave his personal financial guaran-
tee for the purchase price. Hughes turned over the first nine Constellations immediately to the Army Air Corps's Air Transport Command
(ATC) in 1944 and 1945. TWA undertook a wartime training program
for the armed forces that included instruction of ATC pilots and their
crews, airplane mechanics, and radio operators. Hughes used a Constellation to test a simple, lightweight, low-cost radar warning device.
Developed under his direction, the device warned pilots by a red light
and a horn the instant an airplane came too close to the ground or
other obstacles, regardless of weather or light. He adapted this device
to be used first by TWA.

In July 1938, Howard Hughes set a new record by flying a Lockheed 14 called *The New York World's Fair 1939* around the world in three days, nineteen hours, eight minutes, and ten seconds along with his crew: navigators Harry P. M. Connor and Lieutenant Thomas Thurlow, radio engineer and pilot Richard R. Stoddart, and flight engineer Edward Lund. In comparison to Charles Lindbergh's flight from New York to Paris in 1927, which took over thirty-three hours, the first leg of Hughes's flight was about sixteen and a half hours. Hughes claimed that Wiley Post's solo flight around the world in 1933, however, was the "greatest feat." Hughes found the task difficult enough with more modern instruments and a flight crew. Hughes received a hero's welcome with a ticker tape parade down Broadway in New York City but was even more enthusiastically received in his hometown. Tons of confetti choked the air down Main Street in Houston, with crowds estimated at between one and two hundred thousand people. More than seven hundred guests attended a banquet in his honor at the Rice Hotel in downtown Houston.[34]

Hughes's world flight in 1938 was one of the most meticulously

Howard Hughes's reception in Houston following his world flight in 1938. Courtesy of Ernest Sanborn, Vice President, Florida Air Museum, Lakeland, Florida.

planned during aviation's golden age. Hughes made six stops: Paris, Moscow, Omsk, Yakutsk, Fairbanks, and Minneapolis. Typed memorandums provided details as to whom Hughes would meet in various cities, speeches he could say on arrival, details of climate, politics, and geography, places of interest to see, lists of spare parts shipped to different legs of his journey, what altitude he should fly, runway lengths and diagrams, and availability of fuel. He had a list of questions typed in English and Russian in the event of an emergency landing in a remote location. Other lists detailed his radio communications with the U.S. Coast Guard, the U.S. Navy, RCA Communications, the U.S. Signal Corps in Alaska, amateur radio operators, and steamship companies. Hughes obviously had closely monitored and learned from the mistakes of Amelia Earhart's failed world flight in July 1937. One memorandum even detailed the food provided by the Standard Oil Company to be retrieved at Le Bourget Airport in Paris: "12 quarts of pasteurized milk in one quart sealed bottles, three pounds of fried chicken, 15 lbs. of dried ice, five gallons of hot coffee, ready to be poured in the ship's thermos bottles, five hot dinners, individually packed, consisting of lamb chops, baked potatoes, and fresh string beans, also a container of coffee."[35] His staff had prepared statements for Hughes's arrival in Paris:

> We've had a fine smooth trip, but believe me, it's great to be here just the same.

> You have given us a magnificent welcome and we all deeply appreciate this symbol of friendship between two great democratic nations.

> I've been asked by Grover A. Whale, President of the New York World's Fair 1939, to extend to you and to the people of France his sincere good wishes and to tell you that a hearty welcome awaits you when you visit the Fair next year.[36]

By 1940 Hughes owned a controlling percentage of TWA stock, and he would own as much as 78 percent within a few years. In 1939 he paid $315,000 for the introduction of the first pressurized airliner, the Boeing 307 Stratoliner. Hughes then financed and test piloted the Constellation *Star of California* on its inaugural nonstop flight between Los Angeles and New York on February 15, 1946. Shortly afterward, he met young actress Jean Peters, who would become his second wife in 1957. The marriage lasted thirteen years. In 1965 Hughes sold his shares of TWA stock, netting him a profit of $546.5 million dollars.

Hughes is better known for building Hercules HK-1 (commonly and rather comically known as the Spruce Goose, since it was made of wood and never got out of ground effect), the largest wooden flying boat ever constructed. During a taxi test on November 2, 1947, Howard Hughes flew it in ground effect off the coast of Long Beach, California, before settling back down on the channel. From the point of view of test pilots, this short test flight was poorly executed. Technically, the aircraft never flew even though it reached several feet off the water. The aircraft was not intended to be mass produced, contrary to the claims of its critics. The actual cost of the flying boat to the government was $18 million; of course, this was taxpayers' money. However, Hughes put $6 million of his own money into the project. Over four days of testimony before the Senate in 1947, Hughes cleared his company of any charges of mismanagement.

During World War II Hughes completed a total of $100,191,762 in government contracts. His profit on these contracts was only $3,191,354, which did not qualify as excess profits, so he paid no excess profit taxes.

Hughes for a time lost interest in Hughes Aircraft Company. The company had not yet succeeded in putting an aircraft in production. It only represented unattained dreams. Hughes, nonetheless, did not lose interest in his private aircraft, which the company maintained for him. As one of the wealthiest men in the world, he never bothered to file a flight plan or announce his intentions to land to air traffic controllers at either Los Angeles International Airport or Hughes Airport in Culver City, California. He was treated according to a separate standard.[37]

In 1946 Hughes crashed his experimental XF-11, intended for secret high-altitude reconnaissance flights, into a Beverly Hills neighborhood in a nearly fatal accident. The rear blade of the right-hand propeller had reversed in flight, producing a braking action. After recuperating from severe injuries, on April 5, 1947, the forty-one-year-old Hughes test flew a second XF-11 prototype. Hughes had the original concept's eight-bladed propellers replaced with four-bladed propellers. Hughes reported that the aircraft handled well.[38] For the remainder of his life, he remained addicted to codeine after being on morphine. He continued to fly until 1960, and thereafter flew only as a passenger.

Hughes invested in military electronics, weaponry, and the satellite industry. Hughes Aircraft engineers developed an electronic weapon control system, which led to a wartime rise in profits from $400,000 in 1949 to $5.3 million in 1953. Hughes was also then owner of RKO, the motion picture company. In 1953 Hughes established the Howard Hughes Medical Institute, a charitable foundation and major medical research center as well as a tax haven.

Hughes Aircraft built the XH-17, the largest helicopter in the world at that time, which was thirty-one feet high with a rotor diameter of 130 feet—30 percent longer than the wingspan of a B-17. Hughes took an interest in the test flight, but this large rotary craft was not successful. Hughes Aircraft did manufacture more than fourteen hundred OH-6A light observation helicopters in the early 1960s.

Hughes was known to be an impatient individual. When he wanted something, he wanted it that very moment, not later. This was the case whether it was an aircraft, a particular flavor of ice cream in the middle of the night, or a date with a movie star. He courted several leading actresses, including Katherine Hepburn, who was rumored to be dating Hughes at the time of his world flight in 1938. Hepburn presented Howard Hughes with a map of the world with the major flights and ship crossings from around the world, which is on display at the Florida Air Museum in Lakeland, Florida.

By 1975 Howard Hughes's personal wealth was listed as $2.5 billion, making him and oilman J. Paul Getty two of the wealthiest men in the world. As his wealth grew, he became more reclusive. He died on board a private aircraft en route to Houston from Acapulco, Mexico, at age seventy in 1976.

THESE WERE SOME OF THE STORIES OF SEVERAL notable aviation personalities from Texas who shaped the early years of flight. These daring individuals demonstrated the reliability of aircraft and airplane engines each in their own way, whether by setting records or participating in air races; Texans helped convince a disbelieving public that air travel was reasonably reliable and exciting. Beginning in the late 1920s, Texas became more globally connected with the rest of the nation and the world with the rise of the airlines and airmail service.

Chapter 5

Creating a More Connected World

*T*EXAS AIRLINE EXECUTIVES CYRUS R. SMITH, Howard Hughes, and Herb Kelleher revolutionized the airline industry in the United States. Smith (1899–1990) was a graduate of the University of Texas at Austin, major general in the U.S. Air Force, and president of American Airlines from 1934 to 1968. In 1939 *Fortune* magazine described Smith as a "pleasantly profane Texan who worked in shirt sleeves, knew operations, and had ideas about selling. . . ."[1] The career of Houston native Howard Hughes, the largest stockholder of the company that would eventually become Trans World Airlines, is discussed in chapter 4. And Southwest Airlines, under the management of its founders, Rollin King and Herb Kelleher, became a consistently profitable low-cost airline that has gone far beyond the borders of the Lone Star State and the regional boundaries of the southwestern United States. As of March 2011, it is the largest carrier based on the number of domestic passengers boarded, according to the U.S. Department of Transportation.[2] Texas and the country as a whole have benefited from visionary leaders as airline executives.

Texas has served as the headquarters for American, Trans-Texas, Pioneer, Texas International, Continental, Braniff, and Southwest Airlines. In June 1929, Delta Air Service Inc. (later Delta Air Lines) carried its first five paying passengers from Dallas's Love Field to Shreveport, Louisiana, in a Travel Air S-6000B.[3] The various airline companies that came to Texas during the twentieth century found an attractive environment for commercial aviation. Texas's vast open

William Fuller, Airport Manager, Meacham Field, Fort Worth, with a United Airlines stewardess, circa 1930. Courtesy of the William Fuller Collection, History of Aviation Collection, Special Collections Department, McDermott Library, the University of Texas at Dallas.

spaces with large metropolitan centers that were far apart and relatively affluent proved to be an ideal place for airlines to get started and to grow. The building of airports initially required far less infrastructure than railroads or highways; an airport could be built on a single farm or large tract of land rather than requiring vast amounts of land for railroad tracks and roadways. As early as 1922, Texas had more landing fields for aircraft in the United States than any other state, with a total of 162.[4]

Texas has set other unofficial firsts. In 1929 Pan American World Airways (Pan Am) established the first center for instrument flight training for the airlines at Brownsville, which shared with Miami, Florida, the title of international gateway to Latin America. Brownsville also served as an inspection and maintenance base for all flying equipment in the western division of Pan Am. The plant at Brownsville consisted of two steel hangars on the municipal airfield within two hundred yards of the air terminal building, which housed the ticket office, a general administrative office, and a waiting room. One hangar served for general maintenance. The other served for engine overhaul and other repairs, including replacement of upholstery and window glass.[5] As early as 1927, pilots from the Mexican division of Pan Am had been engaged in the study of instrument flying. Pilots who flew from Tampico to Mexico City were accustomed to flying through clouds under instrument conditions at least half of the time.[6]

The first commercial airline to serve Texas was National Air Transport, which would become United Airlines. On May 12, 1926, it carried the first commercial airmail from Love Field in Dallas to Chicago. Passenger service began in 1927. Several regional carriers have also operated in the state, including Western Air Express, Standard Air Lines, Southern Air Fast Express, Amarillo Airport Corporation, Bowen Air Lines, and Muse Air, among others.[7] On October 1, 1930, Temple Bowen, owner of Bowen Bus lines, launched a new air transport service between Fort Worth, Dallas, and Houston. Bowen's fleet of Lockheed Vegas cruised forty miles per hour faster than Texas Air Transport's Travel Airs. Southern Air Fast Express inaugurated airmail and passenger service at Love Field that same year on October 15.[8] Several of these smaller carriers—along with Texas Air Transport, Texas Flying Services, and Gulf Airlines, which were part of Southern Air Transport System of Fort Worth—would merge to become American Airways.

C. R. Smith and the Rise of American Airlines

Born in Minerva, Texas, in 1899, Cyrus R. Smith was the oldest of seven children. He attended public schools in Amarillo and Whitney, Texas. A hard worker, Smith entered the University of Texas at Austin even before graduating from high school. There he studied business administration, law, and economics. Smith became secretary and treasurer for Texas Air Transport beginning in 1928. He learned to fly planes and even to work on them as a mechanic.[9] The following year, Texas Air Transport became Southern Air Transport (SAT), which retained Smith as vice president and treasurer. Later that year, SAT was absorbed into Aviation Corporation (AVCO). In January 1934

Formal portrait of Cyrus Rowlett "C. R." Smith, President of American Airlines, seated at desk, circa 1930s. Courtesy of the American Airlines C. R. Smith Museum, Fort Worth, Texas.

AVCO created American Airways and appointed Smith vice president of the southern division. On October 25, 1934, Smith became president of American Airlines. Over the next three decades, Smith propelled American Airlines, then based in New York, into first place in the U.S. airline industry. He built American Airlines from a small carrier into the global airline we know today. Rather than rely heavily on revenue from carrying the mail, Smith realized that the future of the airline industry rested in carrying passengers.[10]

Over the next several years, Smith was influential in consolidating routes and helping to design the DC-3, the workhorse of the airline industry, by providing its specifications. Smith talked a reluctant airplane designer and manufacturer, Donald Douglas, into building the airplane during a marathon telephone call in December 1934 that cost $335.50. Smith wanted Douglas to expand the DC-2 so that it could transport twenty-one passengers during the day and sleep fourteen at night. Smith insisted that the plane he wanted would only be 15 percent new and 85 percent DC-2. Douglas argued against the idea, saying the market would not justify the development costs. The new model turned out to be 85 percent new and only 15 percent DC-2. Even though it appeared to be an upscale model of the DC-2, the new plane had improved shock absorbers, retractable landing gear that was hydraulically operated, and adjustable propellers of a more advanced design. The DC-3 was far easier to handle, with its swept-back wings and wing flaps that reduced landing speed to sixty-four miles per hour. By 1939, a full 75 percent of the nation's air travelers flew on DC-3s.[11] The model became the single most successful airplane in the history of commercial aviation.[12] The military version was the Douglas C-47.

On June 25, 1936, Smith helped inaugurate DC-3 service with the *Flagship Illinois*, the Douglas Sleeper Transport that flew from Chicago to New York. This gave the airline a head start on competitors and improved sales. Between 1933 and 1937 American Airlines passenger volume tripled; in the next five years, it increased elevenfold. Passenger revenue increased from $1,885,000 in 1933 to $6,598,000 in 1937.[13] American Airlines was the top domestic airline in the United States by the end of the 1930s.

American Airlines had an impressive safety record, but following a fatal crash—in which a deranged passenger may have attacked a pilot (secure cockpits did not yet exist)—Smith came out with a series of advertisements challenging public perceptions of airline safety. The headline was "Why dodge this question: Afraid to fly?" He established a protocol that whenever an incident involved an American Airlines aircraft, a single statement would be issued by the company and then the employees would pull together.

Smith took a leave of absence during World War II to join the U.S. Army Air Forces as a colonel; he also helped organize the Air Transport Command as its chief of staff. He was awarded the Distinguished Service Medal, the Legion of Merit, and the Air Medal. The Distinguished Unit Citation was awarded to the Air Transport Command for its operations between India and China. After the war, Smith returned to American as the company's executive.

On January 25, 1959, Smith led American Airlines into the jet age with the introduction of the first transcontinental jet service. In 1968 he retired as chief executive of American Airlines to become President Lyndon Johnson's Secretary of Commerce. He then returned to American Airlines as interim chairman. Following retirement, Smith remained active in civic affairs in Washington, DC. He died in 1990 at the age of 90 and was buried at Arlington National Cemetery. American Airlines C. R. Smith Museum at Fort Worth is named in his honor.

American Airlines DC-3 next to a horse, circa 1936. Print No. 2007.004.379. Courtesy of the American Airlines C. R. Smith Museum, Fort Worth, Texas.

American Airlines Stewardess College's first class, a DC-6 flying overhead, 1958. Print no. 2007.004.087. Courtesy of the American Airlines C. R. Smith Museum, Fort Worth, Texas.

American Airlines Stewardess College, Fort Worth, 1957—First Flight Attendant Training Center in the World

In 1979 American Airlines moved its headquarters from New York City to Fort Worth, Texas. The new complex included the stewardess college that had been established in 1957 by C. R. Smith. Prior to 1957, stewardesses for American Airlines had trained in a classroom at the airport in Chicago.[14]

The first stewardess college in the world was built on twenty-one acres across from Amon Carter Field, south of Dallas/Fort Worth International Airport. The first class to train in the college graduated in the spring of 1958.[15]

The first floor of the stewardess college consisted of many classrooms with blackboards, movie projectors, electronically operated screens, and mock-ups of airplane galleys. The facility included a kitchen, beauty shop, and a recreation room. At the top of the stairways was a mezzanine lounge. Upstairs there were twenty-seven spacious bedroom suites with fifteen bathrooms, along with storage rooms and self-service laundry rooms. Each trainee had her own desk and built-in vanity.

Personal grooming was part of the curriculum. Each trainee's hairstyle was carefully evaluated and changed, if necessary. Attendants also learned how to put on makeup. Rules were strict. There were curfews and even a guardhouse at the entrance of the driveway. There were also, however, many amenities, including a swimming pool and lounges where trainees could relax, study, and practice songs for graduation ceremonies. According to uniform regulation "don'ts" in the *Stewardess Manual* of November 21, 1960, flight attendants could not wear "unnatural make or make-up applied with water," "rouge or lipstick in excess," or "obvious mascara."

There were between fifty and sixty trainees per class. About 3 percent dropped out or did not graduate from the program. Graduates posed for photographs as though they were high school or college graduates.

All trainees had to be single until the late 1960s, when the Air Line Stewards and Stewardesses Association (ALSSA) and American Airlines ended a protracted contract dispute. The carrier's no-marriage rule had been a major sticking point. The dispute was settled just before the stewardesses were about to go on strike. Under the new contract in August 1968, American's all-female flight attendants finally won the right to marry without forfeiting their jobs.

Bonnie Tiburzi Caputo (1948–), First Female Pilot for American Airlines

Bonnie Linda Tiburzi was born on August 31, 1948, and spent her childhood in Ridgefield, Connecticut. Her father was an airline pilot who owned Tiburzi Airways, a small flying service. Both Tiburzi and her brother became commercial pilots. She took her first flying lesson when she was twelve. After graduating from high school and traveling and working in Europe, Tiburzi tried college for a few months but decided she wanted flying lessons instead. While living in Pompano Beach, Florida, she soloed in the summer of 1969. Within eight months, she had earned her private pilot license. Over the next

Bonnie Tiburzi Caputo, American Airlines Pilot, in uniform.
Courtesy of Bonnie Tiburzi Caputo.

two years, Tiburzi earned her commercial, instructor, instrument, and multiengine pilot licenses.

   In January 1973 a story about the young, beautiful, and slender Tiburzi appeared in *Harper's Bazaar* and caught the attention of a lawyer for the Federal Aviation Administration, who encouraged her to reapply for a flying position at American Airlines. American Airlines called her to Dallas for an interview on February 20. She did so well on her written test and interview that she was told to take a complete pilot's physical examination. Twenty-four-year-old Tiburzi was one of 214 pilots hired from fifteen thousand applicants, making her the first female pilot to work for a major commercial airline. As early as 1929, small regional carriers had hired female copilots, such as Dallas's Edith Foltz (see chapter 7) who flew Ford trimotors for West Coast Air between Seattle and San Francisco.

At the end of 1973, all 214 new hires, including Tiburzi, were furloughed during a downturn in the economy. American Airlines rehired her in April 1976. In 1979 she was promoted from flight engineer to copilot. In 1980, during another slump in the economy, she and two hundred other new copilots were once again returned to being flight engineers. Eventually, Tiburzi regained her copilot status and in 1988 achieved her dream of being promoted to captain. She flew the Boeing 757 and 767 to destinations in Europe and South America.

Female pilots remain a minority in the airline industry, even though women have been flying airplanes for over a century. While women represent about one third of those employed in the fields of science, engineering, and technology, media images of women in technical careers are rare, sending an unspoken message that these fields are primarily for men. In August 2008, of the approximately 10,921 pilots flying for American Airlines, only 478 were women. Of 3,843 pilots serving as captains, 56 were women. In June 2009 Southwest Airlines only had 97 female captains out of 2,982 pilots. Women pilots, both captains and first officers, represent less than 3.5 percent of the total number of pilots flying for Southwest. Hopefully this situation will improve so that women will be able to take full advantage of the flying opportunities that are available to them.[16]

Southwest Airlines, the Airline that Made Flying Affordable in America

Early Southwest Airlines flight attendant uniforms consisted of tangerine-colored hot pants, orange shirts, tall white lace-up leather boots, and wide white belts. The airline was using feminine sex appeal to target male business travelers. Go-go boots and hot pants were quite fashionable in the 1960s, and the original outfits for the hostesses were designed by Juanice Gunn Muse, the wife of Southwest's first president, M. Lamar Muse. These colorful designs were a stark contrast to the more conservative uniforms worn by stewardesses who flew for American and Delta. Interestingly, Southwest was the last airline to hire male flight attendants.

With its "LUV" ad campaigns, Southwest Airlines projected an im-

Southwest Airlines flight attendants with the first three Boeing 737s owned by Southwest in a popular publicity photo, 1971. Courtesy of Southwest Airlines.

age of feminine beauty, youth, and vitality that appealed to the traveling public. One of its early marketing campaigns was "Somebody Else Up There Loves You." During the late 1970s Southwest came out with the slogan "We're spreading love all over Texas," which reinforced the notion that it cared about its people and customers.[17] In 1971 the airline began service between Dallas, Houston, and San Antonio, linking these major urban centers. Harlingen came next.

Southwest noticeably avoided the hub-and-spoke system of scheduling flights in favor of renovating lower-cost satellite airports such as Albany, Chicago-Midway, Orange County, Hobby at Houston, and Baltimore. Traffic would increase a thousand percent in one year in some markets, stimulated by its low fares and welcoming employees.

Early flight attendants' sexy uniforms eventually gave way to shorts, slacks, casual shirts, and comfortable athletic shoes. Most importantly, Southwest Airlines connected families, friends, and business people across the country by making it more affordable for everyone to fly. It played a fundamental role in democratizing commercial aviation in America, which traditionally had been the privilege of the elite.[18] Airline passengers today readily travel by air to sporting events or family occasions.

Southwest's no-frills flights and exclusive use of the Boeing 737 at well-situated, previously underutilized regional airports enabled the airline to keep its operating costs in check, as did its practice of stockpiling aviation fuel at low prices. Although the airline operated Boeing 727s for a short period of time, it soon limited itself to the Boeing 737, a decision that was both cost and safety efficient. Southwest's pilots only need to know how to fly one type of aircraft; likewise, its mechanics focus on maintaining one type. Early on, Southwest offered only peanuts while other airlines served meals.

Southwest Airlines treats its employees well. In turn, they are hardworking and dedicated. Southwest's employees receive stock options, are unionized, and benefit from a flexible work schedule. In contrast to other airlines, through 2012 Southwest has never furloughed one of its employees. It stays lean even in good times, a policy that lends itself to creating a loyal workforce. When fuel prices soared at the time of Iraq's invasion of Kuwait, about one third of Southwest's employees volunteered to take a pay cut to purchase fuel for the airline.

Immediately following 9/11, Southwest Airlines issued refunds to its passengers and started flying again by September 14. It weathered the storm that put a serious financial strain on the entire aviation industry. Above all, Southwest Airlines has excelled because of superior management that continually analyzes ever-changing developments in the aviation industry, especially the price of oil.[19]

Southwest's strategy depends on short turnaround times at airports to keep down its operating costs. Following four and a half years of intense legal battles with Braniff, Texas International, and Continental, Southwest finally won the right to fly within Texas's borders in 1970. These three competitors had tried to exhaust Southwest's financial resources to keep it from ever getting into the air. Failing that, they attempted to restrict Southwest's activities at Love Field, knowing well that if it were forced to operate out of Dallas/Fort Worth International, it would never survive.

Southwest started out as an intrastate carrier, but with the deregulation of the airlines in 1978, it became an interstate carrier. However, it still faced strict regulation through the Wright Amendment of 1979, which limited the routes flown in and out of Love Field. That amendment, by Congressman Jim Wright of Fort Worth, restricted planes flying passengers out of Love Field to locations only within Texas and four neighboring states: Louisiana, Arkansas, Oklahoma, and New Mexico. As traffic improved at Dallas/Fort Worth International, the amendment was modified to add Alabama, Kansas, Mississippi, and Missouri to the Wright zone.[20] For Southwest Airlines, the Wright Amendment was definitely "wrong," in that it restricted travel from its headquarters. Southwest could not fly from Love Field nonstop to the East or West Coast; its passengers faced having to purchase at least two tickets and fly point-to-point, which led to higher costs for both the consumer and the airline. In October 2006, Southwest, American, Dallas/Fort Worth International and the cities of Dallas and Fort Worth all agreed to repeal the Wright Amendment with several conditions. These stipulate that the Wright zone restrictions remain intact until 2014, they lower Love Field's maximum number of gates to twenty from thirty-two, and they keep Love Field a domestic airport.

Herbert "Herb" D. Kelleher (1931–) is a brilliant lawyer who originally came from New Jersey to reside in Texas with his wife, Joan Negley, who was from San Antonio. A graduate of Wesleyan College and New York University, Kelleher entered aviation through providing legal representation to a number of clients who, like him, were entrepreneurial in spirit.[21] One of his clients was a banker who had flown on Pacific Southwest California (PSA) and liked it. Kelleher studied PSA and realized that Texas was similar in geography to California; its major population centers are far enough apart to justify in-state air travel. The quality of customer service of the airlines that operated in Texas could also be improved, from the perspective of Southwest's cofounders.

In 1966 Kelleher had lunch with Texas businessman, pilot, and Harvard Business School graduate Rollin W. King, who introduced the idea of a low-cost carrier that would make flying less expensive than driving. King was very interested in aviation. The idea of an airline connecting Dallas, Houston, and San Antonio was drawn out on a cocktail napkin. Kelleher responded: "Rollin, You're crazy, Let's do it." Southwest Airlines then created its own uniquely branded culture by making flying fun. Its flight attendants became noted for delivering humorous safety announcements prior to takeoff to put passengers at ease. Southwest's advertising campaigns are also noted for their humor.

Today Southwest Airlines operates more than 550 Boeing 737 air-

Herb Kelleher descending Southwest
Airlines' *Spirit of Kitty Hawk* at its
inaugural flight on December 17, 1984,
the eighty-first anniversary since Orville
and Wilbur Wright first flew at Kitty
Hawk, Kill Devil Hills, North Carolina.
Courtesy of Southwest Airlines and
Herb Kelleher.

craft on thirty-three hundred flights per day among seventy-two cities
nationwide. It is a major leader in the airline industry and serves as a
model for other airlines. Much of the tremendous success Southwest
enjoys can be attributed to personality—that of its dedicated employees and that of cofounder and former CEO Herb Kelleher. Kelleher is a
real people person with a great sense of humor. During critical years,
Kelleher showed great skill in dealing with litigation, managing the
airline, and carefully observing the competition. Kelleher also gra-
ciously attributes the success of the airline to the "warrior spirit" of the
employees at Southwest. Luck also played a part. Many experienced
pilots with lots of flying hours were hired when Purdue Air went out
of business just as Southwest Airlines was starting out, making them
available for immediate employment.

Another important ingredient in its formula for success is careful
screening during the hiring of its employees. Pilots with jet training,
which can be acquired through flying for small regional carriers or
the military, are hired on the basis of skill level, experience, and aptitude. Southwest Airlines only employs approximately 20 percent of
all the pilots that it interviews. Above all, Southwest Airlines has an
outstanding safety record: through 2012, it has never had a passenger fatality.[22]

Moreover, Southwest Airlines has maintained an excellent relationship with the Boeing Aircraft Company. Boeing actually financed
Southwest's first aircraft, which had been made to order for Aloha Air-

lines and PSA but were sitting empty on the tarmac in Seattle. Southwest's first planes had interior designs of tropical Hawaiian flowers or San Francisco cable cars because it was not in the financial position to change out the interiors.

In 1973 Southwest Airlines posted its first modest profit. Ever since, it has shown itself to be a true industry leader in terms of profitability. In 1989 Southwest exceeded the billion-dollar revenue mark. In 2011, it posted its fortieth consecutive annual profit. In December 2011, Southwest placed the largest order in the history of Boeing Aircraft Company when it signed up for 208 new Boeing 737s—the airline industry's modern equivalent of the Douglas DC-3—with a list price of approximately $19 billion.[23]

Continental Airlines

Continental Airlines traces its roots back to Varney Speed Lines, founded by Walter T. Varney and his partner Louis Mueller. On July 15, 1934, the first flight by Varney Speed Lines took a 530-mile route from Pueblo, Colorado, to El Paso, Texas, with stops in Las Vegas, Santa Fe, and Albuquerque. Pilot Jess E. Hart flew that route, carrying one hundred letters and no passengers. That same year, Varney ceded control to Mueller.

Robert F. Six, a licensed pilot, began as chief executive officer for Continental Airlines and was responsible for naming the airline in 1937. He would serve as CEO for forty-four years, until 1980. In October 1937, Six moved Continental's headquarters from El Paso to Denver. Continental started out as a tiny regional carrier with four Lockheed Vegas. It would become a major national and global leader in the airline industry.

In 1953 Continental Airlines merged with Pioneer Airlines, adding sixteen new cities in Texas and New Mexico to its routing system. In July 1963 the headquarters moved to Los Angeles. In 1982 the airline merged with Texas International, retaining the Continental name, and began offering service to four continents (North and South America, Asia, and Australia) with a fleet of 112 aircraft. Continental again moved its headquarters, this time to Houston. In 1986 Continental reported its highest one-year earnings, $60.9 million. On June 3, 2003, Continental opened the first phase of its twenty-three-gate Terminal E at George Bush Intercontinental Airport in Houston.

The six-hundred-thousand-square-foot terminal handled all Continental international arrivals and departures in Houston. This phase was completed in 2004.

In 2009 Continental became the first airline in North America to demonstrate the use of biofuel to power an aircraft. During the demonstration flight, Continental's test pilots successfully conducted a number of flight maneuvers, and the biofuel met all performance requirements as compared to traditional Jet A fuel.

There is a growing trend toward the consolidation of airlines in recent years. On October 1, 2010, United and Continental Airlines closed their merger, thereby creating United Continental holdings, a global airline that makes approximately fifty-eight hundred flights a day to 371 airports in the Americas, Europe, and Asia. Continental no longer operates as a separate airline; its headquarters moved from Houston to Chicago. It is still too early to assess the impact of the merger on Houston and its airports in terms of job losses and relocation, beyond potential changes in renovation plans for George Bush Intercontinental Airport.[24]

Airline Captain A. J. High (1923–2013):
Trans-Texas Airways Vice President and
World War II Veteran with 40,000 Flying Hours

Captain A. J. High's airline career spanned Mercury Airlines, Trans-Texas Airways, Texas International Airlines, and Continental Airlines. He also was a certified airplane mechanic and flight instructor for the Convair-240, Convair-600, and DC-9. Born in Cleburne, Texas, in 1923, High took his first airplane ride from a couple of barnstormers in 1938. He then taught himself to fly. Flying before World War II, he notes, was "still a dangerous, learn-as-you-go occupation." He soloed at night on December 1, 1941, flying a J-3 Piper Cub.

On January 28, 1942, he became Aviation Cadet A. J. High at Fort Sam Houston in San Antonio. He received his military wings on November 10, 1942 and flew the Lockheed P-38, the North American B-25, and the Boeing B-17 and B-29. In the last months of the war, he became a flight instructor.

On March 18, 1946, he began his career as an airline pilot. He flew for Mercury Airlines, but this small carrier did not endure. He

Trans-Texas Airways stewardesses sitting on the horizontal stabilizer of a Trans-Texas Starliner, circa 1948. Courtesy of the 1940 Air Terminal Museum.

was hired for the new Trans-Texas Airways in 1947. Trans-Texas Airways was a regional airline started by Houston fixed base operator Aviation Enterprises on October 11, 1947. It operated flights in and around Texas from 1947 to 1968. It was fondly remembered as "Tree Top Airlines," most likely because of its fleet and frequent stops along its routes. In 1953 Trans-Texas Airways served Houston, Dallas, Fort Worth, San Antonio, Brownsville, and El Paso. It also served numerous smaller towns, including Tyler, Corpus Christi, Del Rio, Uvalde, San Angelo, and Beeville. Its aircraft included the Beech 99, DC-3, Convair 40, Convair 600, and the DC-9 jet. On November 1, 1968, the airline became Texas International. It merged with Continental Airlines in 1982.

From 1967 to 1971, High served as vice president of Trans-Texas/Texas International, then returned to piloting. In 1982, the airline merged with Continental Airlines. His last flight as captain was on Continental Airlines on April 7, 1983, the day before he turned 60—

when the Federal Aviation Administration (FAA) required retirement. Captain High then flew as a private corporate pilot for ten years before retiring.[25]

Captain High served as director and chairman of the board of the Houston Aeronautical Heritage Society, the nonprofit group dedicated to restoring the 1940 Air Terminal Museum in Houston. He also volunteered as a museum docent until his death on April 3, 2013.

Braniff International Airways and Braniff College

Braniff International Airways was one of the great airlines of the twentieth century, known for its colorful aircraft and elegant service. On June 20, 1928, Braniff made its first flight between Oklahoma City and Tulsa in a Stinson Detroiter. In 1929 Braniff Airways Inc., a division of Universal, operated between Oklahoma City and San Angelo, Texas, via Wichita Falls, Breckenridge, Abilene, and Amarillo. A second route operated between Oklahoma City and Tulsa and Fort Worth via Wewoka, Oklahoma, and Dallas. The new service was a joint arrangement between Braniff and Texas Air Transport. Its original fleet consisted of four planes, including one eleven-passenger Fokker trimotor equipped to serve meals.[26] On September 1, 1930, Braniff began express and package airfreight services at Love Field in Dallas. The airline was founded officially on November 3, 1930. The first regularly scheduled flights were between Oklahoma City, Tulsa, and Wichita Falls. On May 17, 1934, Braniff began passenger service to Dallas on the Chicago–Kansas City–Tulsa-Dallas mail route.

In 1937 the first ten flying hostesses (flight attendants) were hired by Braniff out of eight hundred applicants. They had to be female, single, between the ages of twenty-one and twenty-six, fluent in Spanish, between five feet and five feet four inches tall, and weigh between 110 and 118 pounds. Ten attendants completed training but only six inaugurated service June 12 on DC-2 flights between Dallas and Brownsville and Dallas and Kansas City and Chicago. Rebecca Garza of McAllen, Texas, was a registered nurse when she became the first flight attendant hired for Braniff. She was one of the original women who served aboard the new fourteen-passenger Douglas DC-2 airplane, which was placed in service in June on Braniff routes between Chicago and Brownsville.

In 1940 Beth Haley of Dallas became the first female hostess hired

Rebecca Garza, first flying hostess at Braniff International Airways, May 1937. Courtesy of the Braniff Collection, History of Aviation Collection, Special Collections Department, McDermott Library, the University of Texas at Dallas.

by Braniff to work in the lobby at the Dallas terminal, Love Field. She provided information to air travelers concerning flights and local transportation, including bus schedules.

Part of what made Braniff a colorful and stylish airline in the 1960s and 1970s were its aviation firsts. In 1965 Braniff became the first airline to hire a couturier, Emilio Pucci, to design its flight attendants' uniforms. It was also known for its silver service, a formal English tea served using fine china and a silver tea set.

In 1968 the company built Braniff College, a $2 million, five-story, 68,475-square-foot modern facility for hostess training in Dallas. It could accommodate up to 144 trainees, but 30 women began their

Braniff flight attendant with silver tea service in hand, circa late 1950s or early 1960s. Courtesy of the Braniff Collection, History of Aviation Collection, Special Collections Department, McDermott Library, the University of Texas at Dallas.

A Braniff flight attendant demonstrating the new look of the 1970s, which included a plastic bubble space helmet. Courtesy of the Braniff Collection, History of Aviation Collection, Special Collections Department, McDermott Library, the University of Texas at Dallas.

five-week training that same year. Its reception area included a sunken lounge with a large fireplace circled by soft cushions on a couch, wall paintings from South America, three-inch-thick white carpeting, and a scenic window. This area was sometimes called the "passion pit," as the young ladies first met with their dates there.[27] Braniff designed each living quarter to suit two or three young women or "girls," painted in its airline colors—primarily yellow, orange, red, blue, and green. Each room had its own balcony protected by iron grillwork. Framed Mexican and South American art hung on the walls. In the "powder puff room," trainees learned the secrets of applying makeup and the importance of having a flawless complexion. Each room had its own bathroom and shower/bathtub, besides a separate dressing room with double-basin sinks and a well-lit mirrored space to apply cosmetics. Other features included an exercise room, a heated swimming pool, a large dining room, and a well-equipped modern kitchen.

In 1965 Braniff began a marketing campaign to paint its aircraft in bold colors, which led to an increase in ticket sales.[28] In 1973 Braniff became the first airline to introduce "flying art," having commissioned world-renowned artist Alexander Calder to design the color scheme for the painting of a DC-8, *Flying Colors*. In 1979 Braniff was the first and only airline to fly the Concorde in conjunction with British Airways and Air France between Dallas/Fort Worth and London or Paris. Despite its firsts, or maybe in part because of them, Braniff declared bankruptcy and closed its doors in 1982.

TEXAS ITSELF, OF COURSE, HAS HAD NOTHING TO do with the management failures of individual airlines, many of which went bankrupt on their own or were absorbed by other carriers. The airline industry is notable for its intense competition. Those airlines that strove managed to thrive and survive. Those that were not competitive disappeared or merged with other airlines. In recent decades, the high-end domestic market for air travel has practically disappeared in the United States. The airlines no longer offer first-class service, only the equivalent of a business class, on most domestic flights. Rather than travel first class on domestic carriers, affluent travelers lease or own private jets. Only on intercontinental flights is there a first class, now equipped with individualized cabins, high-tech seats, and other luxurious amenities. Those airlines that were adaptable to the changes in the market and made new opportunities for themselves grew to even greater heights. During the Great Depression of the 1930s, American Airlines under C. R. Smith came up with new equipment, the DC-3, which appealed immensely to an affluent, air-minded public. DC-3s are still being flown today in more remote areas, such as Alaska. Although currently facing financial challenges with the rise in fuel costs, American Airlines has continued to expand in recent years by extending its relationships with other airlines. It is a true global airline, as is that formed by the merging of United with Continental. By offering affordable flights to the American public, Southwest Airlines in turn has moved far beyond the state of Texas and even the Southwest. It is currently investing in an international terminal at Houston Hobby. Americans fly this Texas-based airline safely all around the mainland of the country, and soon may be traveling as far away as Hawaii, Alaska, the Caribbean, and certain international destinations.

Chapter 6

Flight Training

WITH ITS WIDE-OPEN SPACES, AGREEABLE flying weather, and varied landscapes—especially the spectacular hill country around Austin and San Antonio—Texas is ideally suited for flight training. The U.S. Army selected San Antonio for military airplane test flights in 1910, following initial training by Wilbur and Orville Wright of military aviators at Fort Meyer, Virginia, and College Park, Maryland. Since World War I, flying cadets have trained at Brooks and Kelly Fields in San Antonio. Other Texas airfields have also served as important centers for flight instruction and research, both civilian and military. And many familiar faces in aviation history are associated with Texas flight training. It is through their stories and especially their own words that we can get a glimpse of the challenges cadets faced when earning their military wings.

Flight Training at Brooks and Kelly Fields through the Eyes of Charles Lindbergh

Charles Lindbergh described his training experience at Brooks and Kelly Fields in his best-selling account of his solo flight from New York to Paris, *We* (1927). Lindbergh arrived at Brooks on March 15, 1924, but was not enlisted as a flying cadet until March 19. He was one of 104 cadets who hailed from nearly every state in the country. The barracks were overflowing. Some cadets were even assigned to sleep in cots in the recreation hall. Lindbergh's flight training began on April 1. Each flight instructor had six cadets assigned to him.

Lindbergh trained in a Curtiss JN-4 Jenny, although the 90-horsepower Curtiss OX-5 engine had been replaced by a more powerful 150-horsepower Hispano-Suiza. He thought they were "somewhat tricky" to fly, but "when a cadet learned to fly one of them, well, he was just about capable of flying anything on wings with a reasonable degree of safety."[1] Cadets were usually given ten hours of dual instruction before being allowed to solo. At the end of ten hours, if the cadet was not capable of flying solo, he was in danger of being washed out of the program. At Brooks, an instructor would assign any student who had not mastered the art of flying in that time to another stage commander, who would check out the cadet and make a recommendation. If the cadet failed the check ride, the "Benzine Board," a board of officers, made a final decision. Lindbergh insisted that "there was no disgrace in washing out." In his view, such cadets were simply not adapted to flying. They were sent back to the point of enlistment and advised to take up another occupation, being awarded an honorable discharge. Lindbergh summed up the quality of his training in this way:

> Always there was some new experience, always something interesting going on to make the time spent in Brooks and Kelly one of the banner years in a pilot's life. The training is rigid and difficult but there is none better. A cadet must be willing to forget all other interests in life when he enters the Texas flying schools and he must enter with the intention of devoting every effort and all the energy during the next twelve months towards a single goal. But when he receives the wings at Kelly a year later he has the satisfaction of knowing that he has graduated from one of the world's finest flying schools.[2]

At the advanced training school at Kelly, flying cadets were given longer flights and more cross-country trips than at Brooks. Lindbergh flew to Corpus Christi, Galveston, Laredo, and other Texas cities and towns. Each class then spent two weeks at gunnery school at Ellington Field, between Houston and Galveston. The final few weeks were spent in the pursuit stage practicing dogfights and ground strafing. Flying in formation took up a good amount of time.

Lindbergh made a parachute jump from a De Havilland after flying too close in formation to another plane and damaging his wing. He automatically became a member of the Caterpillar Club, which includes every flyer saved by jumping from a disabled aircraft. The club is named for the parachute, which was made of silk spun by caterpillars.[3] The Irvin Air Chute Company (now Irvin Aerospace) later issued pins in the shape of a caterpillar to all its members.

Standards were extremely high in this rigorous flight-training program. Including Lindbergh, only 18 of the 104 cadets who started the course at Brooks the year before graduated.

U.S. Army Colonel William C. Ocker (1880–1942), an Inventor of Blind (Instrument) Flying and Designer of the Ocker Box

U.S. Army Colonel William C. Ocker developed equipment for the training of instrument flying for the U.S. military at Brooks.

> The removal of the limitations imposed by weather is dependent on two principal factors, the development of suitable instruments for flying during conditions of low or obscured visibility, when the pilot cannot refer to terrestrial objects to keep his ship level, and the education of the pilot in the use of proper instruments.
>
> WILLIAM C. OCKER, *AERO DIGEST*, OCTOBER 1930

> Except for Maj. Ocker's great zeal as a missionary, I doubt whether the course in blind flying would be a requirement in the Army today. I believe that his campaign of education has had more influence in bringing about the use of instruments than that of any other person.
>
> ORVILLE WRIGHT, 1934

On June 24, 1930, William C. Ocker, the "father of instrument flying," successfully piloted the first cross-country flight with only his instruments as his guide. He flew from Brooks Field to Scott Field, Illinois, approximately nine hundred miles. This was not the first blind flight in the world. Although he was better known for his raid on Tokyo in 1942, James Doolittle's most significant aeronautical contribution was performing the first blind flight on September 24, 1929. However, Doolittle and Ocker worked on the concept of blind flying independent of one another.

Ocker's method consisted of convincing military aviators that their senses, when flying blind, were not only of no help but actually caused constant threat of mishaps, injuries, and fatalities. He convinced them that their flight instruments and not their senses were telling the truth and to move their hands and feet in accordance with what they saw on the instrument panel instead of what they saw outside the cockpit. To give instrument instruction, Ocker used a whirling chair and a lighted instrument panel mounted in a box. Ocker worked with Colonel Carl Crane, another Brooks Field instrument flight pioneer. Their partnership resulted in the invention of the preflight reflex trainer, a navigational aid also known as the flight integrator. The two coauthored a book, *Blind Flight in Theory and Practice* (1932).

Ocker sought to improve flight training from his days as a World War I pilot, having earned his wings in 1914. Born in Philadelphia in 1880, he was one of seven children of German immigrants. He entered the Army as an artilleryman in 1900. In 1912 Ocker transferred to the Signal Corps. In 1918 he became an advocate for flight instrument instruction. He flight-tested the bank-and-turn indicator (a device that provides an indication of the direction and quality of the turn) developed by Dr. Elmer Sperry. He identified the phenomenon of spatial disorientation and blindfolded a pigeon to demonstrate that even birds lose their orientation. By 1926 Ocker had developed a solution to counter the effects of vertigo, a disorienting spatial illusion, by adapting the bank-and-turn indicator for use with the whirling Jones-Barany chair. His solution became the world's first blind flying trainer. Ocker's pioneering research led him to invent a hooded pilot cockpit seat to teach aviators to rely on flight instruments rather than on their senses. At times, Ocker's insistence on the importance of instrument training of pilots led to suggestions that he was insane. Although his ideas were not taken seriously at first, the National Advisory Commit-

tee for Aeronautics eventually presented Ocker with an award. In return, Ocker assigned all patent rights to the U.S. government, retaining only the foreign rights to his invention.[4]

The Ocker box played an important part in cadet flight training at
the Kelly Advanced Flying School in San Antonio beginning in 1930.
Then the Mexican division of Pan American Airways in Brownsville
trained with it, and soon afterward all Pan Am divisions adopted
Ocker's hooded cockpit for blind flying training. The Brownsville
training center was the first such center established by a commercial

Blindfolding of cadets in a demonstration of spatial disorienta-
tion at Brooks Field, San Antonio, 1929. Courtesy of the
Edward White II Memorial Museum, San Antonio, U.S. Air
Force.

Ocker box demonstration at Brooks Field, circa 1932. William Ocker in center. Courtesy of the Edward White II Memorial Museum, San Antonio, U.S. Air Force.

airline. Ocker and Crane undoubtedly had a profound impact on aviation safety.

Brooks Air Force Base Facilities for Aviation Medicine and Aeronautical Research

Brooks Field Balloon and Airship School had a large balloon hangar that was still standing in 1942. This huge hangar was torn down during the Second World War due to the increase in flight training using airplanes; at that time, sixteen hangars stood along the flight line.[5] Aside from flight training, Brooks later served as a center for aviation medicine and aeronautical research and instruction. In 1959 the U.S. Air Force moved its School of Aviation Medicine from Randolph Air Force Base to a new $10 million facility at Brooks Air Force Base. The new school offered 256,410 square feet of space on fifteen acres with 433 seats in sixteen classrooms, while the old school at Randolph had six classrooms and room for only 275 students.[6] In more recent years, as many as 7,000 students have studied at the Air Force School of Aerospace Medicine annually. Medical professionals from all branches of service take part in a special course for flight nurses and aeromedical evacuation instructors.

Hangar 9 at Brooks Field is one of the country's few remaining hangars that date from the Great War. In 1970 Hangar 9 was made into an aviation museum and renamed the Edward H. White II Memorial Hangar in memory of astronaut Lieutenant Colonel Edward H. White II, who was born at Fort Sam Houston on November 14, 1930. White was the first American to walk in space, which he did while tethered to the Gemini Spacecraft on June 3, 1965. Along with Gus Grissom and Roger Chaffee, White perished on January 27, 1967, in a flash fire at the launch site in Florida while in training for the first moon flight aboard an Apollo spacecraft. The astronauts' flight heritage was linked closely to the Brooks and Kelly flying schools. The father of astronaut White, Major General Edward H. White, learned to fly at Hangar 9.

In 1995 Brooks was placed on the Pentagon's list of proposed base closings as part of its cost-saving measures, which impacted both civilian jobs and the lives of military personnel in San Antonio. The U.S. Air Force ended more than ninety years of service, research, and training at Brooks in September 2011.[7]

Randolph Air Force Base, the "West Point of the Air Force"

Randolph Air Force Base near San Antonio, with its Spanish colonial revival architecture and unique urban design, stands out as one of the more significant historic sites in Texas. The citizens of San Antonio purchased the two-thousand-acre site for Randolph Field and conveyed it to the United States for one dollar. The magazine *Southern Aviation* described the airfield at Randolph, which would be inaugurated in June 1930, as "the world's largest airport" in January 1930.[8] The U.S. Army selected San Antonio as the site of its biggest airport and flying school because of favorable climatic conditions that allowed training year round. The design is distinctive in that the buildings and streets were laid out in the form of a wagon wheel, rather than the conventional grid.

Spanish colonial revival style gained popularity throughout Texas and the Southwest during the 1920s and 1930s, including in the design of airports. Other airport terminal buildings at El Paso and Brownsville were built using Spanish mission colonial architectural style, a regional style that evolved from an earlier style known as mission revival. Spanish mission revival style developed in the Southwest during the late nineteenth century and reflected the regional Catholic missions of the Spanish colonial period.

Unity in the architectural design of Randolph Field was achieved through the use of Spanish colonial revival as the dominant theme. Its architect, Lieutenant Harold Clark, drew the regional influences of the Spanish missions of San Antonio into his architectural design. Randolph Field's design and construction represented the most innovative approaches to city planning and aviation in their day. Its residential areas have abundant open space and recreational areas, all within a fully functioning military base and airport. The chapel has a copy of the ornate Rose Window from the church at Mission San José, San Antonio.

The administration building at Randolph Air Force Base is known as the Taj Mahal. It was Clark's idea to conceal a water tower within the building because of his concern that a water tower was both unsightly and a potential hazard to aviators. The administration building, reflecting both Spanish Mediterranean and Spanish colonial revival design influences, rises to 170 feet. In 1987 the building was placed on the National Registry of Historic Places.

Randolph Air Force Base is named for Captain William Millican Randolph, who was born in Austin and served on the naming committee at the time of his fatal crash. After serving in the Army as a member of the Second Texas Infantry in World War I, Captain Randolph entered pilot training at Kelly Field, where he received his military wings in 1919. In 1927 he returned to Kelly as adjutant to this advanced flying school. Captain Randolph perished when his plane crashed on takeoff at Gorman Field, Texas, on February 17, 1928. He was survived by his wife and three children. Randolph Air Force Base serves as the headquarters of Air Education and Training Command as well as the personnel center for the U.S. Air Force.[9]

When Randolph opened, officers' quarters included a living room,

An advanced trainer, the AT-6 Texan, with the main administration building at Randolph Field in the background. Photograph by author.

a dining room, a kitchen, three bedrooms, two bathrooms, and a servant's quarters. Flying cadets' rooms were arranged in a way similar to those at West Point: two cadets to a room.

There were eighteen hangars on the field, nine on each side, which housed 275 aircraft. There were also two large aircraft assembly hangars and large shop and maintenance hangars. Their roofs were painted in checkerboard chrome yellow and black for easy visibility from the air. Inside the administration building was a theater with room for seating of one thousand. Athletic fields, a swimming pool, and military hospitals were also built.

The first eight months of training at Randolph were dedicated to primary flight training. This included 150 hours of flying, 60 of which were spent in military trainers. Students learned how to perform basic maneuvers, takeoffs and landings, crosswind takeoffs and landings, and cross-country flying.[10] Photographs taken at Randolph and other airfields reveal the type of training flying cadets received and provide a window for capturing some of their daily life experiences while in training.

Flight instructors at Randolph Field used a variety of methods to instruct cadets. They provided lectures using blackboards to explain aerial traffic patterns. As many as two hundred aircraft could be in the air simultaneously, which presented a problem unless there were stringent regulations. An instructor discussed how to perform a 360-degree overhead approach, one of many maneuvers taught to student pilots during flight training. Flight instructors also used model airplanes to demonstrate how to correct their position when flying in formation. Flying cadets learned the basics of rigging flight controls by examining actual aircraft. When all was said and done, flying cadets sat down to a meal at the Flying Cadet Detachment Mess Hall.

Aviator William P. Mitchell, who earned his military wings in 1942 and became a C-47 transport pilot in France, Germany, and Belgium during World War II, noted in his memoirs that Randolph Field left an "imprint on the cadets."[11] Flying cadets at Randolph had their khaki shirts and trousers dry cleaned, rather than just laundered like other soldiers. The color and shape of Randolph uniforms thus stood out from all the other military cadets; they were always neat and not faded. At Randolph, cadets learned to fly heavier and more complex

Use of airplane models to explain to cadets how to fly in formation at Randolph Field, 1939. The instructor is simulating a shallow dive. Courtesy of the U.S. National Archives, College Park, Maryland.

aircraft and the techniques of formation flying, night flying, and instrument flying. While Randolph was like a "classy hotel," Mitchell described Kelly Field as a "boxcar."[12] Mitchell nonetheless was pleased to have been assigned to Brooks because it meant a greater likelihood that he might become a pursuit pilot, being able to fly AT-6 Texans—advanced military trainers. Mitchell graduated from Brooks on November 10, 1942. However, he was initially assigned to learn to fly the troop carrier C-47 at Del Valle Army Air Base in Austin. Flying a C-47, known casually as "a Gooney Bird," was far less glamorous than flying the B-26 bombers and P-51 Mustangs his cousins flew. Yet it was a safer assignment than flying in the Eighth Air Force, which suffered a high fatality rate.[13]

Bombardier Training in Texas

On May 15, 1942, construction of an Army Air Force Bombardier School began on a plateau about two miles southwest of Big Spring. During World War II, the U.S. Army Air Corps selected bombardiers on the basis of their aptitude. Navigators were credited with above-average intellectual ability. Initially bombardiers had the reputation of men who failed to meet the requirements to occupy the higher prestige positions of navigator and pilot. But by 1943, bombardiers were no longer strictly pilot washouts. Indeed, the bombardier became increasingly central to the Army Air Corps due to its need for precision bombing. Like navigator training, bombardier training first began alongside advanced twin-engine pilot schools.

In 1941 Ellington Field was opened for bombardier training near Houston. But with the humidity of the Gulf coast, it was difficult to peer through the hazy overcast skies with the optical bombsights, so the school was transferred to Midland. There, miles of flat treeless brush and cloudless skies were ideal for carrying out practice bombing raids. At Midland Army Air Field, bombardiers had twenty-three bombing ranges where they could drop their hundred-pound M38A2 practice bombs. These steel containers held three-pound black-powder spotting charges and about eighty-five pounds of sand. As many as one thousand bombs were dropped daily, six or seven days a week. As early as 1934, the Norden bombsight became standard for the U.S. Air Corps.[14]

Ernest L. Clark (1908–2013), Flight Instructor in the Fifties

Ernest L. Clark was born in Louisville, Mississippi, on January 13, 1908. While assigned to Randolph Field, he was an instructor trainee in 1943 and 1944. However, his brief experience there proved not to be a pleasant one. Although he completed the initial phase of the Randolph Standardization School, he became deathly ill with pneumonia. His physician was not sure Clark would pull through. Yet his condition improved and he recovered. In a recent interview, 104-year-old Clark recalled seeing Stearmans, Fairchilds, Ryans, and several B-25s flown at Randolph Field. Clark later became a flight instructor for the U.S. Air Force North Atlantic Treaty Organization (NATO) cadets at Columbus, Mississippi, and at Mission, Texas, from 1955 to 1959. For a detailed reflection in Clark's own words on what it was like to train cadets in Texas, see appendix IV.[15]

Flight instruction for the NATO cadets consisted of approximately 200 hours of ground school, 80 hours of physical training, and approximately 130 hours of flight time rendered by a combined training staff of approximately fifty instructors. Flight training consisted of 30 hours in the T-34 and 96 hours in either the T-28 (propeller) or the T-37 (twin-engine jet). Slightly more than five thousand student pilots were either successfully trained or partially trained (eliminated) at Mission in Clark's time. The USAF (U.S. Air Force) student pilots were either college or university graduates. Some were also USAF Academy graduates or graduates from West Point. In addition to USAF student officers, student pilots from ten other NATO nations were trained. All student pilots had demonstrated an intelligence quotient of nine out of ten to be accepted to the program. The school had not a single fatality during the five-year period Clark was one of its instructors.

The Civilian Pilot Training Program

The University of Texas at Austin served national interests during both world wars by training cadets for military air service. In May 1940 its branch of the Civilian Pilot Training Program opened. The course of study required 240 hours of ground school, which included the study of aerodynamics, navigation, airplane engines, and

Instructor and students in the Civilian Pilot Training Program, January 1942, Meacham Field, Fort Worth. Neg. no. LC-USF 34, photograph by Arthur Rothstein. Courtesy of the Library of Congress, Prints and Photographs Division, FSA/OWI Collection reproduction LC USF 34-024696-D.

communications, along with 35 to 45 hours of flight training at either the Browning or Ragsdale Flying Services in Austin.[16] In 1942, 192 of 225 graduates in the University of Texas Civilian Pilot Training Program enlisted in the U.S. Army Air Corps or Naval Air Corps.[17] Flying cadets also trained at Meacham Field in Fort Worth, as well as in other cities and small towns. The program was established to prepare pilots for military readiness, especially since the military was aware that the training of pilots could not take place overnight. The federally funded Civilian Pilot Training Program was also intended to stimulate the economically depressed light aircraft industry and give a boost to fixed base operators.[18] Of every ten slots, one was reserved for a woman, who had to be enrolled in college. Mary Aletha Miller, for example, trained to be a pilot in the noncollege program of the Civilian Pilot Training Program in Austin.[19] The program was phased out in the summer of 1944, but not before 435,165 pilots earned their licenses from the program's bases all across the country.[20] The program provided an unprecedented opportunity for young women and black aviators to earn their wings, including several who would become Women's Airforce Service Pilots or Tuskegee airmen.

Among the Texans who trained as air cadets at Tuskegee Institute were pursuit pilot Walter McCreary (see chapter 7) and Percy Sutton (1920–2009), who served as an intelligence officer assigned to the 332nd Fighter Group during World War II. Both were from San Antonio. McCreary had attended Phyllis Wheatley High School, where Sutton's father, Samuel Jackson Sutton, was principal. McCreary had earned his pilot license through the Civilian Pilot Training Program in Alabama as a civilian before being militarized at Tuskegee. Sutton—the youngest of fifteen children, all of whom graduated from college—had attended Prairie View College, the Hampton Institute, and the Tuskegee Institute.[21] Tuskegee airmen were held to an even higher standard than most cadets.[22] Other Tuskegee airmen from Texas who earned their military wings at Moton Field are listed in appendix II.

Flight Training of Our Allies in Texas

During the Second World War, Texas served as a major training ground for foreign cadets as well. The building of nearly seventy airfields throughout the state, along with the influx of cadets from across the country as well as from England and Latin America, would change the landscape of the state and transform local communities. For example, the Aguilas Aztecas, the 201st Squadron of the Mexican Expeditionary Air Force, arrived at Greenville in East Texas on August 6, 1944, following a brief introduction and medical examinations at Randolph Field in San Antonio. Thirty-six Mexican fighter pilots received nearly one hundred flying hours of instruction in T-6 Texans and Curtiss P-40s before being assigned to their main base at

Pocatello, Idaho. Mexican fighter pilots flew P-47 Thunderbolts along-side American pilots of the Fifth Army Air Force to liberate the Philippines from Japan.[23]

To help meet Britain's need to train pilots against the threat of world domination by the Axis powers even before Pearl Harbor, 820 Royal Air Force (RAF) cadets received instruction from August 1942 through early April 1943 at Avenger Field in Sweetwater, Texas. At the Fourth of July celebration in 1942, residents of Sweetwater were especially touched by the singing of "Deep in the Heart of Texas" by the young RAF cadets.[24]

Terrell, Texas, became the new RAF site—under the Lend-Lease Act established by President Franklin D. Roosevelt and Prime Minister Winston Churchill—when the U.S. Army Air Corps took over Avenger Field for the Women Airforce Service Pilots program. Approximately 2,300 pilots (mainly British, but also some 125 Americans) trained at the No. 1 British Flying Training School in Terrell, now Terrell Municipal Airport. More than 1,400 cadets earned their wings as single-engine land-licensed pilots. The flying school operated from June 2, 1941, until September 25, 1945. Five additional RAF schools were established—at Lancaster, California; Mesa, Arizona; Miami and Ponca City, Oklahoma; and Clewiston, Florida.

Henry Madgwick (1923–2012) was an RAF cadet from the last flying class to train at Terrell. He was one of three children born to William Henry and Emma Mary Madgwick, milk distributors, of Grayshott, England.[25] He did not finish secondary school, although he knew German, French, and Latin. A college education was not a requirement for flight training in the RAF when it was established in 1918. In 1938 and 1939, Madgwick received some flight training in England, where he soloed in a Tiger Moth at Peterborough after six flying hours. He also attended ground school and did primary training near Cambridge before heading for Canada. His parents were pleased that he was leaving England with all the German bombing raids during the Battle of Britain in 1940. From Canada he and a group of nineteen- and twenty-year-old RAF cadets traveled by train to Chicago, St. Louis, and on to Terrell.

The RAF cadets were surprised by the level of segregation in America during the war. In Chicago, they were warned about going into certain areas and bars. The same was true even in Terrell, although one cadet did have a girlfriend of color. That cadet later married a woman of color and resided in Houston until he died. There was a definite color line in Texas, including at the military training bases. Black workers did all the menial jobs, such as cooking and janitorial work, at the barracks.

Beginning in October 1944, Madgwick completed ten weeks of training at Terrell. At first the cadets had eight weeks of training, then ten weeks, and eventually training was extended to as much as twenty-eight weeks. He soloed the Boeing Stearman PT-17 in five hours and then moved to advanced training in an AT-6 Texan. He also studied navigation, including naval navigation, and flight instruments.

Half of the flying cadets attended ground school in the morning and flew in the afternoon, while the other half did their flight training in the morning and took ground school courses in the afternoon. Ground school included the study of engines, aerodynamics, navigation, flight instruments, armaments, meteorology, and signals—including radio communication. Cadets also spent time on link trainers (flight simulators). Courses lasted six months. Courses one through twelve had fifty cadets in each class. Beginning with course thirteen through course twenty-five, there were one hundred cadets in each class. The failure rate for RAF cadets trying to earn their military wings was approximately 40 percent.

Kenneth John Cawston (1922–1998) trained at Terrell in the fifteenth and sixteenth courses. Cawston was born in Birmingham, England. When war was declared against Germany in 1939, Cawston went to work at an airplane factory. In 1942 he enlisted in the RAF and began flight training in Tiger Moths at Reading, Manchester, Blackpool, Lancashire, and Wales. After experiencing severe rationing, bombing raids, and blackouts, his parents were also pleased to send their son to Terrell. Cawston traveled on the *Queen Mary* to New Brunswick, Canada, and then by rail to Terrell, making stops in small towns and in Chicago along the way. Local residents would come out to greet the young cadets from the United Kingdom at the train station.

At first, citizens of Terrell did not know what to think of these foreigners with their British accents. Soon enough, though, they lined up in front of the base on evenings and weekends, inviting the cadets to their homes, parties, churches, and picnics. The RAF cadets were treated like family members and special guests. The Bass-Rutledge Drug Co. store was a popular stopping ground for the cadets. They bought souvenirs and scarce items to send home to Britain. They saw films at the Iris Theater. They often spent their weekends in Dallas.

Group of Royal Air Force cadets at Terrell, 1943. Kenneth Cawston is standing on the top row on the left, carrying a navigational chart. Courtesy of the No. 1 British Flying Training School Museum.

When Cawston arrived at Terrell on April 1, 1943, he began training as a civilian pilot at the No. 1 British Flying Training School as part of course fifteen, first in PT-17s and PT-18s and then in AT-6 Texans. On December 6, 1943, he earned his wings and the rank of flight sergeant. Once back in England, Cawston resumed flying Tiger Moths until reassignment to the Advanced Flying Unit #II PAFU Calveley, Cheshire, where he began training in the Oxford II. After that, it was on to the Anson I as a staff pilot in Cark, Lancashire, until the end of the war.

During cross-country flights, the RAF cadets practiced flying from Terrell to El Paso, which was about the same distance as from London to Berlin. Having flown to Des Moines, Iowa, on a cross-country training flight, one group of cadets was stranded for five nights due to weather. Henry Madgwick recalled that on those nights each RAF cadet had six young WACs (Women Army Corps), three on each arm, to accompany him to the local bars; he never had to pay for his own drinks. There was safety in numbers, Madgwick pointed out during his interview. The young cadets had a terrific time with so many young American women going through basic training for the U.S. Army in

Des Moines as WACs. On other occasions, Women Air Force Service Pilots (WASPs), particularly those based at Love Field in Dallas, often stopped and refueled their aircraft in Terrell purposely to meet the young RAF pilots.

Upon completing his flight training in Terrell, Madgwick returned to England, where a physician discovered that he was losing his eyesight and was nearly blind in one eye. After only 250 hours of flight time, Madgwick had to give up flying, although he had earned his wings and was a second lieutenant. He then became an interim first lieutenant and physical training instructor for the RAF for the remainder of the war. He spent a couple of years in the reserves before being discharged. Madgwick came to Texas to train as a pilot, but he stayed in Terrell most of his life until his death on March 10, 2012.

In 1946 Henry Madgwick brought Kate Weatherford to England, where they were married. She was the daughter of a dairy farmer in Terrell who owned some fifteen hundred acres. The couple returned to live in Terrell the following year. She passed away in 1993, after 47 years of marriage. He then married a woman with the same first name, Kate Marriot Sanders, whom he cared for until she passed away several years later.

Madgwick worked for Blue Cross and Blue Shield for approximately thirty-five years in Terrell and served as its mayor from 1998 to 2000. Meanwhile, he was involved with the activities at the No. 1 British Flying Training School Museum as its curator, president, and cofounder. He was also a regular visitor to the cemetery at Terrell, where he paid his respects to fallen British RAF cadets, who trained to defend their country only to lose their lives in the process of becoming pilots. Terrell had one Army Air Corps cadet and nineteen RAF cadets killed during flight training. The RAF cadets were buried at the Oakland Memorial Park Cemetery. Madgwick helped the Commonwealth Wars Graves Commission in taking care of the commission's RAF plot. The life stories of Madgwick and his lost comrades underscore that Texas has served as a key training ground for pilots both civilian and military. His body was laid to rest in a plot near his fallen countrymen.

Cawston was among approximately forty of the Terrell RAF cadets who married Texas women. He had left a girlfriend behind in Fort Worth. After the war, her family sponsored him to come to the United States. Cawston immigrated to Texas in 1947, soon becoming an American citizen. In 1948 Cawston moved to Goldsmith, Texas, to

work for Gulf Oil Company. There he met his future wife, Anne Marie
Townsley, through friends. They were married in 1951 and had three
children. Cawston visited Terrell often, especially on Remembrance
Day. He also served on the museum board of the No. 1 British Flying Training School. Upon his death on September 17, 1998, his family spread his ashes at the Terrell Municipal Airport, where he had
earned his wings.

Women Airforce Service Pilots, Avenger Field, Sweetwater

Women aviators trained in Texas to "relieve fighting
men for combat duty" in 1943 and 1944.[26] Over one hundred civilian women pilots from Texas flew noncombat missions and served in
the ferrying command under Nancy Harkness Love and as Women
Airforce Service Pilots under Jacqueline Cochran.[27] Twenty-eight
women aviators between ages twenty-one and thirty-five became the
Women's Auxiliary Ferrying Squadron in the fall of 1942. Each had
at least five hundred flying hours, a commercial license, and a two-
hundred-horsepower engine rating.[28] The first class of the Women's
Flying Training Detachment (WFTD) reported to Cochran at Howard Hughes Field (Houston Municipal Airport) on November 17, 1942.
Four classes trained there before its facility was determined to be too
small for the expanding program. Besides, weather would set in, especially fog, which proved detrimental for flight training.[29] Many early
graduates had more than five hundred flight hours, among other qual-
ifications. Others were initially short of the five hundred hours but
met that qualification by the time they were trained at Houston Municipal Airport. In the fall of 1942, Cochran had negotiated a requirement of only two hundred hours in order for these women pilots to be
admitted to the training program at Houston.[30] She later succeeded
in lowering the entrance requirement to one hundred hours, then
seventy-five, and by summer 1943, thirty-five hours, the minimum required of a private pilot. The women pilots of the ferrying command
and the WFTD merged into one organization, called Women Airforce
Service Pilots, on August 5, 1943. The first class of WASPs graduated
at Ellington Field in Houston in April 1943.[31]

The women cadets who flew for the military were distinct in that
they had to have a pilot's license even to be considered for the pro-

High-altitude flight training of Women Airforce Service Pilots at Randolph Air Field, Aviation School of Medicine, San Antonio, 1943 and 1944. From left to right: instructor Lt. Walter H. Leigh and WASPs Betty Heinrich, Elvira Caroline Griggs, Rita Davoly, Mary Lois Wiggins (center), Lois Lancaster, Mary Margaret Canavan, Robbie Graham Grace, and Carol Webb. Courtesy of the U.S. National Archives, College Park, Maryland.

gram. Once accepted into the program, the rigorous instruction they received was the same as that given to male cadets and included the principles of flight, engines and propellers, weather, instruments, navigation, communications, forms and procedures, mathematics, and physics.[32] Spin training—learning the technique to break a stall in the airplane, stop rotation by applying the opposite rudder, and then recover from a dive—was a normal part of the flight curriculum for all flying cadets, as was the use of parachutes.[33] In 1943 and 1944 WASPs also learned about high-altitude flying in the altitude chambers at Randolph Field's School of Aviation Medicine, where the graduates from Avenger Field were instructed in a simulated manner at twenty-five, thirty, and thirty-five thousand feet.

Jokingly, WASPs at Randolph Field complained about the size of their flying suits before they were issued uniforms. Depending on the type of aircraft, WASPs wore flight suits, baggy mechanic's coveralls—which the women called "zoot suits"—or slacks and jackets with short- or long-sleeved blouses. In 1942 as head of the WAFS, Love approved of simple, rather classically designed uniforms for her WAFS.

Women Airforce Service Pilots at Avenger Field in their winter flight suits
with PT-17 Boeing Cadets (commonly known as Stearmans) on the flight
line in the snow. One WASP is unidentified; Clara Jo Marsh and Ann Loree
are sitting beside Stearman biplanes, January 12, 1944. 342-FH-4A-05356-
36483AC. Courtesy of the U.S. National Archives.

For dress uniforms, WAFS wore gray-green wool gabardine jackets
with squared shoulders, gray skirts, broadcloth shirts, and ties. WAFS
uniforms were utilitarian in nature, not designed for their particular style or beauty. For flying, these civilian women pilots wore gray-
green slacks, blouses, and flight jackets.[34] The WASP trainees initially
wore long tan pants, short-sleeved white blouses, and a general's boat-
shaped cap. For winter flying, WASPs wore leather flight suits that
were lined with fleece.

WASP wings were fashioned from bombardier's "sweetheart" wings
with a shield and stylized ribbon on which the year of their class and
unit could be engraved following graduation. Jacqueline Cochran then
had Santiago blue (a dark shade) dress uniforms designed by Bergdorf
Goodman in New York City for her trainees. The uniform worn for
formal occasions or office wear consisted of a long-sleeved blue jacket
with two pockets on top and two on the bottom, a blue skirt or slacks,
a white blouse, a black tie, a blue beret, and a black purse and shoes.
WASPs wore either a cap or a tan cotton-type helmet, again depending whether they flew an open-cockpit airplane or one with a closed
canopy.[35] WASPs were the first aviators to wear blue uniforms, which

later became standard with the creation of the United States Air Force in 1947.[36]

Air cadets faced an extremely high attrition rate in their quest to become military aviators. Many men and women washed out of the U.S. Army Air Corps or WASP programs before earning their wings. The washout rate of women pilots was comparable to that of male cadets.[37]

Being a private pilot led Ruth Shafer (1922–) of Rochester, New York, to become one of the 1,830 women accepted for military flight training at Avenger Field. Shafer, a member of class 44-W-4, was one of 1,074 women who successfully graduated from the WASP program. She insists that winning her pair of silver wings on May 23, 1944, was the happiest moment in her life, despite having married Air Force Reserve aviator Maurice "Bud" Fleisher in December 1952.[38] For most U.S. women, the happiest moment was supposed to have been their wedding day, not the day they earned their wings.

At eighteen in 1940, Shafer had been too young to enter the federal government's Civilian Pilot Training Program, which had an age requirement of twenty-one. To receive this government-sponsored flight training, one also had to be enrolled in college; Shafer had just graduated from West High School in Rochester, New York. Since there was no one around qualified to teach ground school near Philadelphia and she held a ground instructor's rating, she was hired to instruct college students older than she was in the very program that had refused her entry. Beginning in 1941, Shafer served as a communications officer at a coastal air base at Suffolk, Long Island. She received radio calls about any activity off the coast and relayed that information to the appropriate personnel at the U.S. Army Air Corps base at Mitchell Field. Shafer unintentionally soloed in a Piper Cub on January 14, 1941, after her instructor's stick had come loose, and landed the airplane by herself. She received her private pilot's license on March 11, 1942.[39]

WASP Shafer recalls that the program at Sweetwater was a very strenuous one. The cadets had to study hard to earn their wings. The program was not easy to get through, since an instructor could require additional check rides if he was not satisfied with the quality of their flying. Flying cadets feared being washed out; of the ninety-five cadets that entered her class, only fifty-two graduated. And several male flight instructors resented having to teach women to fly military airplanes. Some of them would have preferred to be flying missions over Europe or the Pacific, rather than being assigned to remote

Sweetwater, where there was nothing but "wind, sand, barbed wire, and women cadets."[40]

After graduation, Shafer tested AT-6 Texans (advanced trainers) and BT-13s (basic trainers) following maintenance at Gunter Air Force Base in Alabama. These were airplanes already in service that had been checked by a mechanic after an accident but needed to be tested before an Army Air Forces cadet or anyone else could fly them. Shafer tested as many as four or five airplanes in a single day. Sometimes she could smell problems before she even got into the airplanes because of a broken or disconnected fuel line. Later, she attended and graduated from the Air Force School of Applied Tactics at Orlando, Florida. She earned her commercial license on January 5, 1945.[41]

Following the deactivation of the WASP program on December 20, 1944, Shafer turned to the few areas in which women pilots could still be employed in aviation. She tried working as a flight instructor and occasionally flying charter flights but could not earn enough to make a living. She then studied to become an air traffic controller. On July 16, 1945, Shafer earned her air traffic control tower operator certificate. She applied for a federal civil service air traffic control position in Philadelphia with the Civil Aeronautics Authority (CAA). The response she received was "Thank you very much, but we already have one," meaning the token female air traffic controller in that region. Shafer's father, airport manager at both Philadelphia International and North Philadelphia Airport, soon learned of an air traffic controller position. Shafer passed a test for the position and served as an air traffic controller at Philadelphia International Airport and North Philadelphia Airport between 1948 and 1952. She had to earn a rating for each field by passing a CAA test, and she worked her way from junior to senior air traffic controller. Although she would have preferred a flying job, air traffic control was an acceptable occupation. She had grown up at the airport, watching traffic operations.[42] Shafer was among the fortunate few women who were hired after the war, when major aircraft manufacturers were shutting down production and thousands of male pilots entered the market following demobilization.[43] She would later work in military towers as an air traffic controller at El Paso and other bases, wherever her husband was assigned.

From February 20, 1943, to December 7, 1944, Avenger Field was the first and only all-women military flying school in the world for the WASP program. Forty miles west of Abilene, Avenger had long wooden barracks painted gray that were divided into two bays, each for six cadets. Their mascot, Fifinelli, a gremlin designed by Walt Disney in 1942, was painted on top of each building.[44]

Cochran, a top air racer and record setter as well as head of the WASP program, had the support of First Lady Eleanor Roosevelt. As the wife of an affluent industrialist, Cochran could make things happen for women in military aviation. She had the connections but also demonstrated highly effective leadership skills. She was determined to start a training program for women, although Love had already started the ferrying command. Cochran had been in charge of U.S. women fliers who transported military aircraft in the Air Transport Auxiliary program (ATA) in England.[45] President Roosevelt then persuaded General Henry H. "Hap" Arnold, Commanding General of the U.S. Army Air Force, to make use of women pilots by relieving male pilots for combat duties. On May 10, 1943, the first twenty-three graduates from Cochran's flight training program in Houston were dispatched to ferrying commands in Wilmington, Delaware; Romulus, Michigan; Dallas; and Long Beach. The second class of women arrived in Houston on June 14, 1943. More graduates would arrive approximately every five weeks until December 1944. Of the 1,074 WASPs, more than ninety entered from Texas (see Appendix III).

EARNING ONE'S WINGS WAS A GREAT ACCOMPLISH-ment for all the young men and women pilots who were trained by the military in Texas and for Texans who traveled to other states, such as Alabama, to learn to fly. Aviators—whether born in Texas, other states, or even other countries—responded to the need for pilots, flight instructors, bombardiers, navigators, and ground crew personnel. World War II–era flight-training programs undoubtedly proved successful, shown by the number of aviators who served their country either at home or overseas. Several patriotic Texans also distinguished themselves by heroic acts of courage, superior aeronautical ability, and leadership qualities during the air war in the global conflict. (See Appendix I: Time Flies in Texas Aviation, especially under the years 1943 and 1944, for brief accounts of individual Texans who earned the Congressional Medal of Honor in air combat.)

Chapter 7

Texas Air Power during the Second World War

*A*FTER WORLD WAR I, MILITARY AIRPLANES WERE transformed from minor war machines to serious tactical instruments such as the B-24 Liberator and the B-17 Flying Fortress. World War I airplanes could damage a military camp, a house, or several buildings. But military planes beginning in the mid-1930s could sink ships or annihilate entire towns by dropping bombs. Airplanes such as the B-29 Superfortress became a threat that could determine the outcome of a global war. However, the airplane most closely associated with Texas during the war is the North American AT-6, or T-6, also known as the T-6 Texan, an advanced military trainer. Highly maneuverable and responsive, this aircraft underscores one of Texas's primary roles in the war effort to defeat Germany, Italy, and Japan: as a major center for primary and advanced military flight training (see chapter 6).

The Texan is a single-engine, low-wing, two-seat airplane. It has a wingspan of forty-two feet, a length of twenty-nine feet, and a height of eleven feet, one inch. It has a six-hundred-horsepower Pratt and Whitney R-1340 engine. Its maximum speed is 210 miles per hour, and it has a range of 870 miles. Yet it was the people who flew it—Texans and Americans from other states—who distinguished themselves in defense of the nation and democracy. Several of the Texas aviators discussed here had modest rural backgrounds. Others came from middle-class families in towns and cities throughout Texas.

Wing Commander Lance Cleo Wade
(1915–1944), Texas's Top Scoring Ace
during World War II

The highest scoring American aviator in the Royal Air Force, L. C. Wade was born in the rural farming community of Broaddus in East Texas in 1915. As a young man he served in the Civilian Conservation Corps during the Great Depression. As part of this New Deal program, Wade drove a team of mules, built roads, and planted trees.[1] In 1933 he learned to fly and applied for cadet training in the U.S. Army Air Corps, only to be turned down due to a lack of education. Undeterred, he traveled to Canada and joined the Royal Air Force (RAF) in December 1940. He was commissioned as an aviator and officer on April 1, 1941. Due to heavy losses during the Battle of Britain, the RAF readily accepted Wade and others like him. Following additional flight training in England, Wade joined the 33rd Aero Squadron in Egypt, where he claimed his first victories on November 18, 1941, by shooting down two Italian Fiat CR.42s over El Eng Airfield. He participated in the heaviest fighting in the Western Desert before finishing his first combat tour on September 17, 1942. He then was assigned to the RAF delegation in Washington, DC. On loan to the U.S. Army Air Corps, he toured training centers and tested aircraft at Wright Field in Dayton, Ohio. In January 1943, Wade returned to duty to conduct flight operations in North Africa as a flight commander with the 145th Squadron of the Royal Air Force. Then he added to his victories by scoring over Tunisia, Sicily, and Italy before finishing his second tour of duty as the top Allied ace fighter pilot in the Mediterranean theater in November 1943. Wade was promoted to wing commander and joined the RAF staff at the Desert Air Force Headquarters only to be killed during a routine flight when his Auster, an Australian liaison aircraft, went into a spin and crashed at Foggia on January 12, 1944. Wade had achieved a total of twenty-five victories, making him one of America's top aces during the Second World War. He is the highest scoring American aviator to have served solely in the Royal Air Force.[2] He also scored more victories than any other Texan ace who flew for the U.S. Army Air Corps. He received the British Distinguished Service Order and Distinguished Flying Cross with two bars, meaning multiple Distinguished Flying Crosses.[3]

General Ira Clarence Eaker (1896–1987), Pioneer Aviator and Record Setter

Over the course of his illustrious career, General Ira Eaker served as commander of the Eighth Air Force in England in 1942 and 1943; as air commander in chief of the Mediterranean Allied Air Forces in 1944 and 1945; as a U.S. Air Force general, earning four stars; as an executive officer in the aerospace industry; and as a syndicated newspaper columnist for military affairs from 1964 to 1982. Eaker led the first U.S. bombing raid in a B-17 against German occupation forces in France at Rouen, northwest of Paris, on August 17, 1942.

The son of tenant farmers Yancy and Dora Eaker, Ira was born on April 13, 1896, at Field Creek, Texas, northwest of Austin. Eaker attended Southeastern Normal School in Duran, Oklahoma, earning high grades. But he loved flying and understood that those officers who flew had a better chance of getting attention and advancing in their military careers faster than those who sat behind desks.[4] In 1917 he enlisted in the army, where he was admitted to officers' training school and commissioned a second lieutenant in the infantry. He trained to be a pilot at Austin (most likely at the University of Texas's School of Military Aeronautics) and then at Kelly Field in San Antonio. He trained in a Curtiss JN-4 Jenny primary trainer and had over seventy-five flying hours by the time he earned his wings in October 1918.[5] He served in the Philippines in July 1919.

On July 1, 1920, Eaker was transferred from the infantry to the air service.[6] He returned for duty at Mitchell Field, New York, in January 1922, where he commanded the Fifth Aero Squadron. From December 1926 to May 1927, Eaker was second in command of the Pan American Goodwill Tour by U.S. Army planes. He flew the *San Francisco*, a Loening OA-1A amphibian biplane, which traveled throughout Central and South America. This flight sought to improve relations with Latin America, foster the development of commercial aviation, and provide operational training for the U.S. Army Air Corps. The twenty-two-thousand-mile journey began in San Antonio on December 21, 1926, and ended 133 days later in Washington, DC.[7] Eaker and other members of the flight crew earned the Distinguished Flying Cross for this goodwill flight.

From January 1–7, 1929, he piloted the U.S. Army's *Question Mark* (not the same aircraft flown by the French flyers Dieudonné Costes

Captain Ira C. Eaker, pioneer military aviator and record
setter, February 16, 1929. LC-DIG-npcc-17056. Courtesy of the
Library of Congress, National Photo Company Collection.

and Maurice Bellonte, discussed in chapter 4) establishing a new
world endurance midair refueling record by remaining aloft for one
hundred fifty hours, forty minutes, and fifteen seconds, nearly six and
a half days of continuous flight. In 1930 he made the first transcontinental flight using midair refueling operations. In 1936 he made the
first transcontinental flight in a P-12 using instruments only (Sperry's
Gyro Horizon and Directional Gyro); he flew the entire way under a
baggy hood. The Gyro Horizon improved pilots' sense of direction
with respect to Earth, which allowed them to fly more instinctively.
The Directional Gyro corrected navigational errors due to the defects
of the magnetic compass during turns and in flight turbulence.[8] Following a series of promotions, Eaker became a two-star general in
January 1942.

As commander of the Eighth Air Force in England, Eaker played a
vital role in convincing Winston Churchill of the need to destroy Germany's war production by having American aviators carry out precision daylight bombing while Royal Air Force pilots bombed at night.
He built up the Eighth Air Force from scratch, going from seven men
and no planes in February 1942 to one hundred eighty-five thousand

Brigadier General Ira Eaker, architect
of strategic bombing. Courtesy of the
United States Air Force.

men and four thousand planes by December 1943.[9] In February 1945,
as air commander in chief of the Mediterranean Allied air forces,
Eaker opposed bombing small German towns where civilians took
shelter from the horrors of heavy bombing raids. Eaker did not want
America to leave a wartime legacy of bombing German sites with no
strategic military or economic objectives where only heavy civilian casualties would result. However, he had no moral objection to bombing
strategic military areas and incurring incidental civilian losses to put
an end to Germany's industrial war production.[10]

During more than thirty years of flying, Eaker accumulated twelve
thousand flying hours. On August 31, 1947, he retired from the U.S.
Air Force, which was established as a separate service by President
Harry S. Truman on July 26, 1947. He then served as an executive
officer for the Hughes Tool Company in Houston and Hughes Aircraft until 1952, followed by a stint at the Douglas Aircraft Company.
Eaker's career suggests that he retired from the U.S. Air Force to work
in the lucrative private sector. Salaries for well-connected ex-military
officers, especially those working for Howard Hughes, were better
than military pay. Hughes Aircraft became the largest manufacturing facility of electronic equipment on the West Coast. It specialized
in radar, lasers, communication satellites, components for guided
missiles and computers, and what became generally known as "avionics."[11] Eaker had first met the millionaire aircraft designer following Hughes's 1938 world flight, when Eaker was a lieutenant colonel
on the air staff and air chief of the Army's Information Division. As

vice president of Hughes Tool Company in Houston, Eaker was tasked with establishing a laboratory that would attract eminent scientists to work on defense issues in what were considered ideal conditions.[12] The extent to which Eaker achieved this remains unclear, but the Hughes name could usually attract the best and the brightest. Eaker was promoted to lieutenant general on the retired list on June 29, 1948.

Over his lifetime, Eaker received numerous honors, including the Silver Star and a Distinguished Service Medal with an Oak Leaf Cluster. He received decorations in Britain, France, the former Soviet Union, Italy, Poland, Yugoslavia, Brazil, Chile, Peru, and Venezuela. In 1970 Eaker was inducted into the Aviation Hall of Fame in Dayton, Ohio.

During the 1970s, with the rise of the women's movement, Eaker favored the idea of incorporating women into the military. On August 27, 1977, he wrote that "women in military service were generally good and sometimes superior to men," recalling lessons learned during World War II.[13] It was Eaker's impression that women kept secrets well because they tended not to frequent pubs to the same extent as men in England. Women, he recalled, drove ambulances and served as fire wardens. Women officers, he insisted, must have equal opportunities for education and training with their male counterparts. He thought the idea of women serving in the military was long overdue.

On October 10, 1978, Eaker received the Congressional Gold Medal "in recognition of his distinguished career as an aviation pioneer and Air Force leader," for his many contributions to aviation and to national security. At the Pentagon, he received his fourth star on April 2, 1985. He passed away in 1987 at age ninety-one.

Walter Lee Dyer (1920–2013):
World War II B-24 Liberator Pilot,
Retired Lieutenant Colonel, Veteran of Three Wars

Walter Lee Dyer was born January 10, 1920, in Stonewall, Oklahoma. In an interview, he recalled that most local traffic in his hometown was by horse-drawn buggy or wagon. When he was four years old, his family moved to a farm in West Texas about thirty miles west of Lubbock. Since boyhood, he was fascinated with airplanes. When he was inducted into the service during World War II, he requested an assignment with the U.S. Army Air Corps, but he was first assigned to be trained as a truck mechanic. Later he applied and was accepted to airplane mechanic training in Yakima, Washington. After graduation, he was sent to Gowen Field at Boise, Idaho, to work on B-17 Flying Fortresses. However, he always envied the pilots. One day a B-17 pilot took him for a ride, and Dyer declared that he wanted to learn to fly like them. He applied for aviation cadet training and was accepted into class 43-K. After ten or twelve hours of flight training in a PT-19, Dyer soloed.

Upon graduation in December 1943, Dyer was sent to an airfield in Fort Worth, where he trained to be a B-24 bomber pilot. He recalled that on one occasion, he, his instructor, and another student were scheduled to fly a particular airplane, but it had maintenance problems. They completed their flight training for the day on another airplane. The next day Dyer learned that another crew had flown that first problematic plane to West Texas, where it crashed. All aboard were killed.

After completing flight training at Fort Worth, Dyer was sent to Salt Lake City, Utah, and to Pueblo, Colorado, for combat crew training. Then he and his crew were sent to Camp Kilmer, New Jersey. On June 17, 1944, they boarded the *Queen Elizabeth* bound for Scotland. Glenn Miller's band played all night long aboard the ship. Miller himself, however, had flown ahead. Later, the bandleader was reported missing over the English Channel.

In England, Dyer was assigned to the 8th Army Air Corps, 2nd Air Division, 389th Bomber Group, 565th Squadron, based at Hethel near Norwich. His group and others flew missions from this base near the North Sea. The 8th Army Air Force had twenty-one B-24 groups and about that many B-17 groups flying out of England. Dyer had flown on Christmas Eve, 1944, but was not scheduled to fly on Christmas. Then he and his men received a call for maximum effort—two thousand planes to fly on the same day. Dyer recalled that the greatest dangers while flying were the weather, flak, and enemy fighter airplanes. Many crews were shot down that day by fighters and flak; Dyer's group lost twelve airplanes and their crew members. He had been aware that other groups suffered losses before the Christmas raid, but that experience made him understand the grave dangers they faced. Some of the people that they had gone to a movie with the night before were killed. It was a day he would never forget.

Another time, Dyer recalled—his twenty-third mission, on October 15, 1944—the target was an oil refinery near Dusseldorf, Germany. Hollywood Actor Jimmy Stewart was flying as command pilot in the lead B-24. After some changes in flight positions, Dyer was assigned to be Stewart's left wing man. They completed their mission and headed back to their home base in England. As they descended, they ran into some clouds, which got so thick that the pilots could not see each other even in close formation. A short time later, they broke out of the clouds to find the formation scattered all over the sky. Somehow, Dyer had crossed over to the right of Stewart's aircraft. It was a miracle that there were no midair collisions.

As pilot in command of a B-24 Liberator, Dyer flew a total of thirty-five missions, thirty-four over Germany and one to France, which had not yet been liberated. Dyer also flew in the Korean War and Vietnam. He completed training to fly the C-45 cargo airplane, the T-39 Sabreliner (his favorite aircraft), and the C-130. After retiring from the Air Force with thirty-seven years of service, Dyer flew commuter airliners, including the Beech 99 and Queen Air. He first flew for Air Texas, based at Meacham Field, Fort Worth, then for West Pacific Airlines at Seattle, Washington. Then he flew for Rio Airways. He was based at Corpus Christi until he was transferred to Wichita Falls. He loved flying the Beech 99 from Wichita Falls to Dallas, Love Field. He flew five trips a day with only two crew members aboard. His last flight as an airline captain was on October 3, 1999. Dyer thought he had indigestion when he let his copilot take over. After they landed, Dyer learned that he had suffered a heart attack and was hospitalized. Even though he could no longer fly, Dyer's enthusiasm for flying was still contagious at the time of his interview. For fifty years of safe flying, Dyer received a Wright Brothers Master Pilot Award from the Federal Aviation Administration in January 2006.

Other Texans Distinguish Themselves in the European Theater

John R. Kane, Colonel, U.S. Army Air Corps, Ninth Air Force, was born in McGregor, Texas, in 1907. He flew one of 179 B-24 Liberators seeking to destroy the Nazi-held oil refineries at Ploesti, Rumania, on August 1, 1943. Kane grew up in the Wichita Falls area and graduated from Baylor University. In 1932 he earned his military wings, having trained at flight schools at Brooks, Randolph, and Kelly Fields in San Antonio.

Despite intense antiaircraft fire, enemy fighter planes, and the extreme hazards of the low-level attack over oil fires and explosions, Kane managed to carry out his mission. By the time Kane left his target, his aircraft had lost an engine, having been struck by antiaircraft fire. Kane crashed in Cyprus on the return leg but survived the ordeal.

Reassigned to the United States, Kane served in various capacities until he resigned in 1954. In 1956 he accepted an appointment as colonel in the Air Force Reserves during retirement. He is the recipient of a Congressional Medal of Honor, two Distinguished Flying Crosses, and five Air Medals, among other awards.

Another Texan, Second Lieutenant Lloyd "Pete" Herbert Hughes, Jr., was a B-24 pilot who did not survive the Ploesti oilfield bombing. His left wing caught fire; he died in the attack. Hughes also received the Congressional Medal of Honor for his conspicuous sense of duty and heroism.

The Flying Tigers

Members of the First American Volunteer Group (AVG), known as the Flying Tigers, were American pilots who helped China fight against the Japanese. When Japan invaded China in 1937, the Chinese nationalist government looked to the United States for assistance and hired a veteran aviator, General Claire Chennault, to recruit airmen from the United States. The Flying Tigers were mercenaries; they received $500 from the nationalist government of China for every Japanese plane they shot down. The AVG had an impressive record in 1941 and 1942, at a time when the outcome of the war looked bleak and good news about the Allied forces was rare. The group lost only ten pilots in combat and the same number in airplane accidents, while it took the lives of approximately fifteen hundred Japanese personnel.

Several Flying Tigers were originally from Texas, including their commander, General Chennault. Chennault was born in Commerce, Texas, in 1893, but raised and educated in Louisiana. In 1942 he thought the best strategy to defeat the Japanese was to destroy Japanese aviation using China as a base. Chennault drew up a written plan for the air strategy in Asia, which he presented to President Franklin D. Roosevelt and Prime Minister Winston Churchill at the White House on May 12, 1943. Flying on a moment's notice, he used his navigation briefcase as a desktop on a flight en route to Washington, DC, writing with a pen that leaked at high altitude. Chennault earned the Distinguished Flying Cross as commander of the Flying Tigers and the Fourteenth U.S. Air Force in China.[14]

The Flying Tigers were named after the ferocious, toothy tiger shark painted on the nose of the AVG P-40s on both sides of its large, distinctive radiator intake. Walt Disney designed the insignia of the AVG for the Flying Tigers—a snarling tiger with its legs extended, showing fangs and claws. Inspired by the design of the No. 112 Squadron of the Royal Air Force, native Texan Charles Bond allegedly was the first American pilot to paint this distinctive tiger shark design on his P-40 Warhawk.

Major General USAF Charles R. Bond, Jr. (1915– 2009), Vice Squadron Leader in the Flying Tigers

On April 22, 1915, Charles R. Bond was born in Dallas to parents of Scottish and Irish descent. His father owned a painting and wallpaper business. Charles hoped to attend Texas A&M University, but the Great Depression hit. He then explored the possibility of attending West Point Academy through the enlisted ranks. Although he earned a ninety-six in a course at Fort Sam Houston in San Antonio, he was unable to gain an appointment. He returned home to work in the painting business. Nevertheless, he was determined to have a military career. He learned that a high school graduate could be accepted as a flying cadet in the U.S. Army Air Corps. In March 1938, he reported to Randolph Field near San Antonio and entered class 39-A for flight training. After six hours of training he soloed in a Stearman PT-13. After nine months, his class moved to nearby Kelly Field. Despite graduating at the top of his class, Bond was assigned to the Second Bomber Group at Langley Field, Virginia. He had hoped to be a fighter pilot, flying single-engine pursuit airplanes. He was assigned to fly co-pilot, assistant squadron operations officer on a B-17, to then Lieutenant Curtis E. LeMay. Under LeMay's guidance, Bond studied all aspects of the B-17. In 1939 there were only fourteen B-17s in the United States, all of them in the Second Bomber Group. In March 1941, he was assigned to the Air Transport Ferrying Command at Long Beach, California. He then ferried aircraft to Montreal for several months.[15]

In the spring and summer of 1942, General Claire Chennault began recruiting for the AVG. Eventually 110 pilots joined, including Bond;

the eldest was forty-three and the youngest twenty-one. The Navy had trained most of the Flying Tigers; six were from the Marines and the rest from the U.S. Army Air Corps. Chennault had permission to recruit from the armed forces. For Bond, the lure of adventure drew him to volunteer to fly in the skies over China and Burma against the Japanese.

Flying in China had its challenges, as Bond noted on February 21, 1942:

> . . . ship started shaking violently. It sounded as though the engine was missing badly. I pulled up in a gentle climb and started out over the bay towards Rangoon. I was determined to get back to friendly soil if I had to swim to it. I throttled back and switched to a full rich mixture. I had my canopy rolled back, my oxygen mask off, and my helmet removed. I was ready to ditch or bail out. The vibration lessened considerably, and the engine began to smooth out. I nursed the plane back to the field and set her down on the runway with a great deal of relief. When I cut the engine in my alert space, I sat there and looked across the nose of the fuselage to reflect and take a deep breath. I saw the problem immediately. There was a one-inch hole right through the middle of one of my prop blades. Somehow a .50 caliber bullet went right through the blade on my last strafing pass on the ground bomber. I had really been in combat—a lot of it, all kinds, and all day.[16]

On May 4, 1942, three Japanese fighters zeroed in on his tail, shooting like mad, according to his diary entry. Bond recalled having parachuted out of a burning plane and landing in a Chinese cemetery. He described his ordeal:

> I felt a burning sensation on my neck and shoulders and suddenly realized that my scarf and flying suit were on fire. I hurried to a small stream flowing through the cemetery and laid down on my back and wallowed in the water. My head ached.
>
> The agony of my burns had me on the verge of passing out. I wanted to die to get out of the pain. I would lie down,

get up, walk around, lie down, get up, hold my hand in the air to reduce the circulation and throbbing pain, cry out loud, and pray.

My helmet had two long rips in it. Apparently the armor plate in the P-40 . . . had barely kept all but a couple of bullets from killing me.[17]

A group of Chinese peasants found him a doctor who treated him. He was thankful to be alive. Bond returned to combat a few weeks later, only to be shot down again on June 12, 1942. On their leather flight jackets, members of the AVG had Chinese lettering with a message informing Chinese peasants that Americans were flying on behalf of the Chinese against Japanese aggressors and urging them to offer assistance.

On June 21, 1942, Bond and a group of men decided to go home. He wanted to get a regular commission. He was honorably discharged on July 4, 1942. In October 1942 he returned to the U.S. Army Air Corps, where he served in various capacities in the United States and abroad.

In 1947 Bond was able to attend Texas A&M University as a thirty-two-year-old among much younger students. He received a bachelor's degree in management engineering. He spent subsequent years at NORAD (North American Air Defense Command) in Colorado Springs. He then served in Thailand during the Vietnam War. He earned the Distinguished Service Medal and was given command of the Twelfth Air Force in Waco, Texas, among other honors.

David "Tex" Hill (1915–2007), Naval Aviator, Flying Tiger, and One of the Top American Aces of the Pacific Theater

David Lee Hill was born on July 13, 1915, in Kwangju, Korea, the son of Presbyterian missionaries. His family moved to Texas when he was six years old. After graduating from Austin College in 1938, Hill completed naval flight school and served in a torpedo squadron (VT-3) on the USS *Saratoga* and in a dive-bomber squadron (VB-41) on the USS *Ranger*.

In 1941 Hill joined the AVG. He reported in July and served as flight leader and then squadron leader of the Second Squadron, flying the Curtiss P-40 Warhawk. As a Flying Tiger, he became one of the top aces who flew on behalf of China, credited with destroying 10.25 Japanese planes.

Hill's first victories came on January 3, 1942, when he shot down two Ki-27 Nates over the Japanese airfield at Tak, Thailand. He claimed two more on January 23 and "made ace" on January 24, when he shot down a bomber and a fighter over Rangoon. In March, he succeeded Jack Newkirk as leader of the Second Squadron.

On May 7, 1942, the Japanese Army began building a pontoon bridge across the Salween River, which would allow them to move troops and supplies into China. Hill led a flight of four new P-40Es, bombing and strafing into the mile-deep gorge. During the next four days, the AVG pilots flew continuous missions into the gorge, effectively neutralizing the Japanese efforts. The Japanese never advanced beyond the west bank of the Salween.

After the deactivation of the Flying Tigers in July 1942, Hill became one of five Flying Tigers to join the Twenty-Third Fighter Group. He was promoted to the rank of major in the Army Air Corps and activated in the Seventy-Fifth Fighter Squadron, later to command the Twenty-Third Fighter Group.

Before returning to the United States in late 1944, Hill and his P-51 Mustang shot down another six Japanese aircraft. It is alleged that he was the first to shoot down a Zero with a P-51. Altogether, Hill destroyed 18.25 enemy aircraft.

In late November 1943, Hill led a force of twelve B-25s, ten P-38s, and eight new P-51 Mustangs from Saichwan, China, on the first strike against Formosa (Taiwan). The Japanese had one hundred bombers and one hundred fighters located at Shimchiku Airfield, and the bombers were landing as Hill's team arrived. The enemy managed to get seven fighters airborne, but they were promptly shot down. Forty-two Japanese airplanes were confirmed destroyed, and twelve more were probably destroyed. The American aviators returned home without any casualties.

In 1945 Hill commanded the 412th Fighter Group, the first jet unit in the Army Air Forces. The group flew the Bell XP-59 and later the Lockheed P-80.

In July 1946, Hill resigned his commission and left active duty. Shortly thereafter, he joined the Air National Guard and became the youngest brigadier general in the history of that service. In 1968 he retired from the military.

Hill's honors include the Nationalist Chinese Order of the Cloud Banner, the Chinese Victory Medal, the British Distinguished Flying Cross, the U.S. Distinguished Flying Cross, two Air Medals, a Silver Star, and the Legion of Merit. On October 11, 2007, David Lee "Tex" Hill passed away in San Antonio.[18] In 2009 the Flying Tigers were accorded veteran status in the United States.

Retired Lt. Col. Walter L. McCreary (1918–), Tuskegee Airman and Prisoner of War during World War II

Black American pilots in Texas fought stereotypes and dealt with the challenges of diversity to help win the right to fly military aircraft during World War II. Until World War II, the only black Americans on air bases were the cooks and janitors. Blacks worked and lived under conditions of segregation. In July 1941, the Army Air Corps began to train black pilots and mechanics at Moton Field at the Tuskegee Institute in Alabama, including several from Texas. The Tuskegee Airmen were a group of slightly under one thousand dedicated and determined young black men. About four hundred fifty of those became the first U.S. black military aviators, among them Walter L. McCreary of San Antonio.[19]

McCreary was born on March 4, 1918, in San Antonio, where he was raised by his grandparents. With an Irish last name given to him by his great-grandfather and a Mexican grandmother, McCreary is of mixed cultural and ethnic background. He graduated from Phyllis Wheatley High School in San Antonio in 1935 and majored in business administration at the Tuskegee Institute (now Tuskegee University) in Alabama, graduating in 1940. In 1941 McCreary entered the Civilian Pilot Training Program. He soloed in a Piper J-3 Cub in late 1941, flew a Waco biplane, and earned his pilot's license as a civilian. He started his military flight training as a cadet in the Tuskegee program in August 1942. After nine months of training, he earned his military wings in March 1943 as a second lieutenant in Tuskegee class 43-C. He then did some operational training at Selfridge Field, Detroit, Michigan.

In January 1944 McCreary was sent to Naples, Italy, where he became part of the One Hundredth Fighter Squadron, 332nd Fighter Group, and flew the P-39, P-47, and P-51. His favorite aircraft was the

Captain Walter L. McCreary, Tuskegee
airman. Courtesy of Walter L. Mc-
Creary, retired lieutenant colonel.

P-51. McCreary flew eighty-nine missions over France, Germany, Italy, Austria, Rumania, Greece, Hungary, and Yugoslavia. Although
he flew some strafing missions in which he shot up enemy airplanes
on the ground, McCreary mainly did his assigned job protecting the
bombers, flying escort. Most white pilots were sent back after completing fifty missions, but the War Department did not know what to
do with the Tuskegee Airmen. They were not rotated back to serve as
flight instructors for white cadets due to the color of their skin.

October 14, 1944, was an eventful day. McCreary was flying over
Lake Balaton in Budapest on a strafing mission, his eighty-ninth,
when his radiator was hit by flak. McCreary knew he had to abandon
ship as he had been trained to do. After he parachuted safely to the
ground, some peasant farmers turned him over to the Germans, who
put him on a train to Budapest. When the train suddenly stopped, Mc-
Creary thought he was going to be shot. McCreary had one opportunity to escape, but to what end? Being a person of color, there was
no way he could blend in with the rest of the European population.
The Germans interrogated McCreary, but actually they already knew
everything about him when he was captured. The *Pittsburgh Courier*
had made it a point to publish biographies of each Tuskegee graduate,
which the Germans had read.

The Germans treated McCreary as an officer in the prisoner-of-war
camp designated for airmen. Stalag Luft III, approximately one hundred miles southeast of Berlin in what is today Poland, held some ten

thousand British and American officers and was run by the Luftwaffe. Upon arrival, McCreary was deloused and issued a new uniform. At first he was listed as missing in action but then designated as a prisoner of war. He was allowed to write and send letters home but not to receive any. The film *The Great Escape* (1963) is based on actual events in that prison camp.

Times were tough in the camp during the Battle of the Bulge in the winter months of 1944 and 1945, when there was not even enough food for the Germans. McCreary did receive a weekly parcel from the Red Cross. Once liberated from the prison camp by the Russians and then General "Blood and Guts" Patton, McCreary was put on a ship back to the United States, where he again encountered segregation.

After the war, McCreary worked at Brooks and Kelly Fields in San Antonio for the U.S. Air Force Security Services, a top-secret operation. From 1953 to 1955 he was assigned to work in Tokyo and then returned to Kelly before working in the Panama Canal Zone. He retired from the Air Force as a lieutenant colonel in 1963 and began a second career as deputy director of finance for the state of Ohio and financial officer for the YMCA until he retired in 1983. Although he lives today with his daughter in Burke, Virginia, McCreary travels each year to his native San Antonio, particularly in the spring.[20]

America's black military pilots and ground crews, known as the Tuskegee Airmen, played an important role in the civil rights movement. After the 332nd all-black fighter group was shown to be the most efficient in the 15th Air Force, President Harry Truman decided to integrate all branches of the armed forces in 1948. The 332nd fighter group consisted originally of four fighter squadrons—the 99th, the 100th, the 301st, and 302nd. (See Appendix II for a list of Tuskegee Airmen from Texas who earned their wings.)

John "Mule" Miles (1922–2013), Tuskegee Airplane Mechanic

Also born in San Antonio was John Miles, a graduate of Phyllis Wheatley High School in San Antonio who attended St. Phillip's Junior College. In 1942 Miles enrolled in the Special Aircraft Mechanic Journeyman Rating School at Tuskegee Institute in Alabama. Throughout the war, he assisted the flight-training program at Tuskegee as a certified aircraft mechanic in the U.S. Army Air Corps. While the pilots in the Tuskegee training program, particularly those who flew multiple missions in North Africa and Europe, have received accolades, these aviators could not have flown escort or strafing missions so successfully without the expertise of their ground crews.

Upon returning to San Antonio in 1945, Miles played baseball for the Kelly Field Brown Bombers until he was signed to play for the Negro Baseball League's Chicago American Giants. He earned the nickname "Mule" from his manager, who boasted that Miles "hit the ball like a mule kicks" when he hit two home runs in one game. In 1948 Miles led the league with twenty-seven home runs. The Chicago American Giants captured the Negro American League title in 1949. Miles completed his professional baseball career with the Laredo Apaches in the Gulf Coast League in 1951. He then returned to work as an airplane mechanic at Kelly Field until retiring in 1971 in San Antonio, where he still resides. In 2000, Miles was inducted into the Texas Black Sports Hall of Fame in Dallas. He passed away on May 24, 2013, at age 90.[21]

Ruth Dailey Helm (1916–), Ferry Pilot for the Women Airforce Service Pilots, Class 43-W-2

Born in 1916, Ruth Dailey Helm grew up in a ranching family in Grapeland, Texas, 130 miles east of Waco. After getting a ride from a barnstormer at age eleven, all she ever wanted to do was learn how to fly. However, her parents insisted that she first get an education. Although attending college was not her first choice, she graduated from Baylor University with a degree in business in 1937. She returned home to help with the family business after her father suddenly died. She made enough money to enroll in the Civilian Pilot Training Program at Tyler Community College, where she earned her pilot's license in January 1939, flying an Aeronca Chieftain she owned. She was one of fifty-nine women in the second class who first reported to Houston Municipal Airport for primary training. Only forty-three graduated. She was always scared to death of washing out of the program; the military's standards were high. Almost as frightening for her was the notion of being absorbed into the Women's Army Corps or WACS, in which women did not fly military aircraft.

After earning her wings at Avenger Field as part of Women Airforce Service Pilots (WASP) class 43-W-2, Dailey was assigned to the Fifth

Ferrying Command at Love Field, Dallas. She ferried open-cockpit PT-13s from Wichita, Kansas, to bases in California and learned to fly the P-63. She also attended pursuit school in Palm Springs, California, where five of forty pilots were women. Throughout thousands of miles of ferrying military aircraft, she only had one incident—she hit ice on the runway during a winter landing at Newark in a P-40. Her aircraft skidded and weathervaned (did a half turn), which buckled the landing gear. What saved her from being dismissed from the program was that a male pilot from Dallas had damaged a P-52 only an hour earlier. After the WASP program was deactivated in December 1944 and World War II ended, Dailey bought another plane and moved to Tucson, Arizona.[22] She later married, raised two children, and then earned a master's degree in business at the University of Arizona. Her last touchdown as a pilot was in 1953. In 1999 she was inducted into the Arizona Aviation Hall of Fame.[23]

Dora Dougherty Strother McKeown
(1921–), PhD, WASP Class 43-W-3, B-29 Pilot,
Bell Helicopter Engineer, and World-Record Setter

Dora Dougherty Strother McKeown was only one of two Women Airforce Service Pilots who had the opportunity to fly and instruct male aviators in flying the B-29. Born on November 23, 1921, in St. Paul, Minnesota, she grew up in Long Island, New York and Winnetka, Illinois. She learned to fly in the Civilian Pilot Training Program as a student at Northwestern University in the summer of 1940. Only 10 percent of those slots were reserved for women.

In 1943, when Jacqueline Cochran called for training civilian licensed women pilots, Dougherty happily applied, graduating from the WASP program's third class. She first was assigned to the Air Transport Command at Dallas, Love Field. Next, she was sent to Camp Davis, North Carolina, where she flew the Curtiss SB2C Helldiver on tow target missions. She then served at other bases where she had the opportunity to fly the following military aircraft: PT-19, BT-13, AT-6, AT-11, UC-61, C-45, C-46, C-47, B-25, B-34, B-17, A-24 (SBD), A-25 (SBC-2), PQ-8, and L-5.

Dougherty was one of only two WASPs who learned to fly the B-29. While she was stationed at Elgin Field, Florida, Lieutenant Colonel Paul Tibbets learned that male pilots were reluctant to fly the B-29 at

WASP B-29 pilots Dora Dougherty Strother McKeown and Dorothea "Didi" Johnson Moorman with Colonel Paul Tibbets, standing in front of *Ladybird.* Courtesy of the Woman's Collection, Texas Woman's University, Denton, Texas.

Clovis, New Mexico. Tibbets recalled, "They said it was unsafe. If you lost an engine, you were dead." By that time, Tibbets had about one thousand flying hours in the aircraft. Dougherty and her good friend Dorothea "Didi" Johnson (Moorman) raised their hands when Tibbets asked for volunteers from among the WASPs at Elgin.[24] Tibbets used these two women pilots to encourage male military pilots to fly the large, intimidating bomber. The idea, Dougherty explained, "was that the men, seeing two girls fly the B-29, would have their male egos challenged and would cease complaining about the B-29." The Army Air Corps painted the WASP insignia—Fifinella, a Disney character—on their B-29 and Col. Tibbets named it *Ladybird.* Neither Dougherty nor Johnson had four-engine experience prior to flying the B-29. Dougherty even passed the ultimate test, when two engines went out on one side.

Dougherty was checked out as pilot in command on a total of twenty-three different airplanes.[25] She earned an airline transport rating with instrument and flight instructor ratings. From 1944 to

1949, she taught civilian pilots and ferried aircraft all over the United States. She graduated from Northwestern with a bachelor's degree, later earning a master of science degree from the University of Illinois. She then worked at an aviation psychology laboratory at the University of Illinois and the Martin Company in Baltimore, Maryland. In 1955 she received her doctorate in aviation education from New York University.[26]

In 1958, Dougherty began working as an engineer for Bell Helicopter in the design of cockpits and management of human factors. Her

Portrait of WASP Dora Dougherty Strother McKeown, 1943. Courtesy of the Woman's Collection, Texas Woman's University, Denton, Texas.

first work was in the Army/Navy Instrumentation Program (ANIP). She worked on developing a contact analog picture of the real world to allow pilots without instrument training to fly helicopters under instrument conditions. Since her boss thought that she should have helicopter training, she got her helicopter rating in 1960 as part of her job. In 1961, Dougherty broke two world helicopter records. The first was the longest nonstop distance in a straight line without payload (405.83 miles or 653.12 kilometers) from Fort Worth, Texas, to Jackson, Mississippi. That was followed by an altitude record in a helicopter (19,385.79 feet or 5,908.86 meters) without payload. She retired from Bell in 1986, a highly gifted aviator and pioneer in the fields of aviation and engineering.[27]

Members of the WASP program did not receive recognition as veterans until 1977; they began receiving veterans' benefits and status in 1979. In March 2010, each WASP earned the Congressional Gold Medal at a special ceremony in the Capitol Building in Washington, DC, belatedly honoring their service to their country. Although Dougherty McKeown did not attend, she recalled that being in the WASP program had influenced her to stay in aviation for the remainder of her life.

Edith Magalis Foltz Stearns (1903–1956),
British Air Transport Auxiliary Pilot
and Naval Flight Instructor

Born in Dallas on August 17, 1903, Edith Magalis Foltz Stearns had a career as a singer before becoming interested in aviation. She attended Dallas High School before getting a musical education at Lenox Hall in St. Louis, Missouri, from 1918 to 1919. From 1920 to 1925 she sang professionally in several theaters in San Francisco. In 1922 she married Joseph Rathelle Foltz, a lawyer and pilot. They had one son, Richard, who was born in 1925.[28] In 1928 she bought an airplane with the intention to fly only as a passenger. She quickly learned to fly the plane herself. She and her husband barnstormed in Oregon, California, and Washington State. Before 1930, Foltz had flown more than thirty hours as copilot on various trimotor monoplanes, cabin airliners, and open-cockpit aircraft on West Coast Air Transport's flights between Seattle and San Francisco. She was among the early commercial women pilots.[29]

Edith Foltz, air racer, with a chart in hand, 1929. Courtesy of the International Women's Air and Space Museum, Cleveland, Ohio.

In the 1929 First Women's Transcontinental Derby, Foltz came in second in the light airplane division, earning $450. In 1933 she applied for a patent for a flying costume that could be utilized either as a skirt or knickerbockers. In 1938, she served as operations manager for Oregon Air Lines. Foltz flew as a ferry pilot for the British Air Transport Auxiliary, 1942–1945, in England under combat conditions. England's first female officer and head of wartime flight operations

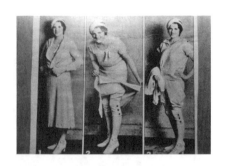

Edith Foltz demonstrating her Foltz-up Flying Tog, a patented design, 1937. Courtesy of the International Women's Air and Space Museum, Cleveland, Ohio.

Edith Foltz Stearns, British Auxiliary Transport Pilot, 1942–1945. Courtesy of the International Women's Air and Space Museum, Cleveland, Ohio.

Allison Elsie King described Foltz and other American women pilots who served for the ATA as "extremely charming" and "brilliant pilots." ATA pilots transported new aircraft, including Hurricanes and Spitfires, from factories to aerodromes for the Royal Air Force.[30] In England, flying military airplanes on ferry duties, women pilots received an average of four thousand dollars per year, which included twenty-five dollars per week payable in U.S. currency to their bank in the United States. On reporting to the Air Transport Auxiliary headquarters, women pilots were issued a complete uniform—jacket, skirt, overcoat, and cap—and a complete flying outfit including helmet, goggles, flying suit, boots, parachute, etc., all of which was returnable on completion of duty.[31] Foltz later returned to the United States where she trained cadets to fly at the Corpus Christi Naval Station.

Tom Danaher (1924–), Fighter Pilot and Hollywood Stunt Pilot

Tom Danaher of Wichita Falls graduated from Dallas High School in 1941, but he had to wait until he turned eighteen to join the Navy pilot training program. He earned his wings at Corpus Christi Naval Station, where he trained in a Vought F4U Corsair.

Since March 12, 1941, Corpus Christi Naval Station has been a primary center for pilot training.[32] On December 1, 1938, Navy Rear Admiral Arthur Japy Hepburn decided on the site based on the area's sparse population, reasonably priced land, and favorable weather. Construction began in June 1940. Graduation rates grew to over six hundred cadets a month following the attack on Pearl Harbor on December 7, 1941.

Danaher became a Marine Corps fighter pilot and flew missions in the Pacific in a Grumman F6F-5N Hellcat. Age twenty-one in August 1945, Danaher gained the distinction of being the last to shoot down a Japanese bomber when he downed three Betties on the last night of World War II.[33]

By the end of World War II, more than thirty-five thousand cadets had received their flight training at Corpus Christi Naval Station. The base also briefly served as a German prisoner-of-war camp until March 18, 1946. In August 1947 the U.S. Navy moved all basic air training from Corpus Christi to Pensacola, Florida, and advanced naval training officially opened on December 1, 1948, at Corpus Christi.

In the postwar years, Danaher did some crop dusting using a Navy N3N biplane trainer. During the Korean War he flew escort for B-29 night missions, including the last B-29 combat mission that struck Pyongyang, North Korea, on July 26, 1953. In 1972 he opened Tom Danaher Airport, also known as Lake Wichita Airport. He has flown as a Hollywood stunt pilot in about two dozen major motion pictures, including *Death Hunt* (1981), *Out of Africa* (1985), *Empire of the Sun* (1987), *Air America* (1990), *Firepower* (1993), *Cliffhanger* (1993), and *GoldenEye* (1995), besides several French and British films. He also flew along the Amazon River for filming of the IMAX documentary, *Amazon* (2000). Danaher has accumulated more than twenty-six thousand flying hours in a wide variety of aircraft, from World War I replicas to the Jet Star he flew in *Cliffhanger*. He allegedly flew across the Atlantic, ferrying aircraft, and often delivering Air Tractors, at least one hundred times.[34] Danaher had a rather unique flying film career, staying in the sky well into his late eighties.

OVER AND ABOVE THE CALL OF DUTY, AIRMEN AND women in Texas made a direct and valuable contribution to the allied war effort during World War II. Texans at home in turn built thousands of airplanes, particularly in Fort Worth, which became a primary center for aircraft production.

Chapter 8

Aircraft Designers
and Manufacturers

EXAS HAS DEVELOPED A TRADITION OF AERO-
space manufacturing and design since the early years
of aviation. Lieutenant Benjamin Foulois (see chapter 1) began making modifications on the U.S. Signal No. 1 Wright
Flyer as early as 1910. Texas Aero Corporation of Temple, Texas, became the first company in the state to receive government approval to
manufacture airplanes, receiving its certificate for the Temple Monoplane on June 22, 1928. It opened an additional facility in Dallas in
April 1929, but then the stock market crashed, followed by the death
of the plane's designer, George Williams, with a student pilot on August 15, 1930. The effects of the Great Depression made the market
for aircraft manufacturers elusive in Texas, although passenger air
travel increased during the 1930s.[1] It was not until World War II that
Texas became a major center for the large-scale production of aircraft. The U.S. Army officially states that 2,743 B-24 Liberators were
built at Fort Worth's bomber plant.[2] North American Aircraft built
12,967 AT-6 Texans, 4,552 P-51 Mustangs, 966 B-24 Liberators, and
299 F-6 aircraft at its plant in Grand Prairie. Texas has also been the
home of such leading aircraft manufacturers as Consolidated Vultee,
Chance Vought, Convair, General Dynamics, Lockheed Martin, Bell
Helicopter, Mooney Aircraft, Globe Swift Aircraft, North American,
and American Eurocopter. Other major employers include Boeing,
Raytheon, and Gulfstream Aerospace Corporation.

Beginning in 1946, the XB-36 and B-36 Peacemaker (see chapter 9), the first intercontinental bomber, was built exclusively by Tex-

ans at the Fort Worth bomber plant, followed by the B-58 Hustler, the world's first supersonic bomber.

In the 1970s a group of engineers at Fort Worth worked on the development of a new advanced tactical fighter that would eventually replace the F-15. On September 29, 1990, the YF-22 was flown for the first time. In 1993 the Lockheed Fort Worth Company produced the F-16 Fighting Falcon, a multirole fighter still flown by the U.S. Air Force's flight demonstration team, the Thunderbirds. On April 23, 1991, the Air Force selected the F-22 Raptor as the new air superiority fighter.[3] Currently Lockheed Martin builds the F-35 Lightning, the world's most advanced multirole fighter aircraft, at its high-tech Fort Worth facility in the former bomber plant.

The Homebuilt Movement in the 1930s: Lillian Holden, Triplane Kit Builder and Codesigner of the American Flea

On a much smaller scale, Lillian Holden of Fort Worth codesigned and comanufactured a triplane kit called the American Flea in her own backyard during the early 1930s. Holden's design resembled an aircraft called the English Flea, so named for the quick manner in which it took off. Inspired by Henry Ford's concept of an affordable automobile for every American family, Holden designed an airplane kit that was both affordable and apparently safe. She sold her first triplanes for only $98, knowing well that there were many young pilots who wanted to own airplanes but could not afford them. She even offered a payment plan for pilots, who could purchase a kit for $12.50 and make monthly payments of $10. Yet even $98 was a considerable sum at the time, and not the cost of the entire airplane.[4] Her later models and more deluxe designs, manufactured under the names Universal American Fleaship or Flea Triplane, sold for between $250 and $350. The low price reflects a certain sense of optimism that she held about the future of aviation, that anyone interested in learning to fly could own airplanes. Holden and her codesigner made between three hundred and five hundred American Flea kits before selling their blueprints, rights to their design, and their company to Ace Aircraft Manufacturing Company. At least a dozen or more were built and flown across the country. None of their triplanes, to her knowledge, were involved in any serious mishaps or crashes. English and

French Flying Fleas, with their staggered wing design, were stall resistant.[5]

To her great dismay, the Ace Aircraft Company never produced any of her model designs. After a long legal battle, Holden eventually recovered her rights and patented the designs. The American Flea was never mass-produced due to a lack of financing, although a few are still flying around today.[6]

Manufacturing during World War II

Beginning in 1941, Texas became a major center for aircraft manufacturing and helped the United States to become the largest producer of aircraft in the world. No country has matched it in mass aircraft production, especially during World War II. Texan men and women worked around the clock at the plants in Fort Worth. Two companies in particular, Consolidated and North American, played

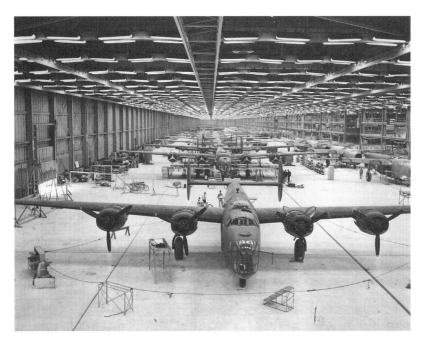

Aircraft production of Consolidated B-24 Liberators. Courtesy of the Cripliver Collection, History of Aviation Collection, Special Collections Department, McDermott Library, the University of Texas at Dallas.

major production roles. In keeping up with the Lend-Lease Act under President Franklin D. Roosevelt, the United States supplied its allies with thousands of aircraft and aircraft designs after fulfilling its own immediate strategic needs during wartime. By the war's end, Texas had produced approximately twenty thousand aircraft at various facilities, including the P-51, the AT-6, and the B-24.

The main plant at the Fort Worth facility, known as "the bomber plant," has 4.9 million square feet under roof and an assembly bay that stretches nearly a mile. It is nearly twelve city blocks long and as

Riveting Rosies at the bomber plant, Fort Worth, Texas, during World War II. Courtesy of the Cripliver Collection, History of Aviation Collection, Special Collections Department, McDermott Library, the University of Texas at Dallas.

Global Swift aircraft production, Fort Worth, Texas. Courtesy of the Mustangs P-51 Collection, History of Aviation Collection, Special Collections Department, McDermott Library, the University of Texas at Dallas.

tall as a six-story building. In November 1943, 30,547 people, drawn primarily from Fort Worth, worked at the bomber plant. The workforce included 11,577 women during the era of Rosie the Riveter. By the war's end, workers at this facility had built 3,034 B-24s and derivative models.[7]

The AT-6 Texan

North American Aviation (NAA) incorporated in Delaware on December 6, 1928. In 1935, it relocated all its machinery and employees to California. As war spread, the company expanded to include a plant in Kansas City, Missouri, for B-25 bombers and one in Grand Prairie near Dallas, Texas, for P-51 fighters and AT-6 trainers (hence the name Texan). The AT-6 Texans evolved from the basic trainer North American built before the war. In October 1944, an

AT-6 set a record for continuous service with five thousand hours of flying time over seven hundred fifty thousand miles. After the war it was renamed the T-6. The North American P-51 Mustang, considered the finest pursuit airplane during World War II, was also manufactured in Grand Prairie. Between 1941 and 1945, more than eighteen thousand aircraft rolled out of the Grand Prairie plant.[8]

The B-24 Liberator

In May 1942, three months ahead of schedule, the first of nearly 3,000 B-24 Liberator bombers rolled off the line of Consolidated Aircraft Corporation's Air Force Plant 4, commonly known as the bomber plant. During its peak period, the employees of the bomber factory at Fort Worth produced 175 B-24s per month. The Consolidated B-24H Liberator was a heavy bomber powered by four 1,200-horsepower Pratt & Whitney radial engines and armed with ten defensive machine guns. Its top speed was 290 miles per hour. The British Royal Air Force in particular favored the B-24, which served a number of important roles, including bombing raids against the Japanese and submarine reconnaissance against the Germans in the North Atlantic.

In March 1943 Consolidated Aircraft and Vultee Aircraft Corporation merged to form Consolidated Vultee Aircraft Corporation (Convair). In 1954 Convair became the Convair Division of General Dynamics. The bomber plant turned to producing the Convair B-58 and General Dynamics F-111 and F-16. Lockheed Martin produced the F-22, and more recently the F-35.

Vought Aircraft Company

The Vought Aircraft Company traces its origins back to New York aviation pioneer and engineer Chauncey (Chance) Vought (1890–1930). In 1912 Vought learned to fly from Swedish aviator Max Lillie, who also taught Katherine Stinson (see chapter 2). He earned flying certificate no. 156. He then began working for various airplane manufacturers, including designer Glenn Curtiss. In 1916 he became chief engineer at the Wright Company in Dayton, Ohio. When the U.S. entered World War I, Vought served as a consultant to the Bureau of

Aircraft Production in Washington, DC, and the Engineering Division of the U.S. Army Air Corps. In 1922 the Chance Vought Company was established. By 1924, Vought had designed twelve different aircraft. Among his most notable early designs was the VE-7 Bluebird, a biplane that was utilized as a primary and advanced trainer. Vought died in 1930, but the company he built went on to manufacture some of the twentieth century's most notable aircraft, including the F4U Corsair, the F-8 Crusader, and the A-7 Corsair II.

The Vought plant in Grand Prairie dates back to World War II, when North American built P-51s, T-6 Texans, and B-24 Liberators there. It was taken over by the Chance Vought Company in 1948. In a fourteen-month period, Vought moved its entire operation—twenty-seven million pounds of equipment and thirteen hundred key employees and their families—to Texas.

In 1953 Vought won the Navy's competition to build a new carrier-based fighter, the F8U-1 Crusader. It is engineered with a special tilting wing, which allows it to achieve short takeoffs and landings consistent with aircraft carrier operations. In 1956 the Crusader set a national speed record by flying over one thousand miles per hour. In 1957 U.S. Marine Corps Major John Glenn, who would later become an astronaut and a U.S. Senator, set a new transcontinental speed record from Los Angeles to New York in a Crusader. In 1957 the Crusader won the Collier Trophy for its contributions to the advancement of aviation science. The U.S. Navy and the U.S. Marines utilized this supersonic fighter over Vietnam. Built in Dallas, the Crusader entered into service in 1957 and was used by the reserves through 1986.

The Chance Vought F4U Corsair was the U.S. Navy's first fighter capable of traveling four hundred miles per hour and one of the finest of its kind in World War II. With its unique inverted gull-wing design and sleek lines, the Corsair is a beautiful aircraft with an impressive record in action. During World War II, pilots flying Corsairs brought down 2,140 Japanese aircraft while only losing 189—an eleven-to-one ratio. The Corsair was constructed primarily of metal, but it also had some fabric-covered control surfaces. It underwent sixteen different redesigns at the Grand Prairie plant.

The Corsair became familiar to the general public through the 1970s television series *Baa Baa Black Sheep*, which portrayed a sanitized version of Major Gregory "Pappy" Boyington. Boyington became an ace with at least twenty-two victories during World War II. He was a recipient of the Medal of Honor, having suffered in a Japanese prison camp after being shot down on January 3, 1944, until he was liberated at the end of August 1945. Corsairs also were featured in the 1951 Hollywood film *Flying Leathernecks*, starring John Wayne. Also, the late baseball player Ted Williams trained Marine pilots to fly Corsairs during World War II.[9]

Roger Smith, a pilot from California, donated a half-scale model of the Corsair named *Baby Blue* to the Vought Heritage Foundation—the organization of retired Vought employees—several years ago. Although it is airworthy, *Baby Blue* has never been flown, in accordance with its builder's stipulations. It has a real engine, and its landing gear is shorter than that of a full-sized Corsair. Made mostly of wood, it weighs a scant 840 pounds. Initially it was on display as a novelty item in the Vought Restoration hangar but then a Vought retiree, Jim Ross, customized a boat trailer and built special boxes for the wings. The dedicated volunteers of the Vought Heritage Foundation have happily taken the model all over Texas. It has been on display at a number of venues, including the minor league park of the Air Hogs baseball team in Grand Prairie, a team that was named for a squadron of World War II pilots. The aircraft makes an appearance at the annual Vought Heritage retiree meeting. It has been in parades such as the Tyler Rose Festival and on display at Commemorative Air Force air shows and fly-ins, as well as for events of the Civil Air Patrol, the local Vought Credit Union, and Lockheed Martin. The retirees' mission is to share the history of the Corsair and the Vought aircraft company. Jim Ross, who serves as *Baby Blue*'s caretaker, enjoys visiting with observers young and old. His favorite comment from former Corsair pilots when they come upon *Baby Blue*: "I remember it being a lot bigger . . ."

Joe Angelone (1922–), Chance Vought Test Pilot, Aeronautical Engineer, World War II Fighter Pilot, and Antique Aircraft Restorer

Joe Angelone's fascination with airplanes began in Alliance, Ohio, where he was born in 1922. The son of an Italian immigrant tailor, he was one of eight children. Like most Americans, he was impressed by Charles Lindbergh. He decided early on that he wanted to be a pilot and later, an aeronautical engineer. Angelone achieved both, becoming a U.S. Army Air Corps pilot and receiving a bachelor of science in aeronautical engineering from Purdue University.

During World War II, Angelone flew a P-47 in the Mediterranean theater. He then flew various pursuit aircraft and bombers before transitioning into jet aircraft. He participated as an engineer in research and development and served as a test pilot while in the United States Atomic Test Group. In 1953 he left the U.S. Air Force and joined Chance Vought as an experimental test pilot. He test flew in electronic, armament, performance, stability and control, structural, and photographic reconnaissance programs. These activities involved various aircraft, including the F7U-1, F8U-1, F8U-1P, and F8U-3. Angelone then worked in several capacities in Vought's Aircraft and Space Divisions, including the Apollo spacecraft environmental control system, spacecraft heat shields, moving base spacecraft simulators, and the XC-142 tilt-wing turboprop vertical takeoff and landing (VTOL) aircraft. His final years at Vought were dedicated to the A-7 program, working on variants such as the two-place version and the U.S. Navy and Air Force forward-looking infrared night-attack versions.

Since the 1960s, Angelone has worked in private aircraft restoration. In 1970 he received an FAA airframe and power plant mechanic's rating. Among his finished projects are the complete disassembly, repair, power plant and accessory overhaul, reassembly, fabric recover, and painting of a 1946 Bellanca Cruiseair and a 1954 Piper Pacer. In 2003 he joined the Vought-173 project and contributes where he can, dividing his time between the V-173, his Bellanca, and the restoration of a 1972 Datsun 240Z automobile.

Along with other Vought retirees, Angelone works on his own schedule of four to five hours on Tuesdays and Thursdays each week. Each retiree selects an area of interest and expertise. Angelone started out working on the propeller for the VE-7 Bluebird, one of company founder Chance Vought's early designs. Vought retirees reconstructed this entire biplane from scratch, since no original parts existed. One side of the fuselage of the VE-7 Bluebird remains open. Thus, the biplane serves as an educational tool for young people and adults. Angelone then worked on the restoration of the propellers for the V-173 "Flying Pancake" and serves as team leader for the plane's restoration.

Mooney Aircraft, Kerrville, Texas: Speed and Safety

Mooney Aircraft is known in general aviation for speed and safety. There has never been a fatal crash in a Mooney as a result of structural or airframe failure. Aviators have set more than 132 official speed records in Mooneys; Mooney engineers also designed the first deicing equipment for a piston-engine aircraft.

In 1925, Al Mooney designed his first airplane—the "long wing" Alexander Eaglerock, the first new aircraft to compete with the low-cost surplus Jenny—for the Alexander Aircraft Company of Colorado Springs, Colorado. In April 1926, he designed a three-place, high-wing monoplane for the Montague Company in Marshall, Missouri. In 1927, Al's brother Art Mooney quit his job as a master carpenter on the railroad and joined Al to build airplanes.[10]

In 1929, Al and Art formed Mooney Aircraft Inc. in Wichita, Kansas. The Mooney brothers recruited businessmen G. C. Yankey and W. L. McMahon to help finance the new company. The first airplane was the Mooney M-18 Mite, which was still in production when the company moved to Kerrville, Texas, in 1953. The M-18 Mite was a certified, all-wood, single-seat airplane with retractable gear and Mooney's distinctive forward-swept tail. Kerrville city officials offered Al Mooney a ninety-nine-year lease on the airport for one dollar per year.

More designs followed. By the mid-1950s, the M20 was in production, using wood for the wing and certain other parts. Al and Art Mooney sold the company in 1955. Art Mooney stayed on in Kerrville, while Al went to work for Lockheed in Marietta, Georgia. Mooney Aircraft has had numerous owners over the years.

Beginning in 1961, an all-metal M20 was introduced to the market, allowing the company to become the fourth-largest light-aircraft manufacturer in the world by 1966. In March 1964 Mooney sales of single-engine piston aircraft exceeded those of other manufacturers. By selling fifty-three units through its distributors, Mooney earned a million dollars that month, a sales record. Mooney models included the Master, the Mark 21, and the Super 21.[11] Production peaked in the late 1970s. In December 1974, employees numbered almost 400 and 129 airplanes were produced. In 1975 production reached 219 airplanes. The company introduced the Mooney 201, which became an immediate sensation, and production grew to 368 airplanes in 1977. By 1979 employment reached 566, and 436 airplanes were built that year. The company delivered its ten thousandth airplane in 1996 and increased competition in the general aviation market on many levels.

Due to the downturn in the economy, Mooney halted production in November 2008. It currently offers owners of Mooney aircraft a ser-

Mooney promotional photograph, circa 1960. Courtesy of
Mooney Aviation Company Inc., Kerrville, Texas.

vice center for maintenance and repairs, along with technical support
and parts for more than eight thousand aircraft still flying.

Texas Instruments

On September 12, 1958, Jack Kilby of Texas Instruments
solved the problem of miniaturization by inventing the integrated circuit. His invention paved the way for handheld calculators, personal

computers, wireless cell phones, and a wide variety of high-tech products that impact our everyday lives. For decades Texas Instruments was on the cutting edge of defense work as the U.S. armed forces have sought more precise and effective ways to target bombing missions. Texas Instruments designed systems to guide missiles more precisely, thereby improving aim and dramatically reducing civilian casualties. The company's laser guidance systems altered the way in which air warfare is conducted. Texas Instruments also helped the military expand its operations to include effective night fighting through innovation in infrared technologies. In 1997 Texas Instruments sold its defense operations to Raytheon for $2.95 billion.[11]

The twentieth century will always be known for the invention of the airplane, but it will also be known as the age of electronics. Between 1957 and 1977, Texas Instruments enabled the United States to become a major leader in space exploration, producing lightweight electronics systems for launch missiles and satellites for NASA. In 1960 the world market for electronic equipment was $24 billion. By 2004, it had increased to $1,175 billion. Kilby's integrated circuit was the basis of the development of these electronic systems. Among the accolades for his invention, Kilby won the Nobel Prize for Physics, the National Medal of Science, and the National Medal of Technology and Innovation.

With the development of side-looking radar in the mid-1950s, the stage was set in early 1957 for the design and development of a revolutionary concept that was destined to have a dramatic impact on the company's defense electronics business for decades.

The Soviet Union had introduced the surface-to-air antiaircraft missile, and there was a greater need than ever to protect aircraft flying over hostile environments. The military was faced with two options: fly extremely high (which would reduce effectiveness) or extremely low during reconnaissance, damage assessment, and close air attack missions. But skimming mountainous terrain at high speeds was often more dangerous than taking a chance on enemy missiles at higher altitudes.

In 1965, Texas Instruments was awarded a contract to develop APN-149, the first terrain-following radar for use on manned aircraft. This technology made it possible for America's aircraft to fly under enemy radar as low as two hundred feet, effectively creating the nation's first "stealth" penetration fleet of fighters and bombers. They arrived at high speeds, completed their mission, and were gone without ever showing up on an enemy's radar screen. During the life of its defense business, Texas Instruments produced more than six thousand terrain-following radar systems for the F-111, the A-7, the F-16, the European Multi-Role Combat Aircraft, the B-1, the C-130, and the HH-53 Pave Low helicopter.

Bell Helicopter: Bartram Kelley (1909–1998), Chief Engineer, Bell Textron

Bartram Kelley had known an early designer of helicopters, Arthur Young, while growing up in Pennsylvania. During World War II, Kelley became Young's assistant at Bell Aircraft in Buffalo, New York. Young assigned his patents to Bell Aircraft and, assisted by Kelley, persuaded Bell to sponsor the development of a helicopter known as Model 30. Following design changes, the Bell 47 (its military version is known as the H-13) first flew on December 8, 1945. In March 1946, it became the first commercially certified helicopter. It was famed for its use as a medical evacuation (medevac) helicopter or flying ambulance, carrying wounded troops from the front lines to the Mobile Army Surgical Hospitals (MASH) located far from the front in the conflicts in Korea and Vietnam. Kelley retired in 1975 and served as a consultant with Bell Helicopter Textron while residing in Dallas until his death in 1998.[12]

In January 1941, Young designed and filed a patent for the development of the first tilt-rotor aircraft. The patent was granted on August 14, 1945. The design integrated the best features of a helicopter and an airplane: the craft could fly like a helicopter with its rotors in the upright position, and then it could tilt the rotors and fly like an airplane. This unique design may well become the outstanding vertical takeoff and landing aircraft of the future. The first flight of the tilt-rotor V-22 Osprey occurred on March 19, 1989.

About one thousand employees assemble the V-22 at Amarillo's Bell Helicopter Textron tilt-rotor assembly plant, which opened in 2000 in partnership with Boeing. Through 2013, more than two hundred V-22 aircraft have been produced—185 for the Marine Corps and 31 for Special Operations. The V-22 Osprey serves as an assault transport for troops, equipment, and supplies, as well as a combat search and rescue aircraft. Due to several crashes, including one during a night mission in Afghanistan in April 2010 that resulted in four fatalities, besides two other crashes in 2000, there has been considerable debate about its use by the military.[13]

American Eurocopter: Celebrating More than 40 Years in Grand Prairie, Texas

Standing proud in his cowboy hat and boots, Texan Sammy Pence, vice president of commercial programs and maintenance at American Eurocopter, is a celebrated icon for the North Texas helicopter company. He became the focus of a marketing campaign by parent company European Aeronautic Defence and Space Company (EADS) entitled "I am EADS." His photograph was taken in the fall of 2004 and published, its caption translated into various languages, through 2007.

Following a term of service in the U.S. Marine Corps as a helicopter mechanic/crew chief, Pence began his career at American Eurocopter in 1978 as a senior aircraft technician in the dynamic component overhaul shop. Over the next twenty-four years, Pence was given jobs at the company of increasing responsibility, culminating in his appointment as vice president in October 2005. He is the first technician at American Eurocopter to have become a vice president.

In 1969 Eurocopter introduced its first helicopter to the American market in order to fulfill such needs as airborne law enforcement, border control, air medical services, oil and gas missions, and select military purposes of the U.S. Army and Coast Guard. Since 1972, it has equipped the first hospital-sponsored air unit to support medical service professionals. In 1978 Eurocopter's Gazelle, the world's first instrument-rated (IRF) helicopter, was assembled and certified in Grand Prairie. The Gazelle has the distinctive Eurocopter Fenestron tail rotor, which differs from conventional helicopter rotors in that it has between eight and thirteen smaller blades that spin at higher speeds. These blades are mounted within an area called a shroud that forms part of the vertical tail fin of the helicopter. It looks like a large fan, as its blade tips are protected.

Less than six months after winning a production contract in 2006, American Eurocopter delivered its first UH-72A Lakota light utility helicopter to the U.S. Army. Beginning in 2008, the U.S. Department of Homeland Security has operated more than seventy American Eurocopter helicopters for customs and border protection. In

Sammy Pence, advertising icon for American Eurocopter, Vice President of Commercial Programs and Maintenance. Courtesy of American Eurocopter, Grand Prairie, Texas.

2008 American Eurocopter delivered its twenty-five-hundredth helicopter to the U.S. market.

Within hours of Hurricane Katrina's landfall on the Gulf Coast August 29, 2005, a rescue mission was organized and underway. Two helicopters from American Eurocopter's own inventory and three volunteer pilots and ground crew were assembled. Frank Kanauka was piloting the EC135 P2, Bruce Webb and Bob Hernandez the EC120. Upon arriving in New Orleans, the volunteer pilots were thrown into challenging situations as they rescued stranded victims, transported medical personnel, and delivered critical supplies along the devastated coast.

American Legend's Legend Cub

On March 11, 2005, the Legend Cub completed its first flight. It is a two-place, single-piston powered aircraft that is manufactured in Sulphur Springs, Texas, as both a factory-built airplane and an airplane kit. It is intended to appeal to recreational flyers. Inspired by the popular Piper J-3 Cub, PA-11, and Super Cub models, the Legend Cub incorporates the latest innovation in design and fabrication. It has conventional landing gear or a tailwheel and flies like a Cub. Since 2005, 180 Legend Cubs have been built and sold, along with nearly 40 kits.

Victor and Joseph Stanzel and the Stanzel Model Aircraft Company, Schulenburg, Texas

Victor and Joseph Stanzel were two Texas farm boys who turned their passion for airplanes into a highly successful model airplane business. Victor was born on January 23, 1910, and Joseph on November 29, 1916, on a ninety-acre farm one mile east of Schulenburg, Texas, between San Antonio and Houston. Their parents were farmers. When their father died in 1918, with no one to work the land, their mother moved the family into a newly constructed residence in town.

Victor did not attend high school, but in 1926 he successfully completed correspondence courses in drafting, mechanical drawing, physics, and practical mathematics through the American School in Chicago. At sixteen, he took courses in tool making, machine school (metal workshop), and machine shop management. Beginning in the 1920s, Stanzel began hand-carving true-to-scale ornamental airplanes from solid wood. He sold these to flight cadets training in San Antonio for $20. He learned that advertising was important and began to subscribe to trade magazines such as *Popular Aviation*, *Model Airplane News*, and *Aero Digest*.

As early as 1929, Victor began making plans to expand the business by designing full-scale amusement park attractions. He developed a full-sized electric powered airplane modified as an amusement ride that he named the Fly-A-Plane Amusement Ride. It was a traditional high-wing cabin airplane attached at one end to a supporting beam. Kids could go for twenty-five-cent rides at a park in Houston.

In 1934 Joseph graduated from high school and became Victor's partner. The manufacture of true-to-scale kit models and the construction of amusement-park rides progressed. One of the most popular designs was the Stratos Ship, completed in 1936. It was a big hit at the 1936 Texas Centennial in Dallas, the Great Lakes Exposition in Cleveland, Ohio, and the New York World's Fair in 1939.

The Stanzel brothers then launched a unique business designing engine-powered model aircraft, which continued throughout the 1940s and 1950s. The Stanzel brothers designed and constructed eighteen unique engine-powered aircraft models for control-line flying and free flight. Their work encompassed more than twenty patents. At one time as many as 125 housewives from Schulenburg were employed in manufacturing the model airplanes.

Dr. Leo Windecker (1921–2010), Innovator in Composite Aircraft Design

Dr. Leo Windecker was not an aeronautical engineer but a dentist who incorporated composite materials into the design of a new light airplane, the Windecker Eagle, the first of its kind in the world. Windecker was born on July 9, 1921, at Gull Lake, Saskatchewan, Canada. His family moved to Texas when he was seven. In 1939, he entered the University of Texas at Austin before being drafted into the Army. After serving as a medical technician in the South Pacific, suffering from shell shock following a bomb attack by the Japanese, he was discharged honorably with a Purple Heart and received a commendation for his laboratory work. He graduated with the 1948 class of the University of Texas Dental School in Houston.

Windecker's interest in composite materials in his dental practice led him to think he could build an airplane that was lighter, less expensive, and stronger than the aluminum airplanes he learned how to fly. After attending aeronautical lectures at the University of Houston, Windecker began experimenting with fiberglass, polyester resin, polyurethane, epoxy, and airplane wings in his garage.

In 1958 Windecker won a research grant from Dow Chemical Company to build an airplane using plastics. Within two years he built a plastic-wing monocoupe, which was flown successfully. He then founded Windecker Industries, which became Windecker Research in Midland, Texas. In 1965 he tested composite wings at the Cessna Aircraft Company. Windecker recorded twenty-two U.S. patents and numerous foreign ones, which were primarily assigned to Dow Chemical Company. In 1967 the Windecker 1 flew. Although a prototype crashed during spin trials, the Windecker Eagle became the first composite airplane to receive FAA certification on December 18, 1969. Five production aircraft were built, but there was not yet a viable com-

Dr. Leo Windecker, designer of the world's first composite aircraft, 1967. Courtesy of Theodore R. Windecker.

The Windecker Eagle, first composite aircraft in the world. Courtesy of Theodore R. Windecker.

mercial market for this type of aircraft. The technology was licensed to larger companies, including Lockheed Martin, Northrop, and the De Lorean Motor Company. The entire cost to develop the Windecker Eagle was only $2.75 million, less than a quarter of what manufacturers have spent to develop similar composite aircraft. In 1970 Windecker went on to work with the U.S. military on the development of the first stealth aircraft, one that could not be detected by radar. The original Windecker Eagle is at the National Air and Space Museum in Washington, DC.[14]

Leland Snow (1930–2011) and Air Tractor

Besides being an aeronautical engineer, crop-duster, designer, and manufacturer, Leland Snow was also a co-owner of Air Tractor, the world's leading manufacturer of agricultural aircraft. In addition to their use in agriculture, Air Tractors carry chemicals to extinguish forest fires. A government version of the Air Tractor has also been used by the Department of State's Bureau of International Narcotics and Law Enforcement Affairs in the war against drugs in Colombia.[14]

Born on May 31, 1930, in Brownsville, Texas, Snow was among the first aviators and aeronautical engineers in the country to recognize the need for improvement in agricultural aviation. He designed and produced the Snow S-2 series of agricultural airplanes, which eventually became the basis for aircraft made by Thrush, a manufacturer in Georgia. Snow was largely responsible for the development of more agricultural airplanes than any single individual in the world.

Even before kindergarten, Snow constantly drew airplanes. By six, he bought ten-cent balsa wood airplane kits. At nine, he built his own Seversky P-35 model that he launched off the porch of his home near Santa Rosa, Texas. At fifteen, he became acquainted with two local flight instructors who helped him get a job after school and on weekends washing and refueling airplanes in return for flying time. He soloed by sixteen and earned his pilot's license at seventeen. He and a couple of friends engaged in "pumpkin bombing" to entertain themselves while growing up. There were plenty of pumpkins to load up in the Piper Cub J-3, which they would use to "bomb" barns, tractors, and anything that moved.

By his early teens, Snow had decided on a career in aircraft design. Texas A&M's engineering department had a wind tunnel, so he pursued his studies there. He used his Aeronca, which he had rebuilt, to commute on weekends between Harlingen and Bryan-College Station, some 330 miles, often in fog and drizzle.

During his freshman year at Texas A&M, Snow became interested in parachuting. In the 1940s, parachuting was considered by most people to be either daredevilry or simply crazy. Parachutes were not up to the standards that they are today. He once jumped some 700 feet over campus, where his parachute opened at 350 feet. He missed all the buildings and landed in front of the administration building. Little did he know that in 1999, years after leaving office, President George H. W. Bush would parachute onto the Texas A&M campus to dedicate the library in his name. Snow graduated in May 1952. During his junior and senior years, Snow crop-dusted. He then continued his studies in aeronautical engineering at the University of Texas at Austin, avoiding the draft during the Korean War.

Snow immediately began the 1952 crop-dusting season. Due to his inexperience, he was not aware of the seasonal effect windshields have on open cockpit airplanes. These shields mainly were designed to deflect rain, not wind, since pilots who fly open-cockpit airplanes still wear goggles. He quickly learned as the dust (insecticide, herbicide, or fertilizer) pulled forward through the fuselage, landing on his face. In the fall of 1953 Snow departed for Nicaragua with a fellow pilot from Clovis, New Mexico, in a leased Piper PA-12 Super Cruiser. His

S-1 proved well suited for the mountainous terrain. He improved some wing struts, covering everything with fabric, which made the struts more streamlined. The standard load for the S-1 was eleven hundred pounds, which was also standard for the Stearman biplane. The S-1, with only 250 horsepower, could carry the same load as the Stearman with a 450-horsepower engine. Snow crop-dusted in Nicaragua until 1955. By then, he was busy planning the S-2 and providing guidance to two employees who worked in production of his second model. By crop-dusting again in 1957, he was able to hire a third employee.

Early that year, he applied to the Federal Aviation Administration (FAA) for the S-2's type certificate authorizing manufacture, which was received in October 1957 after further improvement of its landing gear. Snow chose to improve the wing structure by demonstrating that the spar strength could carry fourteen thousand pounds of pesticide on the wings. After loading eleven hundred pounds of dust in the hopper as required by the FAA, Snow took off. At 160 miles per hour in hot, humid air, there was an explosion. The left wing separated from the fuselage during the high-speed dive and pullout. The airplane began to spin wildly, throwing sacks of dust into the air. Snow waited a few seconds before pulling the ripcord. He suffered a slight injury to his neck due to the instant opening of the parachute canopy. Losing the S-2 was a tough blow, since money was running out.

Snow moved to the rural community of Olney in North Texas in January 1958, which had offered a loan to get production and FAA certification of the first S-2. The FAA apparently issues certificates for manufacturing and following production. Every aircraft manufactured has to have an airworthiness certificate. The first loan was for $18,500. The S-2 had an aileron flutter during testing, which did not help certification efforts when the FAA learned about it. After some structural changes and furloughing two employees in the spring, the S-2B finally received certification on July 31, 1958. Snow now qualified for a larger loan of $50,000. Snow made demonstration flights to get business going. By 1959, he had made a total of 30 agricultural aircraft. In 1998 Air Tractor made 120 aircraft, which were sold all over the world.

In 2009 Air Tractor stole the show at the Paris Air Show, according to *Aviation Week* and other aeronautical journals, including *Trade-a-Plane*, which featured the company's armored government model used in the war against drugs in Colombia. Other models of Air Tractor include the AT-502, AT-602, AT-802, and the new prototype

Leland Snow with Lisa McCord, a modern-day Rosie the Riveter who works at the Air Tractor Factory in Olney, 2009. Photograph by author.

Air Tractor, Olney, Texas. Photograph by author.

AT-1002. The AT-802 has been particularly successful in fighting forest fires. The model number depicts the number of gallons held in the aircraft's hopper. Air Tractor celebrated its fiftieth anniversary in 2008.

Air Tractor is one of the great success stories in the history of aviation in Texas. It currently has 201 employees who, since July 2008, own the company. Its employee stockowner plan allows employees to sell their stock back to the company on retirement. This ownership plan could serve as an outstanding model for other airplane companies. Snow showed up for work on a regular weekly basis until he passed away while jogging in early 2011. He and others left a legacy of more than a half-century of excellence in innovation in aviation.

SINCE THE SECOND WORLD WAR, TEXAS HAS NO-tably been at the forefront of aircraft manufacturing in the United States. Over the years, Texan engineers have developed numerous designs, many with exceptional capabilities. This innovation helped the United States achieve victory in World War II and predominance in aircraft manufacturing during the postwar years.

Chapter 9

Red, White, and Blue All Over
Texas Air Power in the Cold War and the Space Age

FOLLOWING WORLD WAR II, THERE WERE TWO superpowers: the United States and the Soviet Union. The two countries competed against one another in a global struggle to dominate the Earth, air, and space. Aerospace leaders, along with influential politicians, helped to defend national interests during the Cold War and in the push to put the first man on the moon. Vice President Lyndon B. Johnson advocated in April 1961 for the United States to move forward with "a bold program," while taking every necessary precaution for the safety of the active participants in space flights.[1] On November 10, 2010, the International Space Station (ISS) marked its tenth anniversary of continuous occupation. Launched on October 31, 2000, and monitored from NASA Johnson Space Center, the ISS has proven to be a showcase for international cooperation.

The B-36 Peacemaker, the first long-range intercontinental bomber used by the U.S. Air Force, manufactured by Convair exclusively in Fort Worth, served as a deterrent during the initial years of the Cold War. It had a unique design—it was propeller driven, meaning there were propellers at the back of the wing. The B-36 was the nation's principal nuclear weapons carrier in the arsenal of the Strategic Air Command at Carswell Air Force Base in Fort Worth. It was the successor to the B-29 Superfortress. Fortunately, the B-36 never needed to be used in combat. From its base in Hurst, Texas, Bell Helicopter Company's Hueys changed the nature of the use of aircraft during the Korean and the Vietnam wars.

On October 4, 1957, the Soviet Union launched the first Earth satellite, Sputnik l, initiating what became a race between Cold-War rivals to be the first to go to the moon. Americans suddenly became aware of a new frontier. Senator Lyndon B. Johnson, a masterful politician, recalled "the profound shock of realizing that it might be possible for another nation to achieve technological superiority over this great country of ours."[2] Johnson spearheaded legislation to bring the space project to Texas, suggesting that Houston was an ideal location with its mild climate, port status, and university research facilities.

When the Cold War expanded into Korea and Vietnam, Bell's Huey helicopter, ideally suited for air mobility and medical evacuation, became symbolic of these "hot wars." These conflicts were the first in which helicopters were used extensively.

The space race, the B-36, and the Bell Huey helicopter epitomized America's struggle to maintain world peace while attempting to achieve technological and military superiority during the Cold War.

Beryl Erickson and Gus Green, Convair B-36 Peacemaker Test Pilots

Convair, an aircraft manufacturer that came from the merger of Consolidated and Vultee in 1943, is best known for the massive B-36 long-range bomber that it produced at its Fort Worth factory for more than seven years. It had a wingspan of 230 feet, height of 47.5 feet, and length of 163 feet (the size of an Olympic swimming pool). It had six three-thousand-horsepower engines and cruised at three hundred miles per hour. Convair test pilots Beryl A. Erickson and Gus Green first test flew the Convair XB-36 at Carswell Air Force Base in Fort Worth on August 8, 1946.

Chief Test Pilot for the Convair XB-36, Beryl A. Erickson, had twenty-one years of flying experience. He was a transoceanic aviator and navigator. He joined Convair in San Diego in 1941 to test fly many different types of aircraft, including the JATO (jet-assisted takeoffs) for large aircraft, especially Convair's PB2Y-3 Coronado patrol bomber. He also did much of the developmental flying for Convair's B-32 Dominator and contributed to developing Convair's B-24 Liberator heavy bomber as well as the B-58 Hustler, which flew twice the speed of sound and was produced at the bomber plant in Fort Worth.

The copilot on XB-36 test flights was thirty-three-year-old G. S.

Convair B-36 Peacemaker. Courtesy of aviation photographer Thomas Norris.

"Gus" Green, chief of flight operations at Convair's Fort Worth division. Green found the huge XB-36 to be similar to a Curtiss Jenny he learned to fly at fifteen in his hometown of Cleburne, Texas. He flew for the Texas Air Transport School. Between 1930 and 1935, he was a pilot for a Dallas oilman, co-operator of a flying school, and a cotton-duster. In 1935 he went to Ohio to do research on aviation fuel. In 1939, Green became chief pilot for a flying service and an instrument flight school in Fort Worth. In May 1943 he became a pilot for Convair's Fort Worth division. During World War II, he test flew nearly three thousand B-24 Liberators and numerous B-32s built at the bomber plant in Fort Worth.

On March 26, 1947, Erickson was at the controls of the XB-36 with Green as his copilot when the right main landing gear suddenly collapsed. The retracting hydraulic strut exploded, which ripped the main brace from the huge wing spar. The right main landing gear swung side to side. Erickson and Green were confident they could still land the airplane despite the wind blowing at thirty to thirty-five miles per hour. Erickson chose, though, not to risk the lives of his entire crew during an emergency landing, so the twelve crewmembers parachuted to safety. With no way to dump the twenty-one thousand gallons of fuel on board, Erickson and Green flew around to burn up fuel. With the hydraulics inoperative, Erickson and Green landed the plane without brakes and with no nose-wheel steering. The pilots still could use the rudder and aileron controls to steer the huge plane, which rolled to the edge of the runway and off into the soft ground before stopping. The aircraft still had eight thousand gallons of fuel on board. The successful landing preserved the government contract for succeeding B-36 models in production at Fort Worth's bomber plant.

The B-36 Peacemaker served its mission until the Air Force replaced it with the B-52 in the mid-1950s. On August 11, 1954, Convair delivered the last model to the Strategic Air Command in Fort Worth. During its peak years, some thirty thousand employees worked at Convair and Carswell Air Force Base. On average, fourteen thousand of Fort Worth's one hundred twenty-eight thousand workers worked under one roof to produce this Texas-made bomber.

J. Robert Ford (1922–2011): Bombardier, 1942 Recipient of a Distinguished Flying Cross, and Member of the Caterpillar Club

Twenty-year-old J. Robert Ford of Austin was the recipient of the Distinguished Flying Cross in 1942 as a bombardier for sinking a Japanese troop vessel in New Guinea.[3] The B-24 housed a crew of ten. The bombardier normally manned the forward guns in the front canopy.

During the 1950s Ford served as a radio operator for the B-36 Peacemaker. Ford flew through mushroom clouds off the coast of the Bikini Islands at least five times after detonation of an atomic bomb. Despite inquiries during his physicals at Veteran's hospitals, Ford claimed that he did not suffer any ill health effects from repeated exposure to radiation.

On the afternoon of February 13, 1950, Ford and his fellow crew members under the command of Captain H. L. Barry took off from Eielson Air Force Base in Anchorage, Alaska, en route to their home base at Carswell Air Force Base in Fort Worth following a practice flight to Russia. Their B-36 carried a ten-thousand-pound "Fat Man"

U.S. Army Air Corps Bombardier J. Robert Ford with his wife, Frances Ford, circa 1942. Courtesy of the Ford family.

bomb, which did not have the necessary plutonium core to cause an atomic explosion. Around midnight three of their six engines developed carburetor icing and suddenly caught fire. The crew detonated the bomb at four thousand feet over the Pacific to prevent it from falling into enemy hands. Then the crew began to bail out, one after another. Captains W. M. Phillips and T. F. Schreler, Lieutenant A. Holie and Staff Sergeants E. W. Pollard and N. A. Straley went first and landed in the Pacific, never to be seen again. The remaining twelve men, including Ford and Barry, managed to reach Vancouver Island, British Columbia. Ford landed in a tree, hung up for five hours in darkness until daybreak, not knowing how high he was from the ground on that freezing night. He finally released himself. He kept walking and yelling out until he joined a party of four led by Captain Barry. The group of survivors built a teepee out of a parachute and made a fire. They tried to dry their clothes and get warm, but it was another miserable night. After about forty hours on the ground, Captain Barry's party managed to reach the coast, where they were rescued by a Canadian fisherman.[4]

By bailing out of the disabled B-36, the surviving crew automatically gained membership in the Caterpillar Club, which dates back to the 1920s. Aviators who survive a parachute jump from a disabled airplane earn a caterpillar pin (see chapter 6).

Hueys: "But They Kept on Flying"

The story of the Huey helicopter began in the winter of 1950 and 1951 during the Korean conflict, the first war in which helicopters were used extensively. Model 47, designed by Arthur Young and his assistant Bartram Kelly, was developed in Buffalo, New York. It was used in the Korean War as a medevac helicopter or flying ambulance, carrying wounded troops from the front lines to the Mobile Army Surgical Hospitals that were far from the front, depicted in the popular film and television series *MASH*. Model 47G was the first model designed and developed entirely at the new Bell plant at Hurst, Texas, between Fort Worth and Dallas. Approximately 80 percent of the helicopters used in Korea were Bell designs. Some twenty-five thousand persons were rescued in Korea.

Beginning in the mid-1950s, the U.S. Army began to search for a replacement for the Bell Model 47. The new Bell model's designation, HU and later UH, accounts for the nickname "Huey." Early model Hueys could carry three stretchers for patients and a trained medic inside, besides the pilot and crew. The HU-1B had an enlarged cabin to allow it to carry five wounded plus a medic or seven equipped troops.

Development on the Huey design was completed in 1959 at the Bell Factory in North Texas well before the handful of U.S. advisors went to Vietnam, which led to U.S. involvement in that civil war. The original military order was for 173 helicopters, which was completed in March 1961. Fourteen of those had dual controls and were used as instrument trainers for Army Aviation flight training. The first Hueys to operate in Vietnam in April 1962 were the medevac HU-1As. As U.S.

involvement in Vietnam increased, so did the number of Hueys. Production began again in March 1961 and extended into 1965, with over 1,000 manufactured for the U.S. Army. Marine Hueys arrived in May 1965. The Navy used Hueys in a similar manner.

Roy P. Benavidez (1935–1998): Medal of Honor Recipient

The primary role of the Bell Huey helicopter was to fly into battles to retrieve the wounded during the Vietnam conflict. Many came under fire and were shot down. Dustoff pilots (the name stands for "dedicated unhesitating service to our fighting forces") earned reputations for bravery, risking themselves and crew by using their aircraft to remove wounded soldiers from the jungles and rice paddies of Vietnam during intense firefights. The use of the Huey under fire resulted in the awarding of several Congressional Medals of Honor, including one to Roy Benavidez (1935–1998) of San Antonio.

On May 2, 1968, Staff Sergeant Benavidez, a Green Beret, heard a call to "get us out of here" over his unit's radio while based in Loc Ninh, South Vietnam. He heard "so much shooting that it sounded like a popcorn machine." A twelve-man Special Forces team including three Green Berets answered the call. Sergeant Benavidez hopped aboard a Huey to fly to the scene, little knowing that he was going to spend the next "six hours in hell."

When Benavidez jumped off the helicopter, he was shot in the face, head, and right leg, but he continued toward his fellow troops, finding four dead and others wounded. He carried survivors onto the helicopter, but its pilot was killed by enemy fire as he attempted to take off. The helicopter crashed and burned. Benavidez removed the injured troops from the damaged helicopter. For the next several hours, he organized return fire, called in air strikes, administered morphine, and recovered classified documents, despite being shot in the stomach and thigh and hit in the back by grenade fragments. He then was bayoneted by a North Viet Cong soldier, whom he killed with his knife. Finally, he shot two enemy soldiers, as he carried the wounded aboard another Huey evacuation helicopter.

When he arrived back at Loc Ninh, Sergeant Benavidez was unable to move or speak. He was about to be placed in a body bag when he spit into a physician's face to signal that he was still alive. He was then evacuated for surgery in Saigon. Benavidez retired from the military in 1976. He was awarded the Medal of Honor in 1981 by President Ronald Reagan.

Edward H. White II (1930–1967), First American to Walk in Space

With the launch of a Soviet R-7 on April 12, 1961, placing Yuri Gagarin and his Vostok spacecraft in Earth's orbit, the Soviet Union initially led the space race. On May 25, 1961, President John F. Kennedy told Congress that the United States should commit itself to "landing a man on the Moon and returning him safely to Earth" before the end of the decade. One historic step in getting to the moon was walking in space. Edward H. White II became the first American to walk in space on June 3, 1965.

Born November 14, 1930, in San Antonio, White received a bachelor's degree from the U.S. Military Academy and a master's degree in aeronautical engineering from the University of Michigan. He also received an honorary doctorate from the University of Michigan. White was a test pilot for the U.S. Air Force, selected in 1962 to pilot Gemini 4. The Gemini program was designed to test the new technologies and skills astronauts would need to walk on the moon.

During Gemini 4's mission (June 3–7, 1965), White walked in space, beginning over the Pacific Ocean near Hawaii and ending over the Gulf of Mexico. The walk initially had been planned for Gemini 6, but the mission was accelerated to Gemini 4 after Russian cosmonaut Alexi Leonov performed the first space walk on March 18, 1965. White's June 3 walk, or "extravehicular activity" (EVA), lasted approximately twenty-two minutes, during which White was tethered to the space capsule by a twenty-five-foot-long line, often referred to as an "umbilical cord." He moved around with the help of a hand-held self-maneuvering unit that consisted of two small gas tanks of compressed air, which could propel him in space when released in small bursts.[5] The visor of his helmet was gold-plated to protect him from the unfiltered rays of the sun.

The Gemini 4 spacecraft orbited around the Earth sixty-two times and was the first space flight directed by Mission Control in Houston. As the first American to walk in space, White felt great pride. He remarked to a reporter for *Life* magazine: "I felt red, white, and blue all

Astronaut Edward H. White II, first American to walk in space, 1965. Courtesy of the Johnson Space Center, NASA.

over."[6] Learning how to walk in space was both physically challenging and something to be proud of. White and his crew stayed in space for four days, longer than all previous U.S. space flights added together. The Soviets made even longer flights, but White's walk in space in 1965 represented aviation's ultimate achievement: man's ability to go beyond the confines of our own planet.

White was later selected as command pilot for the Apollo 1 mission, which was to be the first manned flight of the Apollo program. Then tragedy struck. During a preflight test in preparation of Apollo 1 on January 27, 1967, a flash fire at the launch pad swept through the command module, taking the lives of the three Apollo 1 astronauts—Virgil "Gus" Grissom, Roger B. Chaffee, and White. This tremendous loss set the space program back at least two years. Yet engineers at the National Aeronautics and Space Administration (NASA) and other personnel persevered.

Johnson Space Center

The first mission control center for unmanned and manned space programs was built in Florida in 1957 and housed equipment for the Mercury and Gemini programs, which placed astronauts in suborbital and orbital space. In 1965 mission control was transferred to Houston under President Lyndon Baines Johnson. The Johnson Space Center was home to the NASA Astronaut Corps and responsible for their training. Mission operations control directed all future space missions following their launch from Cape Canaveral, Florida. Probably no other single moment in the twentieth century was as historically significant for humankind as the lunar landing on July 20, 1969. The United States definitively shed its image of being second to the Soviets in space exploration with Apollo 11's landing on the moon.

On July 20, 1969, thirty-six-year-old flight director Gene Kranz entered the mission operations control room in Houston thinking that he and his team were "meant for this day," the date of the first lunar landing by the crew of Apollo 11. The United States surged ahead of the Soviet Union upon fulfilling President Kennedy's pledge to go to the moon and return safely by the end of the decade. The Apollo mission control room at Johnson Space Center—which monitored the Mercury, Gemini, and Apollo space missions—is now a National Historic Landmark. It is where flight personnel first heard "Houston, we have a problem" during the Apollo 13 crisis. The massive Saturn V rocket now rests on its side at the Johnson Space Center.

Alan Bean (1932–): Astronaut and Artist, First Moonwalker from Texas

Five more lunar landing missions followed, through December 1972. On November 19, 1969, astronaut Alan Bean became the first native Texan to walk on the moon, as part of the crew of Apollo 12. This was his first space mission and humankind's second lunar landing. Born in Wheeler in 1932, Bean graduated from Paschal High School in Fort Worth in 1950. During his senior year, Bean won an ROTC scholarship to the University of Texas at Austin. Five years later, he was awarded a bachelor of science degree and was commissioned ensign in the U.S. Navy. In 1956, Bean completed flight train-

Mission Control, Johnson Space Center, celebrating the conclusion of the Apollo 11 lunar landing, July 24, 1969. Image S-69-40023, JSC. Courtesy of the Johnson Space Center, NASA.

ing and was awarded his naval wings. Bean spent three years as a test pilot, but he was also very interested in art. He pursued his passion by enrolling in night art classes at St. Mary's College of Maryland. In 1963, Alan Bean was selected by NASA as an astronaut. He was the lunar module pilot on the Apollo 12 mission.

In 1973, Bean began to fly in space again as spacecraft commander of Skylab Mission 2. He spent fifty-nine days in space and traveled over twenty-four million miles. In 1975 he then was selected as backup spacecraft commander for the joint American-Russian Apollo-Soyuz Test Project. He was assigned chief of operations and training and acting chief astronaut until the first flight of the space shuttle. While at NASA, Bean helped establish eleven world records in space and astronautics. He has received the Robert C. Collier Trophy and the Yuri Gagarin Gold Medal, among other medals and honors. In 1981 Bean resigned as a NASA astronaut to devote full time to painting. In his lunar paintings, Bean recreates his impressions of humankind's early lunar exploration, including images of fellow astronauts, lunar landscapes, and views of the Earth from the moon.[7] His works of art have been exhibited all around the world and are in many private collections.

Skylab, a Working Laboratory in Space, and the Space Shuttle Program

The United States launched its own space station, Skylab, into orbit on May 14, 1973. The Skylab project remained in space for six years, although astronauts were on board only for a total of 171 days. In 1979 this orbital workshop burned up on reentry.[8]

NASA's major efforts then led to developing reusable spacecraft that could travel back and forth between Earth and space. On April 21, 1981, NASA launched the first space shuttle, *Columbia*, from Cape Canaveral. The space shuttle program launched satellites, undertook a wide variety of scientific and technological experiments, and launched and repaired the Hubble Space Telescope. Approximately eighteen thousand people worked at the Johnson Space Center in 2009, including a corps of about 110 astronauts who learned how to maneuver in weightless conditions. NASA astronauts also practiced simulated space shuttle missions to test their emergency procedures and problem-solving skills.[9] The space shuttle program proved to be one of America's great technological achievements of the twentieth century.

Despite tremendous success, the space shuttle program was not without its losses. On January 28, 1986, the space shuttle *Challenger* exploded into a giant fireball upon launch, killing its crew of seven.

Space Shuttle *Endeavor* riding piggyback on a Boeing 747 over Houston near NASA's Johnson Space Center. Courtesy of the Johnson Space Center, NASA.

This tragedy stunned the nation and the world. A presidential commission later determined that the destruction of the O-ring seals on one of the solid rocket boosters failed to prevent hot gases from leaking through the joint during the propeller burn of the rocket motor. It should have been an identifiable problem, especially in cold weather. The temperature that day was below freezing. On January 28, 2011, Dr. Hans Mark, the John J. McKetta Centennial Energy Chair in Engineering in the Department of Aerospace Engineering at the University of Texas at Austin and former deputy director of NASA, remarked in an interview on the twenty-fifth anniversary since the *Challenger* explosion that those individuals within NASA who were responsible did not heed the signs that were apparent. This tragedy led to changes within NASA's operations.[10] Nevertheless, on February 1, 2003, the Space Shuttle *Columbia* and its crew were lost on reentry, apparently after a chunk of foam insulation on the fuel tank had damaged the underside of its left wing during launch on January 16. Unknown damage that breached the protective panels on the wing's leading edge allowed heating from reentry to cause high-speed aerodynamic breakup of the *Columbia* at an altitude of about two hundred thousand feet over East Texas.[11]

Rick Douglas Husband (1957–2003), Astronaut from Amarillo on the Space Shuttle Columbia

Among the seven astronauts whose lives were lost on space shuttle *Columbia* was Commander Rick Douglas Husband, a NASA astronaut who was born on July 12, 1957, in Amarillo, Texas. He died when space shuttle *Columbia* broke apart over East Texas and the crew perished during reentry, sixteen minutes prior to its scheduled landing on February 1. He is survived by his wife and their two children. The international airport in Amarillo is named for its native son.

Husband graduated from Amarillo High School in 1975. He earned a bachelor of science degree in mechanical engineering from Texas Tech University in 1980 and a master of science degree in mechanical engineering from California State University, Fresno, in 1990. In May 1980, Husband was commissioned a second lieutenant in the U.S. Air Force and attended pilot training at Vance Air Force Base (AFB), Oklahoma. He graduated in October 1981 and was assigned to F-4 training at Homestead Air Force Base, Florida. He logged over thirty-eight hundred hours of flight time in more than forty different types of aircraft. Husband was pilot on STS-96 *Discovery* (May 27 to June 6, 1999) and crew commander on STS-107 *Columbia* (January 16 to February 1, 2003). The crew on STS-96 performed the first docking with the International Space Station and delivered four tons of logistics and supplies in preparation for the arrival of the first crew to live on the station early the following year. The mission was accomplished in 153 Earth orbits, traveling four million miles in nine days, nineteen hours, and thirteen minutes. The sixteen-day STS-107 was a dedicated science and research mission. Working twenty-four hours a day in two alternating shifts, the crew successfully conducted approximately eighty experiments.[12]

Also among those lost in the STS-107 *Columbia* disaster was India's first female astronaut, Kalpana Chawla. She received a master of science degree in aeronautical engineering from the University of Texas at Arlington in 1984 before going on to earn her doctorate in aerospace engineering at the University of Colorado at Boulder.[13]

THE SPACE SHUTTLE PROGRAM LEFT A LEGACY OF both great triumph and tragedy. Between April 21, 1981, and July 21, 2011, it flew 135 missions. The program also helped build the International Space Station, which was assembled in space beginning in 1998 and occupied by its first crew in 2000. It remains a testimony to international cooperation among sixteen nations into the twenty-first century. It is the most complex facility ever constructed in space. The second mission control room at Johnson Space Center monitors the International Space Station, which continues to be manned cooperatively by NASA, the European Space Agency, and the space agencies of several other countries, including Russia, Canada, and Japan. Its mission is ongoing. The space shuttle's final flight, *Atlantis* STS-135, was launched on July 8, 2011, and landed safely on July 21, 2011. This final flight marked the end of an era in manned space travel for the United States.

Epilogue

Aeronautical Achievements, Education, and the Future of Air and Space Travel

HE HISTORY OF AIR AND SPACE IN TEXAS IS LIKE a tapestry with many rich textures and patterns. Several common threads or patterns in the various stories stand out: a sense of courage, perseverance, independent-mindedness, willingness to take risks, and entrepreneurialism as well as the determination not to allow obstacles stand in one's way, whether they be race, gender, financial constraints, government regulations, or physical limitations. These personal traits or characteristics are not necessarily unique to Texas; they are a large part of the human spirit. Aviators, astronauts, and other individuals from around the world have made great contributions and personal sacrifices to be a part of aviation or air and space. Nevertheless, there were incredible acts of personal self-sacrifice on the part of several Texans: from the thirty-two-year-old World War I ace William Erwin, who searched for his fellow air racers but then spun to his death during the Pacific Air Race in 1927, to the Medal of Honor recipients who flew B-24 Liberators at treetop level on approach to attack the oil refineries at Ploesti, Romania, during World War II or those Dustoff pilots and crew who flew the seriously wounded in helicopters in Vietnam. Other individuals in Texas also demonstrated remarkable aeronautical and military leadership skills, particularly General Benjamin Foulois and General Ira C. Eaker, who both advanced aviation at a time when the military had not been fully convinced of the utility of the airplane. Foulois and Eaker both showed great management skills and the ability to get things done. Ultimately, these two pioneer aviators and army generals played a vital role that led to the creation of a separate U.S. Air Force in 1947. Airline executives C. R. Smith and Herb Kelleher, moreover, made significant contributions to the airline industry through their leadership skills and sense of innovation. A number of women aviators in Texas, too, have played an integral role in the expansion of aviation since its early years. There were also many other colorful, creative, and daring aviators, astronauts, airline executives, designers, and aviation enthusiasts who helped to make aviation in Texas what it is today.

Texas has been a major provider of aerospace services, including general aviation, industrial aviation, commercial aviation, and the space industry. The state boasts several major international airports, including Dallas/Fort Worth, Dallas Love Field, and Houston George Bush Intercontinental Airport. Dallas/Fort Worth is the third busiest airport in the United States. Congestion there has been reduced since 1989—making it safer for passenger travel on commercial airlines—by Fort Worth Alliance Airport, an industrial airport with state-of-the-art facilities. With its long runways, connecting railroad tracks, depots, and access to major highways, Alliance serves as an inland port for international trade.

Texas is the home of more major U.S. airlines than any other state: American Airlines is based at Dallas/Fort Worth, Southwest Airlines at Love Field, and the former Continental Airlines (which began to merge with United Airlines in 2010) at Houston. Texas has also been the home of Braniff Airlines, Pioneer Airlines, Trans Texas Airways, and Texas International. Geography—that is, the presence of metropolitan areas far from one another—truly made commercial aviation attractive to the various budding airlines. By 2010 commercial aviation services and related activities amounted to $44.9 billion in revenue for Texas; it increased labor income by over $20 billion, and provided more than seven hundred thousand jobs.[1]

General aviation also thrives in Texas. Texas is third in the nation in terms of numbers of licensed airplane, helicopter, and glider pilots. In 2008, it had 48,849 aviators certified by the FAA (Federal Aviation Administration), behind only California and Florida.[2] In 2010, that number grew to 50,932 FAA-certified pilots.[3] Texas has some 387 airports, more than any of the other contiguous states; 26 provide passenger service for commercial airlines. General aviation is vital in disaster relief, law enforcement, border patrol, search and rescue operations, and firefighting. Medevac helicopter pilots provide emergency services by transporting patients from remote locations to hospitals in a timely, life-saving manner. General aviation enhances the quality of life of individuals, including many business travelers who enjoy the freedom of private or corporate aircraft.

Aviation in the state creates thousands of jobs and supports billions of dollars in economic activity in Texas. Each year business and flight support activities at its airports improve how businesses operate and serve to help retain major companies in the state. General aviation activities and expenditures associated with airports, businesses, and visitor spending by itinerant pilots accounted for $14.6 billion in economic activity in Texas in 2010. It supported more than fifty-six thousand jobs and paid $3.1 billion in salaries, wages, and benefits.[4]

Equally important, general aviation provides an important source of innovation or invention that impacts our everyday lives. Instruments such as the GPS came from general aviation. Dr. Leo Windecker's composite engineering innovations also began in general aviation. Some general aviators operate flight schools or flying services called fixed base operations or FBOs—businesses that may offer flight training, aircraft sales and maintenance, aircraft parts, aircraft parking, and aviation fuel at Texas's more than three hundred fifty airports. Together, general and commercial aviation accounted for $59.5 billion in 2010 in Texas, supporting seven hundred seventy-one thousand jobs, and providing $23.2 billion in labor income.[5]

What makes the history of flight in Texas most distinctive from other states is that Texans, including many "adopted" Texans, have embraced its aviation heritage to a large extent. Since the time of the Great War, individuals like Stuart McLeod Purcell have documented the types of aircraft aviators have flown. There are numerous aviation museums and events, great appreciation for the many jobs that aerospace generates, and, of course, Space Center Houston, a top tourist attraction that draws people from all over the world and serves as NASA's official visitor center.

Interestingly, only Texas celebrated its centennial of both powered flight and military flight in 2010.[6] On March 2, 2010, there was a reenactment of Lieutenant Benjamin Foulois's first military flight at Fort Sam Houston in San Antonio. A reproduction of a Wright B flyer taxied in the parade field as another Wright flyer flew overhead during a well-attended public ceremony. The Bob Bullock Texas State History Museum in Austin celebrated this event with a special museum exhibit, *Tango Alpha Charlie: Texas Aviation Celebration*, from September 10, 2010, to January 9, 2011. Some 5,000 visitors viewed this tem-

Pioneer Flight Museum's Fokker Dr 1. Courtesy of Thomas D. Gaylord, Pioneer Flight Museum, Kingsbury, Texas.

porary exhibit; many aviation objects, including an AT-6 Texan, are permanently on display within the museum.

Several Texas pilots and aviation enthusiasts dedicate their time to restoring antique aircraft for a living, as a hobby, or as museum volunteers. At the Old Kingsbury Aerodrome in Kingsbury, a rural community east of San Antonio, a group of volunteer pilots devotes much of their time to restoring original vintage aircraft to flyable condition. The Aerodrome is home to several entities, all supporting the building and flying of early aviation aircraft—defined as earlier than 1939. Vintage Aviation Services (VAS) builds replicas and restores early aircraft for paying customers, while the Pioneer Flight Museum (PFM) builds and restores early aircraft to keep in the museum's collection. The volunteers work under the guidance of trained professionals— Steve, Chris, and Roger Freeman, three brothers who grew up in California and learned their trade from their father. Both Roger and Chris worked on the filming of the Robert Redford aviation film *The Great Waldo Pepper*. Commissioned by the Hong Kong Aviation Historical Society, the volunteers also built and flew a Farman biplane like the one flown by French aviator Louis Paulhan. Their biplane is on display at Hong Kong International Airport.

Pioneer Flight Museum's replica of a World War I SPAD. Photograph by aviation photographer Jo Hunter, 2008.

One can view the start-up of the World War I triplane engine run up on youtube.com under Old Kingsbury Aerodrome Fokker Dr 1 Triplane Engine Run (HD), a video from the Old Kingsbury Aerodrome Spring Air Fair in 2009. The building of a SPAD XIII took the volunteers approximately four years and was completed in 2009. SPADs were flown by French and all U.S fighter squadrons during World War I, including American ace Eddie Rickenbacker. A historic reproduction was built with some original parts, including the main fuel tank, cockpit instruments, and the engine—a 220-horsepower V-8 Hispano-Suiza motor. These various historic reproductions made at Kingsbury are true works of art.

The Commemorative Air Force (formerly known as the Confederate Air Force), based at Midland, also plays a vital role in the preservation of vintage aircraft, particularly "war birds" dating from World War II. The CAF was established in 1961 as a Texas nonprofit corporation to collect, restore, and preserve World War II fighter planes. Founder Lloyd P. Nolen (1923–1991) purchased a Curtiss P-40 Warhawk in 1951, which he kept at his Rebel Field in Mercedes, Texas. He and four friends then bought a P-51 Mustang in 1957, which they restored. Nolen, who could not meet the minimum vision requirements to be a military aviator, received a special waiver to become a flight instructor during World War II.

The name Confederate Air Force was discovered painted on the side of the P-51 Mustang. The founders adopted the name supposedly "as a joke," but it had racist overtones. In 2002 the group changed its name to Commemorative Air Force to reflect the growing diversity and change in sensibilities among its newer members. Yet a few members still refer to the organization as Confederate Air Force.

During the 1970s the CAF established "wings," or chapters, across the country. The organization currently has approximately nine thousand members. There are forty-four wings and members in twenty-eight foreign countries. After their museum was relocated to Harlingen in 1968, the CAF moved its fleet to Midland in 1991. In 2005 the CAF expanded its mission to collect, restore, and preserve military aircraft from all wars involving the U.S. It currently has approximately 177 aircraft, including the B-29 Superfortress, Consolidated B-24 Liberator, B-17 Flying Fortress, and the Bell P-36 King Cobra. The American Airpower Heritage Museum at Midland has over forty thousand square feet of exhibits, one hundred thousand artifacts, and an extensive library, including an oral history collection. The CAF flies its vintage aircraft—such as *Fifi*, a rare B-29 Superfortress—to airports and major air shows around the country as both a living museum and a testament to the group's mission to preserve aviation's rich past. Its members also gather the oral testimonies of veteran military

Commemorative Air Force "war birds," including a Douglas A-26 Invader, Consolidated B-24 Liberator, B-17 Flying Fortress, and other aircraft perform at the Labor Day Air Show at the Greater Southwest International Airport in Fort Worth, September 4, 1971. Courtesy of the *Fort Worth Star-Telegram* Collection, Special Collections, the University of Texas at Arlington Library, Arlington, Texas.

aviators for posterity. The CAF does an outstanding job in the historic restoration and preservation of military aircraft.[7]

Robert Vajdos (1965–), National Champion for Restoration of World War II Aircraft

Robert Vajdos, Jr., was born in El Campo, Texas, in 1965. He is the son of Robert Charles Vajdos, a World War II B-25 pilot and native of Louise, Texas. At fourteen, the younger Vajdos worked with his father on the restoration of an Aeronca Champ airplane. He learned to fly a Cessna 150 at fifteen. Then he bought his own Aeronca Champ. By the time he graduated from high school in 1983, Robert knew that he wanted to work in the restoration of vintage airplanes. He enrolled in the Texas State Technical Institute, earning his airframe and power plant (A&P) airplane mechanic's license in 1985. Vajdos has restored a number of different types of vintage aircraft, but he specializes in Boeing Stearman biplanes. Among the planes he has restored is a 1939 open-cockpit Stearman biplane flown by aviation adventurer Gustavus "Gus" McLeod to the magnetic and geographic North Pole, respectively, in 1999 and 2000. Vajdos rerigged the entire airplane and rebuilt its wings.

In 1995 Vajdos won an award as champion restorer of a World War II trainer, another Boeing Stearman, at the EAA Airventure Oshkosh, the largest and most prestigious general aviation air show in the United States. He won the same award the following year for restoring an Innerstate L-6. His father worked with him restoring airplane wings up until his death in 2008. With forty-five hundred flying hours, Vajdos also flies vintage military aircraft for the Lone Star Flight Museum in Galveston.

Dedicated aviators like Vajdos have done much to advance general aviation in Texas, which plays a critical role in the economy and society, as well as the landscape. General aviation includes industrial aviation, meaning the utilization of aircraft to help industries such as agriculture, law enforcement, and health care. Air Tractor, based in Olney, Texas, produces the world's most extensive line of agricultural aircraft, eight of which are FAA certified. More than two thousand industrial aircraft have rolled off the assembly lines of Air Tractor since operations began in 1958. Police helicopters monitor traffic flow in major cities like Fort Worth, Dallas, and Houston. They occasionally assist in tracking down criminals, and in search and rescue missions. Medical helicopters operate from airports and fly aircraft that are used to transport critical patients to emergency medical facilities.

Fort Worth Police Department Air Support Unit

Since 1968, two Bell Jet Ranger helicopters have covered an area of 368 square miles and a population now over seven hundred thousand in Fort Worth, Texas. The helicopters fly an average of twenty-five hundred hours per year. Each year the unit receives an average of three thousand calls—missing children, car chases, bank robberies, prowlers, and other cases. The helicopters have been directly under the command of the Fort Worth Police Department since 1985. Two mechanics maintain its two Bell helicopters.

Guy del Giudice (1966–2010), Chief Helicopter Pilot for CareFlite, Dallas/Fort Worth

CareFlite is the oldest joint-use helicopter medical transport program in the United States. Since its founding in 1979, it has safely airlifted over half a million patients. CareFlite's emergency medical services (EMS) helicopters serve more than one hundred counties within a one-hundred-fifty-mile radius of Dallas/Fort Worth. CareFlite is also the only service in North Texas that operates under instrument flight rules (IFR), meaning that its helicopters are equipped with the proper flight instruments to fly during times of bad weather. The company also provides fixed-wing air ambulance service for transports beyond the range of its helicopter fleet and an extensive ground ambulance emergency response system.

Medical helicopter pilots know they are accepting the most dangerous job in commercial aviation. They fly at a moment's notice, often only a few hundred feet above the ground. Sometimes pilots take off in clear skies only to encounter thunderstorms or fog midflight. Birds can also be a problem. CareFlite helicopters usually fly between 160 and 173 miles per hour but sometimes fly even faster. They land on highways and city streets, in backyards, and in other areas where they immediately go to work to help save lives just like EMS ambulance drivers. Doctors rely on them to get their critical patients to medical facilities quickly.

CareFlite's chief helicopter pilot, Guy del Giudice, was a highly experienced emergency medical helicopter pilot who in 2010 had five thousand flying hours. Born in Glendale, California, in 1966, Guy grew up in Jasper, Indiana, and attended Indiana State University where he earned a bachelor's degree. He learned to fly helicopters during the early 1990s at Sky Helicopters of Garland, Texas. He attained aviation's highest rating, an air transport pilot (ATP) license. Since 2001, del Giudice saved more than a thousand lives as a CareFlite helicopter pilot.

Tragically on June 2, 2010, forty-four-year-old del Giudice and twenty-three-year-old mechanic Stephen Thomas Durler of Dallas perished in a crash during a maintenance flight check near Grand Prairie airport in a Bell 222. The Bell 222 had recorded an excellent safety record. It was CareFlite's first fatal accident, although there have been increasing reports of air ambulance accidents in recent years. The National Transportation Safety Board determined that the cause of the crash had to do with failure of the main rotor head components, according to the investigative report of March 14, 2011.[8] There is no way for pilots, even experienced ones, to recover from the failure of the main rotor head components at altitude.

William Bussey (1943–), DDS, Hot Air Balloonist, U.S. National and World Record Holder

Dr. William Bussey has described the thrill of hot air ballooning as "primitive, it's ancient, it's safe. It's colorful. It has the mystique of the old. It has wicker and fire." Bussey is a dentist in Longview, Texas, an avid hot air balloon pilot, and official world record holder of fourteen world and twenty-nine U.S. national hot air balloon records for distance and duration. He is also the founder of the Great Texas Balloon Race and the first person to organize a "balloon glow," at the 1980 Great Texas Balloon Race on the grass by the Longview Mall. At a balloon glow, balloonists fire their burners to inflate their colorful balloons at twilight or at night. Spectators are amazed by their glowing beauty and learn how air balloons operate. Balloon glows are now a part of hot air balloon festivals and events around the world.

Bussey worked several jobs—apartment manager, post office janitor, waiter, assistant private investigator, and others—before he graduated from the University of Texas at Austin with a bachelor of arts degree in history and headed to the University of Tennessee College of Dentistry in Memphis. At that time, this dental school and Kentucky were the only two accelerated programs running year round. His years there were rewarding. While he helped support himself by doing lab work, he had time to be president of the Student American Dental Association and join the Xi Psi Phi Dental Fraternity. Upon graduation he received the International College of Dentists award for most outstanding student, as well as other honors. Bussey was strongly impressed by the graduation speech given by Dr. Arthur Guyton, author of *Medical Physiology*. He remembers that powerful speech and the incredible accomplishments of Dr. Guyton. Incidentally, the dean told Bussey that he would never graduate because he did not have sufficient funds for his education. Bussey claims that those discouraging words gave him even more determination. The same dean ultimately presented him with the most outstanding student award, and twelve years later, his school loans were paid in full. Graduation day was December 15, 1968. Two weeks later Bussey became a captain in the United States Army Dental Corps. He was stationed in Fort Lewis, Washington.

Bussey became interested in ballooning in the late 1970s while skiing in Aspen, Colorado, when he saw two hot air balloons tethered on a rugby field. He became fascinated with the burning fire, the beautiful fabrics, the wicker baskets, the connection with aviation, and the colorful history of ballooning. This led to a distinguished career in hot air balloon events all over the United States and around the world. Bussey received the prestigious Spirit of Albuquerque Award, and has flown in Japan, Mexico, Canada, and the Middle East. He has also been a guest of the Sultan of Malaysia. For his many accomplishments he received the Montgolfier Diploma, the highest international award in ballooning. The award is named for the Montgolfier brothers, who invented the first hot air balloon in France in 1783. He also received the Shields-Trauger Award, the highest honor in this sporting activity in the United States. In 2007 he became enshrined in the Texas Aviation Hall of Fame in Galveston, the first and only hot air balloonist to be so honored.

Bussey has logged over three thousand hours flying hot air balloons. He is a competitive pilot who won thirty-five championships. He finished in the top three places in more than one hundred events; he is a perennial top ten competitor at the U.S. National Championships and has represented the United States in world competition three times. In 1986 Bussey set his first world record. Since then, he set his U.S. and world hot air balloon records. A summary of some of the most important record-setting flights and details about taking a hot air balloon ride can be found on his website: www.balloonadventures usa.com.

H. Ross Perot, Jr., (1958–) and the Bell Long Ranger II Model 206L-1 Spirit of Texas

H. Ross Perot, Jr., learned to fly helicopters after graduating in 1981 from Vanderbilt University, where he majored in business administration. His father, independent Texas politician H. Ross Perot, gave him flying lessons as a graduation present. After learning to fly from his instructor, W. "Dub" Blessing, the younger Perot set his eyes on becoming the first aviator to fly around the world in a helicopter in 1982. Perot by then had accumulated five hundred flying hours. Rather than allow this aviation record to fall into Australian hands, the twenty-three-year-old decided to make the attempt with an experienced copilot, Jay Coburn. Coburn had flown helicopters during the Vietnam War.

Perot's flight instructor, Blessing, made sure that the two helicopter pilots went through extensive survival training, particularly water evacuation, at state-of-the-art U.S. Navy facilities in Pensacola, Florida. Both were submerged in a tank wearing full flight gear and dark goggles to simulate the lack of vision that would be encountered in a real night emergency.

The *Spirit of Texas* departed Dallas on September 1, 1982, and returned to Love Field at Dallas on September 30, 1982. It took twenty-nine days, three hours, and five minutes to fly twenty-six thousand miles. A Hercules C-130 with three Navy SEALs trailed behind the helicopter and carried fuel, parts, and other supplies. A special 151-gallon auxiliary fuel tank was added to ensure the maximum range necessary to make the long overwater legs of the journey. Total fuel on board the Bell Long Ranger II was 260 gallons.

Weather is almost always an issue along the dangerous leg of the Aleutian Islands in the Pacific. Since the Soviet Union, prior to the fall of the Berlin Wall, would not allow the two pilots to land within two hundred miles of their coastline, Perot and Coburn were forced to land and refuel on a platform on a container ship in the Pacific during twelve-foot swells, something neither pilot had ever done before. The team prepared by placing a former Coast Guard helicopter pilot on the ship to advise them. From 250 miles away, Perot and Coburn picked up the nondirectional beacon signal installed on the ship as a navigational aid. On his first attempt, Perot made one pass over the ship and then circled to land. The motion of the ship in the heavy seas required the deck crew to secure the helicopter skids to the platform.

Some of their flying was done close to the ground where there was not only spectacular scenery but also animal life in its natural setting. Several helicopters, including a Bell UH-1H Huey and the Bell Long Ranger II Model 206L, *Spirit of Texas*, were put on display at the Smithsonian's new Steven F. Udvar-Hazy Center at Dulles Airport in 2010.

Testing the Limits of Aviation— Jeana Yeager (1952–), Copilot on the Voyager

On December 23, 1986, a unique aircraft named *Voyager* completed a nonstop flight around the world without refueling, the first of its kind, in nine days, three minutes, and forty-four seconds. Aviators Dick Rutan and Jeana Yeager, the craft's designer Burt Rutan, and crew chief Bruce Evans shared the Collier Trophy, aviation's most prestigious award, for this accomplishment.

Retired U.S. Air Force Lieutenant Colonel Richard Rutan was pilot and Yeager was copilot on this flight. Yeager was born in Fort Worth, Texas, in 1952. She received her private pilot license in 1978. She worked in California as a drafter or a technical artist and a surveyor. Dick Rutan completed his military flight training in a T-38 at Laughlin Air Force Base, Del Rio, Texas, in 1966. He was the recipient of five Distinguished Flying Crosses, sixteen Air Medals, a Silver Star, and a Purple Heart in Vietnam. The flight was conceived over lunch with Dick, his aerodynamicist brother Burt, and Yeager in 1981. Burt sketched his ideas for an airplane that would fly nonstop around the world without refueling on a restaurant napkin. Both Dick and Yeager had flown and set aviation records using Rutan's ingenious designs, but this world flight was a different matter.[9]

The flight of *Voyager* tested the abilities of aircraft designer Burt

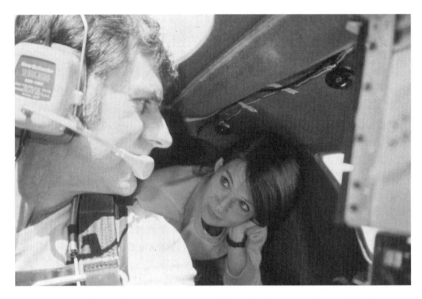

Dick Rutan, pilot, and Jeana Yeager, copilot, during a 1986 test flight in *Voyager*, prior to setting their world aviation record. Courtesy of the Jeana Yeager Collection, James G. Gee Library Special Collections Department, Texas A&M University–Commerce.

to develop a composite aircraft capable of flying around the world without refueling. Rutan utilized a composite material made of one-quarter-inch paper honeycomb and ultralight graphite for the airplane. Like coal and diamond, graphite is mainly carbon. Drawn into fibers, heated, and pressed, it becomes the mechanical equivalent of Superman's fist. It is half the weight of steel and five times as strong.

Three-quarters of *Voyager*'s total weight was composed of fuel. The aircraft had eight fuel tanks on each side of the airplane and one in the center. Weight and balance were an important factor in the success of this flight. The pilot shifted fuel from tank to tank during the flight to keep the airplane in balance. Every item on the plane, including food, was weighed before takeoff. To lighten the load, Yeager even cut off her long hair to save every ounce of weight. When the plane took off it had 7,011 pounds of fuel on board. When it landed there were 106 pounds of fuel left.

Dick Rutan was the more experienced pilot of the two. He did not trust Yeager to fly the aircraft while it was fully loaded with fuel because it was unstable. But when he was too exhausted to fly safely, she would take over. She flew it approximately 15 percent of the time.[10]

Weather, wind, and geography determined *Voyager*'s route around the world. A westbound course was selected to take advantage of the low-altitude easterly trade winds in equatorial regions. Most of the route was over water to avoid both turbulent air and the red tape of overflight clearances. *Voyager* flew an official distance of 42,212 kilometers (24,986 miles) at an official speed of 186 kilometers per hour (116 miles per hour). Flying *Voyager*, Rutan and Yeager established eight absolute and world-class records. The aircraft and its engines are permanently on display at the National Air and Space Museum in Washington, DC.

The late Scott Crossfield, one of the greatest American test pilots, best summed up the *Voyager* flight:

> The most remarkable people in aviation were the Wright brothers, who disdained institutions, solved all their own problems, paid for everything out of their own pockets, and brought the miracle of Kitty Hawk to us all.
>
> The Rutans and Yeager disdained institutions, mortgaged everything but their dignity, gave six years of their lives creating a most ingenious flight against all kinds of hazards, all on their own. They subjected themselves to nine days of the most exquisite torture anyone has ever volunteered for in their life, and did an incredible job that no government could do—NASA couldn't do it, the military couldn't do it. There was no prize, no money, and they are still paying off their debts. Theirs is one of the most remarkable aeronautical feats in history.[11]

The Collier Trophy

The Collier Trophy is the most prestigious award in the field of aviation. Since 1911, it has been awarded to those who have made "the greatest achievement in aeronautics or astronautics in America with respect to improving the performance, efficiency and safety of air or space vehicles, the value of which has been thoroughly demonstrated by actual use during the previous year." The award is named after Robert J. Collier, who asserted that "The flying machine should be unselfishly and rapidly developed to its potential for America's economic advancement."[12] Collier was the first private citizen to purchase an airplane from the Wright brothers. Texans who have received the Collier Trophy include Howard Hughes and his crew for their 1938 round-the-world flight, Alan Bean, and Jeana L. Yeager. In 1990 the Bell Boeing Team won this prestigious award for the development of the V-22 Osprey, the world's first large-scale tilt-rotor aircraft.

Aeronautical Education and Training Centers

The space race and the Cold War stimulated the growth of research laboratories and educational centers. There are many opportunities in the fields of aerospace and aeronautics in Texas. From ground crews, flight attendants, and pilots to aerospace engineers, mission control specialists, and astronauts, Texas schools provide opportunities for advancement in fields related to the aviation and space industries. With greater emphasis being placed on STEM (science, technology, engineering, and mathematics) subjects in our public elementary and secondary schools, the future of the field looks bright with interested young minds becoming involved at earlier ages and continuing their education through to the highest levels. There are a variety of programs for students who demonstrate a desire to work in the aerospace industry, whether in piloting, manufacturing, or providing a variety of services.

Texas A&M, Department of Aerospace Engineering

As early as 1928, Professor W. D. Bliss, head of the Mechanical Engineering Department at Texas A&M, recognized the importance of the airplane and introduced a course on aerodynamics. In 1930 Professor W. I. Truettner, a graduate of the University of Michigan, came to teach the course. A graduate course on advanced aeroplane design was soon added to the curriculum.

Prior to 1939 the College Airport (now Easterwood) was only suitable for light aircraft. Between 1942 and 1943, nearly $1.75 million was spent to improve the airport. Civil aeronautic authorities spent $1.4 million, and the college provided some money to pave the three runways and taxiways.

In 1939 the Civilian Pilots Training Program, a federally funded program, allowed forty students to take ground school courses and complete flight training for their private pilot licenses. Beginning in the summer of 1940, forty-five students were enrolled and the college was certified as an advanced flying school. Through the Works Progress Administration and the War Department, plans were drawn up to improve the airport. New courses were also introduced, which allowed those students who had completed their junior year in mechanical engineering to graduate in one year and qualify as junior aeronautical engineers. The first class of 1941 consisted of seventeen mechanical engineering students who enrolled in ten hours of elective courses in the new Department. During 1942–1943, the Aeronautical Engineering Department became the first in the Southwest and the fourteenth in the country to be accredited by the American Engineers' Council for Professional Development.

After World War II, the flight-training program was phased out. Its number of graduates increased over the years until it reached a peak in 1947 as a result of the GI Bill. In 1948 the number of graduates declined from eighty-seven to seventy-three; its lowest number of graduates was in 1954 when there were only nine.

In 1950–1951, Fred E. Weick, Distinguished Professor of Aeronautical Engineering and Director of the Personal Aircraft Center of the Texas Engineering Experiment Station, designed and developed the construction of AG-1, an agricultural airplane intended for crop dusting, spraying, seeding, fertilizing, and disease control. In 1954–1955, modified versions of the plane were developed. These were AG-2 and AG-3.

In 1959–1960 the name of the department was changed from Aeronautical Engineering to Aerospace Engineering. The first commercial test using its wind tunnel was run in July 1960. Bell, Temco, and Vought have used the wind tunnel for testing their designs. NASA also used it to test the Gemini capsule. An additional instruction facility was built in the form of a smoke tunnel.

The program at Texas A&M benefited from the Apollo space program, which spurred interest and led to the hiring of additional faculty in the late 1960s. The number of students who graduated grew again in the 1980s. Between 1990 and 2009, there were 1,338 graduates. Hopefully the program will continue to satisfy many of the needs of the aeronautical industry in the space age.

The aerospace engineering program at Texas A&M is distinctive in that it is well balanced, with strengths in areas including fluid dynamics, materials and structures, stability and control, and propulsion. It is a major research facility with commercial and hypersonic wind tunnels, flight simulators, and laboratories. It ranks within the top 15 percent of universities in the country that offer programs in aerospace engineering; however, it has experienced problems in recent years recruiting and retaining women students. Despite this failing, a number of its graduates have gone on to have distinguished careers in the aeronautical industry. One of its most outstanding graduates was Leland Snow, founder of Air Tractor.

University of Texas at Austin's Aerospace Engineering Program

The Department of Aerospace Engineering Program at the University of Texas at Austin is always ranked by *U.S. News and World Report* as one of the top ten programs in the United States. With more than thirty faculty members, students in this program have unique opportunities to be engaged in hands-on endeavors as part of the Longhorn Rocketry Association, the Unmanned Aerial Vehicle Team, or the Armadillo Satellite Team (which works on a small, three-unit cube satellite that was designed and built by students). Students design, build, and fly while developing their team leadership skills. Students and faculty are engaged in the study of a variety of topics, including aerothermodynamics, composite design and structural materials, guidance and control systems, and aircraft design. The program at the University of Texas is based around atmospheric flight and space flight.[13]

In 1981 the University of Texas established the Center for Space Research. Results of its research have provided practical applications to questions regarding agriculture, the fishery industry, mapping of ocean circulation, weather forecasting, and the environmental impact of oil spills, exploration, and drilling.

Rice University, Rice Space Institute

In 1963 Rice University established the first Space Science Department in the United States following a speech by President John F. Kennedy on its campus in September 1962. More than 150 faculty and research staff members from twenty departments now comprise the Rice Space Institute. Its areas of study include space weather, astronomy and astrophysics, space technology, space history and public policy, space education and public outreach, and space remote sensing. In recent years Rice University has increased its efforts to develop educational materials and activities to engage K–12 students in space exploration. The mission of Rice Space Institute is "to engage interdisciplinary research and education at all levels to achieve the vision of making the universe smaller and to chart the course for the next generation of peaceful uses of space."

Sasakawa International Center for Space Architecture, University of Houston

The Sasakawa International Center for Space Architecture (SICSA) is a unique research and design entity. It offers the world's only master of science degree in space science architecture. Founded in 1987, it has a permanent $3 million endowed program provided by the Japan Shipbuilding Industry Foundation. Its mission is to plan and develop programs that will advance peaceful and beneficial uses of space and space technology on Earth and above. Its students conduct research and design for habitats in space and other extreme environments. The master's degree program, established in 2003, responds to the interest of aerospace engineers, social scientists, and other specialists employed by NASA and other space agencies. Most retain their regular jobs while pursuing graduate work. Dr. Larry Bell, professor of architecture and holder of an endowed professorship in space architecture, founded SICSA and heads the graduate program in space architecture.

University of Texas at Arlington

Aerospace engineering actually predates the University of Texas at Arlington (UTA) to the 1930s, when this institution was called the North Texas Agricultural College—its name from 1923 to 1949. At that time, faculty offered courses in airframe and engine maintenance. In 1939 the Navy's V-12 College Training Program began and U.S. entry into World War II led to an expansion of the vocational aeromechanics training program. In 1959 Arlington State

College, as the institution was known from 1949 to 1967, offered a four-year bachelor's degree in engineering. In 1967 UTA became part of the University of Texas system; it now has over thirty thousand students.[14]

In 1964 the aerospace program began within the joint Aerospace and Mechanical Engineering Department. Its first degrees were granted in 1965. Subsequently in 1971, an autonomous Aerospace Engineering Department was established, but then in 1992 it merged back into the Mechanical and Aerospace Engineering Department. Presently, the program is one of the largest within the College of Engineering in terms of student enrollment; it has thirty-eight full-time faculty members.

Besides being the fourth largest metropolitan area in the country, the Dallas/Fort Worth region enjoys the second highest concentration of aerospace economic activity. Thus, the aerospace engineering program at UTA enjoys close proximity to major aerospace corporations, as well as many auxiliary companies. UTA students benefit greatly from co-op and internship opportunities, as well as finding potential employment. Students also have the option to pursue a more flexible advanced degree and continuing education opportunities, including distance e-learning. Opportunities are also abundant for corporate-funded research and development.

The faculty is engaged in aerospace education from the undergraduate through the doctoral level as well as in K–12 and public outreach. Faculty members participate in weeklong summer programs organized by the College of Engineering to introduce middle school to high school students to science and engineering. A Girlgeneering summer camp focuses on girls, with female aerospace students taking the lead and serving as role models. These initiatives were started in 1998 and have enrolled a total of over a thousand students.

The faculty is actively engaged in promoting underrepresented minorities and women in their research. These efforts are funded by the NSF Louis Stokes Alliance for Minority Participation and the McNair-SOAR programs. These initiatives have successfully engaged highly qualified students to participate in cutting-edge research. Many have published articles in archival journals, leading the way to acquiring advanced graduate degrees.

The aerospace program has strengths in multidisciplinary research, collaborating within the campus and with other academic institutions, industry, and government agencies. Its cutting-edge research activities are broadly based, covering various aspects of aerospace engineering and even beyond. These include advanced composites and structures, aerospace vehicle design, and air refueling; detonation-based power and propulsion; electronics cooling; guidance, navigation, and control—including GPS-based systems; hypersonic aerodynamics; hypersonic thermal protection systems; robotics and unmanned, autonomous systems; space debris; and synthetic fuels. All these areas have an undergraduate component. A special feature of UTA is its comprehensive aerodynamic test facilities from low-speed to hypersonic. Finally, among UTA's alumni are two space shuttle astronauts: Robert L. Stewart, who flew on both the *Challenger* and the *Atlantis*, respectively in 1984 and 1985; and the late Kalpana Chawla (1962–2003).

University of Texas at El Paso

The WINGS program at the University of Texas at El Paso helps prepare math and science teachers to motivate students. Boeing also sponsors teachers to attend space camp and hosts the Space Exploration Educators Conference to engage classroom, college, and museum educators around the country. The Boeing Company is partnering with K–12 educators across Texas to inspire the next generation of explorers by supporting programs that enhance math, engineering, and science curriculum. The Center for Space Exploration Technology Research at UTEP promotes research and education in aerospace and energy engineering. Its faculty and students share a particular interest in advanced propulsion, in situ resource utilization, aerospace structures, and green technology.

The Future of Space Travel

Space travel no longer rests solely in the hands of government agencies. On October 4, 2004, *SpaceShipOne* flew to the border of space, becoming the first privately funded vehicle to exceed an altitude of 328,000 feet twice within a two-week period, thus claiming the $10 million Ansari X-Prize. This event spurred the idea of greater access to space for private citizens, as well as promising greater innovation and efficiency than government-sponsored programs.

Richard Garriott (1961–),
Sixth Private Astronaut in the World

Certain daring individuals, nonetheless, are unwilling to wait for government initiatives to travel into space. Richard Garriott, born in Cambridge in the United Kingdom on July 4, 1961, was the sixth private citizen to fly into space. Garriott was born while his father was at Cambridge University on sabbatical from Stanford University. His family then moved back to California until his father was accepted as a NASA astronaut in 1965. Then the family moved to Arizona, where his father learned to fly jets, as did all astronauts at the time. In 1966 the Garriott family moved to Nassau Bay, just outside the front gates of NASA.

Richard Garriott's passion for space travel began early on, inspired by his father, Dr. Owen Garriott, a scientist and NASA astronaut in the 1970s who flew on two missions. However, the younger Garriott's poor eyesight ruined his chances for a career in NASA, because perfect vision is a requirement for its astronauts. The devastating news that he would not be able to join the exclusive space club like his father, neighbors, and adult friends he had grown up with in Houston was delivered by a physician in a matter-of-fact manner when he was thirteen. But poor eyesight did not deter Garriott from pursuing a successful career in computer game design, private space travel, and other extreme adventures.

Garriott found instant success in the launch of his Austin-based computer game development company, Origins Systems Inc. This company and Garriott became most famous for the Ultima Online project, a massively multiplayer online role-playing game. Garriott also worked on other video game projects but maintained his interest in space travel.

During the 1990s Garriott helped found the company Space Adventures. Since private citizens are not allowed to fly on NASA missions, Space Adventures works with the Russian Federal Space Agency to send clients to the International Space Station aboard small Soyuz rockets. Garriott attended the University of Texas at Austin for a couple of years, where he dedicated himself to developing video games, but he dropped out to pursue a full-time, highly successful career in developing video games as a programmer. Garriott had intended to be the first private astronaut by funding a $200,000 research study

Richard Garriott,
private astronaut.
Courtesy of
Richard Garriott.

for the Russians to consider bringing private citizens into space in the 1990s. He thought that a pressurized module would fit in the back container of the shuttle, but NASA was not at all interested. With the dot-com financial crisis and 9/11 in 2001, his personal wealth plummeted and he had to take care of financial matters on Earth first. He recovered financially to pursue his dream of traveling in space. In 2007 Garriott left his job as a computer game developer to begin the yearlong training process to spend time in space. On October 12, 2008, Garriott joined an orbital spaceflight, a spaceflight in which the spacecraft makes at least one full orbit around the Earth.[15]

Garriott dealt with the fear factor of traveling into space by being thoroughly familiar with procedures during training with the Russians, who, he notes, have not lost an astronaut in over thirty-five years. Russians work in small teams, so when critical information is learned it is passed directly on to those involved with the preparation of launches. The scientists and engineers, in other words, are all the same individuals involved with training and launch procedures. He found the Russians to be congenial and their approach to research very cost effective.

Garriott described his takeoff in the Soyuz as very smooth and elegant, not unlike a ballet movement, rather than a sports car taking off when the light turns green. He spent two weeks in space. The capsule itself was very confining, cold, dark, and claustrophobic; if there were to be an emergency, he doubted that things would go well because it would be difficult to get out. However, the launch into space itself was surprisingly silent, lasting only eight and a half minutes before all the fuel burned and the vehicle shut down. Being in space did not seem very far from Earth. He was approximately 250 miles up, about the distance between Houston and Austin. Yet he was traveling at seventeen thousand miles per hour, and either sunrise or sunset was taking place every forty-five minutes. Garriott could make out great detail from space, such as the Golden Gate Bridge in San Francisco, Lake Travis in Central Texas, and Galveston along the Gulf of Mexico. Literally he had a physical reaction to seeing the scale of the Earth, known among astronauts as the "overview effect." He could also better appreciate plate tectonics—how the landmasses of the various continents had at one time fit together.[16]

While in space, Garriott took on commercial projects, corporate sponsors, and other small assignments to show the commercial potential of "space tourism." Garriott worked with the British National Space Center to develop space outreach programs for students, which included regular radio broadcasts while Garriott was in orbit and a competition by students to design experiments for Garriott to carry out in space. Garriott also worked with the Nature Conservancy to take photographs of Earth from space to identify environmental change. In 2009 Garriott received the Sir Arthur C. Clarke award for his outstanding individual achievements in space exploration.

Space Adventures offers space tourism opportunities to the public. It seeks to send private citizens into space for prices ranging from $102,000 for a suborbital spaceflight (which is a flight into space that does not complete one full orbit of the Earth like Garriott's mission did) to $100 million for a future trip to the moon. Garriott hopes to lower the price for a suborbital flight to around $50,000. Space tourism is gaining popularity as more and more companies seek new ways to offer space experiences to a broader audience.

In addition to his space flight, Garriott has participated in several extreme adventures, such as traveling to Antarctica to search for meteorites, traveling down the Amazon, and even diving down to see the *Titanic* first hand. His next adventure will be space diving, in which he will travel to the edge of space in six minutes and then step out of a space vehicle and dive back to Earth using a high-tech space suit and a parachute. Garriott currently serves on a NASA advisory board for commercial space travel.

Armadillo Aerospace

John Carmack, born August 20, 1970, is a visionary computer programmer and rocket enthusiast. Carmack favors private initiatives to reach space, something that he had wanted to do. In 2000 he became the financial founder of Armadillo Aerospace, based in Mesquite, Texas, an aerospace company that develops reusable rocket-powered vehicles. Russ Blink, Neil Milburn, and Phil Easton have also been involved in its activities since day one. Armadillo Aerospace currently has five employees. The company selected a whimsical name that depicted the local flavor of Texas. Armadillo Aerospace started out by building hovering vehicles. It has built and flown probably more than twenty different vehicles in varying forms, as well as helping one of its customers, Rocket Racing League, outfit two aircraft with rocket engines to do flight demonstrations. Armadillo Aerospace has also built vehicles for NASA to do terrestrial lunar-lander-style flight testing. In addition, it has done a great deal of research on its own vehicles to provide payload services for the commercial sector at prices well below the cost of an expendable rocket. Currently Armadillo Aerospace is working on a thirty-four-foot tall, twenty-inch diameter vehicle that is capable of reaching very high altitudes depending on the payload.[17]

In 2008 Armadillo Aerospace participated in the Northrop Grumman Lunar Lander Challenge (NGLLC) and won the Level 1 competition by sending a lunar lander (a prototype for a future model that will hopefully carry humans or supplies regularly to the moon) 160 feet into the air, keeping it in flight for at least 90 seconds, then landing it in a different, exact location, and repeating this process again. In 2009 Armadillo Aerospace won the Level 2 NGLLC prize, extending their lunar lander's flight duration to 180 seconds.[18]

Carmack and his team hope that the reusable rocket-powered vehicles created by Armadillo Aerospace will lower the cost of space travel so that more people can engage in space tourism. Space Adventures will use an Armadillo Technologies rocket for its next suborbital spaceflight, taking passengers sixty-two miles into the sky. The use of an Armadillo rocket has cut the price of suborbital spaceflights in half, to $102,000. Armadillo Aerospace hopes that the future integration of reusable rockets in commercial space travel will further reduce the cost of private space flights.

Orbiting Outpost

Five space agencies representing fifteen countries cooperated to build the International Space Station. As NASA's prime contractor for the station, the Boeing Company designed and built all the major U.S. elements and is responsible for incorporating all new hardware and software—including components from international partners. Boeing also provides engineering work to maintain the station. Boeing prepared every U.S. component in the station for space flight at the Space Station Processing Facility at Kennedy Space Center, Florida. Boeing employees in Houston; Huntsville, Alabama; Huntington Beach, California; and Kennedy worked with NASA on the project. NASA itself spends approximately two billion dollars a year to operate the station.[19]

The 2005 NASA Authorization Act designated the U.S. segment of the space station as a national laboratory, making it available for research by other federal agencies and the private sector. The research conducted on this one-of-a-kind orbiting lab helps improve life on Earth and teaches us valuable lessons needed to tackle the challenges of long-duration space flight.

Multiple connected solar cells, known as a solar array, power the International Space Station. The U.S. solar array surface is more than thirty-eight thousand square feet, big enough to cover eight basketball courts. The space station has more living space than a conventional five-bedroom house.

On July 21, 2011, NASA launched STS-135 *Atlantis*, marking the end of the shuttle program and 135 missions since April 12, 1981. U.S. astronauts such as Shannon Walker now travel to the International Space Station on Russian spacecraft, at least until commercial companies can carry astronauts safely into space. Walker served as flight engineer (copilot) on a Russian Soyuz spacecraft, TMA-19, which launched on June 15, 2010. After 161 days at the International Space Station, she served as flight engineer again on her return to Earth on November 25, 2010. Walker, born in Houston in 1965, graduated from Westbury Senior High School in 1983. At Rice University, she received a bachelor of arts degree in physics in 1987, a master of science, and a doctorate in space physics in 1992 and 1993, respectively. Walker joined the astronaut corps in May 2004.[20]

What Now?

The United States is developing a new generation of rockets and a spacecraft based on the Apollo and Space Shuttle programs. The new aircraft will incorporate the best features from past vehicles with the latest technology to enable mankind to travel further into space. Orion was the name of one new vehicle, but it is already considered somewhat antiquated, as technology and ideas about space travel are evolving quickly. NASA is working more with putting capsules back on the top of a variety of rockets to reach space. A variety of different private companies in Texas are playing a major role in getting people back into space.[21]

Besides federal budget cuts, humanity still has other obstacles to overcome and to consider before returning astronauts to the moon and going beyond to Mars. There are concerns about the effects of space travel on human physiology. Fears have even been expressed that astronauts who travel for months at a time may not be able to walk on Mars by the time they reach their destination because their bones could become too brittle. The loss of bone mass is one of the biggest challenges facing space travelers in the future.[22] Our bodies need physical stress to maintain good health. Astronauts are unable to get the kind of workouts they get on Earth. Space travelers have to ensure they receive proper nutrition and spend time every day doing exercise.

NASA's 2009 class of fourteen astronauts was selected from more than thirty-five hundred applicants. Among them are test pilots, flight surgeons, a flight controller, a molecular biologist, a Pentagon staffer, and a CIA intelligence officer. Each has an advanced degree in science, engineering, or mathematics. These men and women have their eyes set on being the first astronauts to return to the moon (including one becoming the first woman astronaut to walk on the moon), visit near-Earth asteroids, and ultimately travel to Mars. Training for deep space, these astronauts will take an outdoor survival course in Maine, spend two weeks living underwater in a laboratory, endure altitude chambers, and be challenged by having to face months of confinement and isolation.[23]

Yet, as we have seen, aviators and astronauts in Texas have overcome many challenges in the past and will continue to do so in the future. Texans, in a rich variety of ways during these past one hundred years, have worked for the overall good of aviation and space exploration, public safety in air transportation, national defense, and the advancement of scientific knowledge that someday will return mankind to the moon and beyond. Automation and hypersonic launch vehicles (meaning they travel multiple times faster than the speed of sound) also are on the horizon in the future of space travel.

Back on Earth, perhaps an all-composite aircraft is on the drawing board of an aerospace engineer to advance commercial aviation, even beyond Boeing's amazing 787 Dreamliner. Composite aircraft, first developed in Texas, reduce weight and drag and are more cost efficient by reducing the amount of maintenance over the lifetime of an aircraft. Composite aircraft are lighter, resulting in lower fuel consumption. United Continental Holdings is the first airline in the United States to get Boeing's newest airplane, the 787 Dreamliner. On September 28, 2012, United Airlines flew its first Boeing 787 Dreamliner to Houston from the Boeing production line at Everett, Washington, where it will begin its first commercial flights on a jet that will give passengers greater comfort and save on fuel. Its inaugural flight with paying passengers took place November 4, 2012, from Houston George Bush Intercontinental Airport to Chicago O'Hare. United's Dreamliner will initially carry passengers between United hubs, including Chicago, Houston, and Newark before being dedicated primarily to international flights.[24]

Many aviators, aviation enthusiasts, and air travelers alike in Texas will continue to turn their heads toward the sky in the hopes for a better future, greater convenience, comfort, entertainment, and the expectation that perhaps more affordable space travel for private citizens will become possible in the near future.

Appendix I
Time Flies in Texas Aviation

1910

February 18   Frenchman Louis Paulhan becomes the first person to demonstrate the airplane in Texas.

March 2   Lieutenant Benjamin D. Foulois soloes in a Wright Flyer at Fort Sam Houston, San Antonio. This is the first flight in the military airplane dubbed *Signal Corps No. 1*. He makes four flights that day, lasting seven and a half minutes, ten minutes, twenty-one minutes, and twenty-one minutes, respectively. On the fourth flight, the gasoline feed pipe breaks.

March 3   Otto Brodie flies a Curtiss pusher-type aircraft fifteen to twenty feet in ground effect at the fairgrounds in Dallas, making the first flight in North Texas after working all night with mechanics readying the aircraft to fly.

April 10   In Houston, Leslie L. Walker builds and flies a monoplane using a French design. His Bleriot has a forty-horsepower, four-cylinder concentric-valve Kemp engine.

April 24   Father of naval aviation and aircraft designer Glenn Curtiss flies several exhibition flights at San Antonio, including one with a passenger, at a height of seven hundred feet and a speed of forty-five miles per hour.

August   Philip O. Parmalee pilots the Wright Flyer at San Antonio while his passenger, Lieutenant M. S. Crissy, holds the U.S. Army's first aerial bomb.

August 8   Lieutenant Foulois installs tricycle landing gear on the Wright Flyer at San Antonio. Previously, the Wright Flyer had a brake skid, not wheels. Foulois also adds a safety belt.

1911

January 12   French aviator Roland Garros performs the first powered flight at a racetrack in Fort Worth with seventeen thousand spectators. Garros flies a Bleriot XI as a member of the Moisant International Aviators.

March 3   Lieutenant Foulois and civilian pilot Parmalee complete a 106-mile nonstop cross-country flight in a Collier Wright from Laredo to Eagle Pass, Texas, in an attempt to prove to ground forces the usefulness of the airplane. The flight lasts two hours and ten minutes. Parmalee, with Foulois as a passenger, sends and receives radio messages and drops written messages to army units during this flight near the Mexico/Texas border, according to the *Aircraft Year Book* (1950).

September 17–November 5   Calbraith P. Rodgers completes the first transcontinental flight in a Burgess-Wright biplane called the *Vin Fiz*. He travels the 3,390 miles from Sheepshead Bay, New York, to Pasadena, California, in forty-nine days. At least twenty-three stops are in Texas, including the first airplane flight in Austin on October 20. Rodgers crashes at least fifteen times—including an incident at Kyle, Texas—besides experiencing numerous other mishaps. Rodgers's transcontinental flight does not demonstrate the reliability of the airplane, but it does introduce the airplane to many communities.

1912

April 14   Matilde Moisant, following a flight at Dallas, noses her Bleriot over to prevent harm to her admirers at Wichita Falls.

July 4   Residents from Odessa gather to view the Pliska airplane built by John W. Pliska, a blacksmith in Midland.

1913

• The Burgess H at Texas City, home of the First Aero Squadron, is the first U.S. military airplane to have the engine and propeller mounted in front (USAF Museum Dayton).

March 5   The First Aero Squadron is established in Texas City, Texas.

May 29   Lieutenants T. D. Milling and W. C. Sherman set the world endurance and distance record of 220 miles in four hours and twenty-two minutes from Texas City to San Antonio in a Burgess tractor powered by a seventy-horsepower Renault engine.

1915

April 20 | Lieutenant Bryon Q. Jones and Lieutenant Thomas D. Milling perform a reconnaissance flight from Brownsville in a Martin aircraft.

August 26 | Lieutenant Bryon Q. Jones, with Morrow (no first name listed) as observer, takes off from Brownsville to look for bandits operating in the area around Santa Maria, Texas.

November 19 | The First Aero Squadron begins the first cross-country flight by the Army Air Service. The route extends 439 miles from Fort Sill, Oklahoma City, to Fort Sam Houston, San Antonio.

1916

March 19 | First reconnaissance missions are flown into Mexico by the First Aero Squadron following the raid on the garrison town of Columbus, New Mexico, by Francisco "Pancho" Villa on March 9, 1916.

June 18 | H. Clyde Balsley, fighting for France with the famed World War I volunteer air unit Escadrille Américaine, becomes the first American aviator to be shot down in air combat. He survives his crash near Verdun, France. Balsley had painted a white lone star, the symbol of Texas, on the fuselage and wheel hubs of his Nieuport 11.

1917

April 30 | The University of Texas at Austin establishes the School of Military Aeronautics, which opens on May 21. Edgar G. Tobin is the first of 5,958 cadets admitted to the ground school. By July 235 cadets are enrolled. Their coursework includes airplane engines, aerodynamics, gunnery, aerial observation, and signals (Morse code).

May 17 | Kelly Air Field at San Antonio is activated as Camp Kelly, to be renamed Kelly Field on July 30. Air Service mechanics, pursuit, bomber, and observation flying training is held here until 1943.

August 1 | A group of eleven young cadets assembles at Kelly Field to attend ground school at the School of Military Aeronautics before earning their wings. Cadet Sydney J. Brooks, a San Antonio native, would become Kelly's first fatality. Only one of the eleven cadets would make it overseas: Hugh Brewster of Fort Worth would shoot down two German planes in September 1918 while flying a SPAD VII with the 49th Pursuit Squadron.

October (to November 1918)   The British, U.S., and Canadian governments enter into reciprocal agreements to train military pilots for combat. Canada agrees to train U.S. pilots in return for the use of three airfields in the Fort Worth area.

October 19   Love Field is established at Dallas for military flight training by the U.S. Air Service. The name honors Moss Love (1879–1913), who perished in an accident in San Diego in 1913.

November 1   Ellington Field is established at Houston to provide bombing instruction to early aviators.

December 8   Ground is broken for a new San Antonio airfield. Brooks Field would officially open in February 1918. Balloon and airship training as well as flight and observation training would take place here. Brooks Field is the center for primary flight training, while Kelly serves for advanced flight training.

1918

February 16   Brooks Field is activated as a U.S. Army Air Corps base.

1919

May   The "Gulf to Pacific" Squadron of de Havilland Four military aircraft under the command of First Lieutenant R. O. Searle completes a round-trip, cross-country flight of 3,300 miles from Ellington Field to the Pacific coast and back. They fly an average of 101 miles per hour (*New York Times*, May 28, 1919). That same month Colonel G. C. Brant also flies one of the de Havilland army biplanes from Houston to Belleville, Illinois, in seven hours and thirty-three minutes.

October 27   Walter Beech learns to fly a Curtiss JN-4D Jenny as a cadet at Rich Field, Waco. Beech later becomes a major airplane designer and manufacturer of the Travel Air and Beechcraft in Wichita, Kansas (Walter and Olive Beech Collection, Wichita State University Library, Special Collections).

1920

August   The Air Corps Training Center is established at San Antonio, Texas. Frank P. Lahm commands the school, which includes primary and advanced flying school and the School of Aviation Medicine. Lahm would be appointed assistant to the chief of the Air Corps with the rank of brigadier general in July 1930.

1921

- Vincent J. Burnelli (1895–1964), who was born in Temple, begins to design aircraft with wing-shaped fuselages in New York. Burnelli is obviously an original thinker, but his aircraft designs never become mainstream.

1922

- Texas, with 164 airfields, has more airfields than any other state in the United States. Of these, 12 are federal, 8 municipal, 5 commercial, and 139 unimproved (*Aircraft Handbook* for 1922).

1924

- Flying Douglas World Cruisers, the U.S. Army Air Service completes the first around-the-world flight, which includes stops at Love Field on September 19, Sweetwater on September 20, and El Paso on September 21. The flight takes 175 days with 74 stops. Total flying time is 371 hours and 11 minutes. Total distance: 26,503 miles. Frederick L. Martin commands the flight. Some ten thousand spectators show up at Love Field to greet the world flyers.

April 23   The National Balloon Race begins at San Antonio, to be won by W. T. Van Orman landing at Rochester, Minnesota.

1925

- Mayor H. C. Meacham had provided $3,000 from his personal finances to build a small house and dig a well for the airfield north of Fort Worth, which is named for its early benefactor.
- Grace McClelland and Mat Watson offer one-dollar airplane rides in two five-passenger Lincoln Standard L.S.5 biplanes, which operate from the parade ground in northwest Austin at Camp Mabry.

August 17   William G. Fuller, U.S. Army Air Corps World War I veteran
pilot, is assigned to manage Fort Worth Municipal Airport at
Meacham Field.

1926

- S. Webb Ruff, a student at the University of Texas at Austin,
signs up twelve students to take a ten-hour flying course. They
form the University Flying Circus. This group of university flyers will give thousands of Texans their first airplane flights,
mostly operating around towns with populations under five
thousand. Ruff would later describe his own group as rather
reckless and heavy drinkers. Many would leave towns with
their hotel bills unpaid, according to a letter he would sign on
June 7, 1957. (Florence Hester Wood, "Early Commercial Aviation in Texas, 1904–1954," MA thesis, University of Texas at
Austin, August 1957, pp. 73–75.)

May 12   The National Air Transport Company establishes airmail service between Dallas and Fort Worth. The first northbound
flight carries 486 pounds of mail. This is considered the first
airmail service flown in Texas, although airplanes had carried
mail as early as 1912.

December 21 (to May 2, 1927)   The Pan American Goodwill Flight through
Mexico and Central America and around South America and
back through the Caribbean begins at Kelly Field, San Antonio.
Through this flight, the United States seeks to enhance its relationship with Latin America, pioneer the expansion of commercial aviation, and provide valuable training for the U.S. Army
Air Service.

1927

- Hollywood movie stars Buddy Rogers, Richard Arlen, Clara
Bow, and May McAvoy shoot the great silent film *Wings* at
Camp Stanley, a remote field north of San Antonio. Hollywood
motion picture director Lucien Hubbard uses a large number
of troops from Kelly Field and Fort Sam Houston, along with
forty-five aircraft from Kelly Field. *Wings* is notable for being
the first large-scale drama of military aviation during World
War I. (Office of History, San Antonio Air Logistics Center,
Kelly Air Force Base, Texas, *A Pictorial History of Kelly Air
Force Base, 1917–1980.* U.S. Government Printing Office, 1964.)

- A month after Captain William M. Randolph returns to Kelly Field as adjutant to the advanced flying school, he perishes when his plane crashes at Gorman Field, Texas. He is survived by his wife and three children. Randolph was born in Austin, Texas, and attended Texas A&M University before entering the U.S. Army in 1916. He received his wings from the Kelly Field flying school in 1919.

August 27   During a nationwide tour, Charles A. Lindbergh, the world's most famous aviator, stops at Love Field, where he is greeted by some seventy-five thousand people (*Dallas Morning News*, August 28, 1927).

November 27   Temple Bowen and his brother organize Texas Air Transport, which uses Travel Airs designed by Walter Beech. Texas Air Transport and Gulf Air Lines would later merge to form Southern Air Transport.

1928

February 6   An airmail pilot lands with the city of Houston's first airmail in a black and gold Pitcairn biplane at W. T. Carter Field (today, Houston Hobby). The same day, a pilot for Texas Air Transport, L. S. Andrews, carries the first airmail to Austin in a Waco aircraft, despite fog and rain. The Texas Air Transport Company begins operations that month.

June 8   Texas Air Transport begins passenger service from Meacham Field.

July 28   The world's first glider tow by an airplane is accomplished at Meacham Field. The two pilots are Earl T. Akin of Breckenridge and S. Webb Ruff of Austin. Eddie Stinson and other individuals pull on the glider when the group of men decide to tow it behind an airplane. William Fuller, airport manager for the city of Fort Worth, witnesses and verifies the event.

October 1   Texas Air Transport offers another airmail route, this one between San Antonio and Laredo.

1929

- Safeway Airlines (later sold to American Airlines) is established in Dallas, headquartered at the Love Field hangar leased by Bryon Good. Born in Carrollton, Texas, Good left the farm during World War I, becoming a skilled pilot and mechanic. Other privately owned airplanes also used this fixed base operation (named Good & Foster after Good's deceased partner, Harry C. Foster). Good & Foster operates three gasoline trucks for the U.S. Army airplanes stationed at Love and Hensley Fields. Monthly sales run about fifty thousand gallons of gasoline and five hundred to six hundred gallons of oil.

- At Meacham Field, Cyrus R. Smith forms Southern Air Transport through the Aviation Corporation's purchase of Texas Air Transport. This merger and that of several other aviation companies will eventually become American Airlines ("Southern Transcontinental Line is Inaugurated," *Southern Aviation*, November 1930).

- A dozen women from Texas organize the Woman's Flying Club of Houston. Their president is Katherine Pollard, and their ages range from eighteen to seventy. Ten are flying students working on getting their pilot licenses. Two are private pilots. The primary purpose of the club is to fly, learn about flying, and enjoy the fellowship of other flyers and fledglings.

March 9   Pan American Air Terminal opens at Brownsville, now Brownsville International Airport, becoming the first airport of international entry in Texas.

March 10   Charles Lindbergh inaugurates international service in a Ford trimotor aircraft by flying airmail from Brownsville, Texas, to Mexico City.

March 28   Amelia Earhart earns her transport license, aviation's highest credential, at Brownsville. She claims to be the fourth U.S. woman to receive one.

May 19–26   Reginald Robbins and James Kelly set a new world and U.S. endurance record of 172 hours, 32 minutes, and 1 second in a Ryan Brougham, a single-engine monoplane they named *Fort Worth*, having taken off from Meacham Field in that city (Russell Plehinger, *Marathon Flyers* [Detroit: Harlo, 1989], 79, 125). They land when a propeller blade cracks and begins vibrating severely, after seventeen fuel contacts that transfer 1,510 gallons. They cover an equivalent of 12,900 miles.

June 1   Delta Air Service (later Delta Air Lines) carries its first five passengers on what would become a daily flight from Love Field via Shreveport and Monroe, Louisiana, to Jackson, Mississippi, and Birmingham, Alabama, in a Travel Air S-6000B.

October 15 Braniff International Airways begins service to Dallas, Fort Worth, Oklahoma City, Tulsa, Wichita Falls, Abilene, San Angelo, and Amarillo. The new service is a joint arrangement between Universal Air Lines and Texas Air Transport.

October 15   Southern Air Fast Express Inc. begins mail and passenger service between Love Field and Los Angeles. Texas has four established airmail routes: Dallas to Galveston, Dallas to Brownsville, Houston to New Orleans, and Dallas to Chicago ("Aviation Progress in Lone Star State," *Southern Aviation* November 1930).

1930

- Twenty-four-hour weather service becomes available at Love Field. The Dallas Weather Bureau provides pilots with information about wind velocities and direction, upper air currents, and weather conditions at anticipated landing fields.
- Eighteen-year-old Margaret Thomas of Dallas becomes a member of the Curtiss-Wright Exhibition Company for one year. She is selected from among eighty young women pilots (*Southern Aviation*, March 15, 1930). She began to fly at fifteen, accumulating two hundred flying hours prior to selection. She flies a Travel Air Speedwing from Wichita, Kansas, to Miami, Florida, where the team practices flights in preparation for its nationwide cross-country tour. She performs aerial demonstrations of various types of aircraft, including the Travel Air Mystery Ship and the early Wright and Curtiss flyers. The following year, she begins flying as a demonstration pilot for Privateer, a company in Florida.

June 21–22   Randolph Field outside San Antonio is dedicated for military flight operations. Its importance in military training leads to its nickname, "West Point of the Air."

June 24   William C. Ocker, known as the "father of instrument flying," successfully pilots the first cross-country flight with only his instruments as his guide. He flies from Brooks Field to Scott Field, Illinois, a distance of about nine hundred miles.

September 4   French flyers Captain Dieudonné Costes and Captain Maurice Bellonte complete the first nonstop flight between New York and Dallas. (*Southern Aviation*, "The Dallas Visit of the Question Mark," Oct. 1930, p. 41.)

September 15   Austin airport is dedicated. It covers 340 acres and is considered a modern landing field with boundary lights and runways.

October 1   Temple Bowen, owner of Bowen Bus lines, launches a new air transport service between Fort Worth, Dallas, and Houston.

October 15   Two prominent women pilots, Elinor Smith and Ruth Nichols, take part in the dedication of Southern Transcontinental airlines at Love Field, Dallas (*Southern Aviation*, November 1930).

November   Officials of the Aviation Department of the Dallas Chamber of Commerce claim that Love Field is the world's busiest airport, based on their figures of total flights (6,095) and passengers (13,676) that month (*Southern Aviation*, November 1930, 22).

1931

May 17   Bowen Air Lines adds Austin to its routes between Dallas and San Antonio, introducing a newer and faster Lockheed Orion, a six-place, low-wing monoplane that cruises at 175 miles per hour.

June 16   Amelia Earhart arrives at Love Field in a new Pitcairn Autogiro, having wrecked another on departure from Abilene a few days earlier during her national tour.

1932

- Marie McMillan of McMillan-Johnson Flying Service in Greenville, Texas—a widow, licensed pilot, and mother of a daughter—sets a new world women's altitude parachute record by jumping 20,800 feet at the National Air Races in Cleveland, Ohio.

1933

- Texas native Wiley Post flies solo around the world in seven days, eighteen hours, and forty-nine minutes while making only eleven stops in the Lockheed Vega *Winnie Mae*.

1934

August 5   Frances Harrell Marsalis of Del Rio, Texas, crashes her Waco aircraft at the finish line of the fifty-mile feature closed-circuit pylon race at the Women's National Air Derby at Vandalia (Dayton), Ohio, resulting in her death.

1935

- Howard Hughes breaks the speed record in a landplane by flying 352.3 miles per hour in his Hughes IB Racer, also known as the H-1. This sleek aircraft, hand built from aluminum and wood, pioneers the development of high-speed, radial-engine aircraft, influencing important single-engine fighters flown in World War II.

1936

June 25   American becomes the first airline to fly the Douglas DC-3 in commercial service. By the end of the decade, American will be the nation's number one domestic air carrier in terms of revenue passenger miles. President Franklin D. Roosevelt would award designer Donald W. Douglas the 1936 Collier Trophy in recognition of his design.

1938

- Howard Hughes and his crew complete a world flight in the Lockheed 14 in three days, nineteen hours, and eight minutes.
- The North American AT-6 Texan serves as an advanced trainer at U.S. Air Force schools from 1938 until 1956. At Randolph Air Force Base near San Antonio, the AT-6 is used for the basic phase of flight training from 1943 until 1951. Over ten thousand of these aircraft are produced.

May 15–21 Mrs. Joan F. Shankle (1908–1964) of San Antonio flies the U.S. mail, the largest cargo to date. She carries 114 pounds of mail, including 4,446 letters, from Amarillo to San Antonio during National Airmail Week. Shankle has ten years' flying experience and holds a transport license, aviation's highest rating. She was married to World War I Texan flyer Clarence E. "Dutch" Shankle in 1928. Her husband taught her how to fly in Boston, Massachusetts, where she earned her flying certificate in September 1929.

1939

- Reed Pigman founds American Flyers, a flight school that offers instrument instruction, at Meacham International Airport. It becomes one of the most successful flight schools in the country.

1940

- Globe Aircraft is founded to build Swift aircraft at Fort Worth in 1939. The Swift GC-1 began production at the Bennett Aircraft Corporation in Fort Worth.
July 29   Civilian Pilot Training Program opens at Austin High School. The University of Texas signed a government contract to launch the Civilian Pilot Training Program for forty college students.

1941

- Love Field serves as headquarters and base for the men and women of the Fifth Ferrying Group of the Air Transport Command.
- Following the entry of the United States into World War II after Japan's attack on Pearl Harbor on December 7, 1941, hundreds of thousands of American servicemen and women are ordered to military installations throughout Texas. The Army Air Corps is one of the major agents of change in Texas after 1940, building many military installations and airfields throughout the state.
February 25   Air Corps Commander General Henry H. "Hap" Arnold issues an order for the development of troop gliders and the procurement of suitable training gliders. Many glider pilots train and graduate from the South Plains Army Air Base at Lubbock; other Texans complete glider mechanics courses at Sheppard Field at Wichita Falls.

1942

- Jack Ridley (1915–1957), who was born in Garvin, Oklahoma, earns his military wings at Kelly Army Air Field in San Antonio. He is assigned as a test pilot to the Consolidated Vultee (later Convair) plant at Fort Worth, where he test-flies B-24 bombers. He is also assigned to develop the B-36 intercontinental bomber, which later becomes the primary aircraft of the Strategic Air Command during the early years of the Cold War.

August   The B-36 project, contracted to Consolidated Aircraft, is transferred from the company's San Diego division to its Fort Worth plant.

October   Florene Miller Watson joins the Women's Auxiliary Ferrying Squadron (WAFS), having received a telegram instructing her to show up at her own expense in Wilmington, Delaware. Born in San Angelo, Texas, on December 7, 1920, she had learned to fly along with her brothers in a single-engine Luscombe owned by her father in 1940. The last number of her private pilot license (no. 30195-40) indicates the year she earned it. By December 7, 1941, she is instructing male cadets in the War Training Program at Lubbock and Odessa. By 1942 she has one thousand flying hours and is a sophomore at Baylor University. The following year, she is named commanding officer of the WAFS stationed at Love Field. During World War II, Watson serves as an experimental military pilot and also tests radar equipment. By the time the Women Airforce Service Pilots (WASPs) are disbanded in December 1944, she has flown every type of aircraft that the Army Air Corps flies and delivers: training, cargo, fighter, and twin- and four-engine bomber (from Sarah Byrn Rickman, *The Originals*, 122).

1943

• The first class of WASPs arrived at Sweetwater, Texas, to train at Avenger Field.

January 5   The Second Women's Auxiliary Ferrying Squadron (WAFS) is formed at Love Field. February delivery includes 161 B-24 Liberator Bombers, 12 PB2Y-3 Coronado patrol bombers, 61 PBYOA-10 patrol bombers observation amphibians, 15 A-31RA-31V-72 Vengeance attack bombers, 12 A-35 Vengeance attack bombers, 11 C-87 Liberator Express transporters, 3 AT-19 Reliant advanced trainers, 372 BT-13BT 15SNV-1/SNV-2 Valiant basic trainers, and 21 L-5 Sentinel liaison planes.

March 18   First Lieutenant Jack Mathis (1921–1943) of San Angelo, Texas, serves in the U.S. Army Air Corps, 359th Bomber Squadron, 303rd Bomber Group. As lead bombardier of his squadron, he is seriously wounded by the enemy while flying through intense antiaircraft fire. Knowing that the success of his mission depends upon him, Lt. Mathis drags himself back to his bombsight and releases his bombs before expiring at his post. Lt. Mathis is awarded the Congressional Medal of Honor posthumously on July 12, 1943.

August 1   John R. Kane, Colonel, U.S. Army Air Corps, Ninth Air Force, born in McGregor, Texas, in 1907, flies one of 179 B-24 Liberators seeking to destroy the Nazi-held oil refineries at Ploesti, Rumania.

October 11 Colonel Neel E. Kearby, U.S. Army Air Corps, born in Wichita Falls, would receive the Congressional Medal of Honor in 1944 for his heroic actions at Wewak, New Guinea. Col. Kearby shoots down six enemy aircraft even though he is outnumbered twelve to one and running low on fuel.

December 17 Second Lieutenant John C. Morgan, U.S. Army Air Corps, 326th Bomber Squadron, 92nd Bomber Group, brings back the B-17 in which he flew as copilot with its crew, despite the aircraft's having suffered a frontal attack that placed a cannon shell through the windshield. The pilot's skull was split open by the .303 shell, leaving him in a crazed condition but still trying to fly the airplane. Officer Morgan completes the vital bombing raid over Germany and returns to base in England with his crew. For his heroic performance, copilot Morgan receives the Congressional Medal of Honor. Morgan was born on August 24, 1914 in Vernon, Texas.

1944

- Convair's delivery to the U.S. military for February includes 454 B-24 Liberators, 60 PBY-5A Catalina patrol bombers, 68 A-35B Vengeance attack bombers, 16 C-87 Liberator express transports, 23 AT-19 Reliant advanced trainers, 310 BT-13SNV-2 Valiant basic trainers, and 125 L-5 Sentinel liaison planes, totaling 1,061 aircraft. This is the largest February delivery made by Convair during World War II. The figures include both San Diego and Fort Worth plants.

April 17   Howard Hughes and Jack Frye (aviator and chairman of TWA from 1934 to 1947) fly a Lockheed model C-69 Constellation from Los Angeles (Burbank), California, to Washington, DC, in record time: six hours and fifty-eight minutes. Frye was raised on a fifteen-thousand-acre cattle ranch near Wheeler, Texas.

1945

- Convair's February delivery includes 99 B-24 Liberator bombers, 17 B-32 Dominators and TB-32 heavy bomber trainers, 65 PB4Y-2 Privateer patrol bombers, 12 PBY-5 and -6 Catalina patrol bombers, 6 TBY Sea Wolf torpedo bombers, and 154 L-5 Sentinel liaison planes.
- Convair's April delivery includes 130 B-24 Liberators, 50 PB4Y-2 Privateer patrol bombers, 151 L-5 Sentinel liaison planes, 14 TBY Sea Wolf torpedo bombers, 11 B-32 Dominators and TB-32 heavy bomber trainers, and 26 PBY-5 and -6 Catalina patrol bombers.

1947

- Pioneer Air Lines begins service at Love Field.
- Texas Engineering & Manufacturing Company (Temco) acquires assets of bankrupt Globe and continues to produce the Swift. Designed before U.S. entry into World War II, the B-36 Peacemaker is manufactured by Consolidated Vultee Aircraft Corporation. Chance Vought produces the F4U Corsair and the F6U Pirate, followed by the F7U Cutlass and F8U Crusader.

October 11   Trans-Texas Airways begins service at Love Field.

1948

- Chance Vought moves its parent corporation to North Texas, taking fifteen hundred key employees and thirty million pounds of equipment from Stratford, Connecticut, to Dallas by rail and truck. The company eventually employs sixty-five hundred. On April 19, 1949, Chance Vought opens its plant.
- Lyndon Baines Johnson (1908–1973) campaigns all over Texas for the U.S. Senate race in a Sikorsky helicopter called *The Flying Windmill.*

December 8   A B-36 Peacemaker completes a ninety-four-hundred-mile nonstop flight from Fort Worth to Hawaii and back to Fort Worth without refueling.

1949

February 27 (to March 2, 1949)   Captain James Gallagher and his crew of thirteen fly their Boeing B-50 Superfortress 23,452 miles to complete the first nonstop around-the-world flight, starting and ending in Fort Worth. The flight lasts ninety-four hours and one minute and requires four in-flight refuelings.

March 26   The first jet-equipped Convair-built B-36D intercontinental bomber flies at Fort Worth. As many as 385 B-36 aircraft would be produced at the bomber plant in Fort Worth.

1951

- (Until 1954) U.S. Navy Blue Angels are based at the Naval Air Station in Corpus Christi. The Blue Angels are the U.S. Navy's flight-demonstration team, which serves to maintain public interest in naval aviation and as a recruitment tool.
- Lawrence Bell, President of Bell Helicopter, moves the helicopter factory from Buffalo, New York, to Hurst, Texas, building a $13 million facility in the Dallas/Fort Worth area. It begins production of the Bell Model 47.

January 16   The B-36 Peacemaker makes its first appearance in Europe when six land at Lakenheath, England. The B-36s complete the seven-thousand-mile flight from Fort Worth in about twenty-four hours of flying time.

1952

September 1   A tornado descends on Carswell Air Force Base, causing estimated damages of $50 million. Seventy B-36 Peacemaker bombers are badly damaged.

September 17   A Bell Helicopter Model 47D sets a world distance record for its class. Test pilot Elton J. Smith flies it nonstop from Hurst, Texas, to the Bell Aircraft headquarters in Buffalo, New York—approximately 1,217 miles—in twelve hours and fifty-seven minutes.

1953

- Mooney Aircraft Inc. moves from Wichita, Kansas, to Kerrville, Texas.

April 25   Dedication ceremony of Amon Carter Field at Fort Worth.
May 20   World's First hotel helioport is established at Fort Worth.

1954

- Production begins of B-58 Hustler, the world's first supersonic bomber, at General Dynamics at Fort Worth. This aircraft would not enter combat during its Cold War–era operational career. B-58-type aircraft produced at Fort Worth numbered 116, including eight test models, which were converted to trainers.
- Bell's Huey Cobra is introduced to the public.
- Paramount Pictures films *The Strategic Air Command*, starring Jimmy Stewart and June Allyson, at Carswell Air Force Base in Fort Worth.

1955

- The Bell UH-1, later UH-Iroquois, becomes the first helicopter built in Texas as well as the first mass-produced turbine-powered helicopter. The Army chooses Bell Helicopter out of twenty companies to build its first turbine-powered helicopter. The first F8U Crusader is completed at Vought.

1956

- Jan Collmer, a native of Dallas, earns his wings at the Naval Air Station in Corpus Christi. A 1963 University of Texas at Arlington graduate in mathematics, Collmer would fly for the Navy until 1966, earning the rank of Lieutenant Commander. He would become an air show performer in 1981, known for his snap roll on takeoff, a vertical torque roll, an engine slide off, and snap roll on final approach. He would perform these maneuvers near ground level, thrilling the crowds at air shows.

November 11   Convair's Chief Test Pilot Beryl A. Erickson flies the U.S. Air Force's first supersonic bomber, the delta-wing Convair B-58 Hustler, which is capable of speeds over one thousand miles per hour.

1957

- The world's first special facility for flight-attendant training, the American Airlines Stewardess College, was built in Dallas/Fort Worth.

July 1   William "Bill" Wheat starts working for Mooney Aircraft. He had taken his first aircraft ride in 1948. He was a prior station manager for Trans-Texas Airlines, a regional carrier that began in Houston. Wheat did production flying, which means that design changes were implemented based on his test flights. Up to age eighty, Wheat still performed maintenance flight checks for Mooney along with another pilot who got paid to fly.

1958

July 29   Stanley Feller begins working for Mooney Aircraft in Kerrville. He would retire on November 4, 2008, marking his fiftieth year. Feller worked his way up in the company, from a mechanic who had never seen an airplane to shop foreman in the sheet metal fabrication department. He has worked in the engineering department, final assembly, and the hammer house. He has worked as a drop hammer operator and as a stretch and hydro press operator. These large presses turn sheets of aluminum into airplane parts. Feller is a native of the White Oak community in nearby Fredericksburg.

1959

- The Lockheed Electra (L-188) joins the American Airlines fleet, where it remains until 1971. The Electra holds seventy-five passengers and has a four-engine propjet.

1960

- The first all-metal Mooney aircraft is introduced.
- Lyndon Baines Johnson uses aircraft as a backdrop for his successful campaign speeches.

July 1   Texas Air National Guard is founded, but its origins date back to World War II. It is a separate reserve component to the U.S. Air Force.

1961

May 26   A crew of the 43rd Bomb Wing flies a B-58 Hustler nonstop from Fort Worth to Paris to set new records for travel from Washington to Paris and New York to Paris, respectively three hours, thirty-nine minutes and forty-nine seconds at an average speed of 1,048.68 miles per hour and three hours, nineteen minutes, fifty-one seconds at an average speed of 1,089.36 miles an hour.

November 19–20   Constance Wolf sets three hot air balloon National Aeronautic Association records in the Feminine Class A-6 Balloon. She takes off from Big Spring, Texas, and lands in Boley, Oklahoma, in a free hydrogen balloon manufactured by A. Riedinger, Augsburg, Germany. Duration: 40 hours 13 minutes. Altitude: 4,144.37 meters (13,597 feet). Distance: 585.786 kilometers (363.99 miles).

1962

March 5   A crew on the B-58 Hustler sets three new records: Los Angeles to New York in 2:00:56.8 at an average speed of 1,214.71 miles per hour, New York to Los Angeles in 2:15:48.6 at an average speed of 1,081.77 miles per hour, and a round-trip record of 4:41:11.3 at an average speed of 1,044.96 miles per hour.

April   The first Bell HU-1A helicopters arrive in Vietnam. Later renamed UH-1A and known as Hueys, they airlift wounded soldiers to medical facilities, improving their chances of survival by approximately 25 percent.

September 12   President John F. Kennedy's speech at Rice University encourages Americans: "We choose to go to the moon."

September 18   B-58 Hustler sets two new official world altitude records with a flight reaching 85,360.84 feet.

1964

- The Hughes Syncom III, the world's first geosynchronous satellite, is launched by a Thor-Delta launch vehicle. Communications satellites often use geosynchronous orbits (orbits that allow satellites to remain above the same location on Earth).
- Durrell U. "Dee" Howard (1920–2009) invents the first successful jet engine thrust reversers, which are first adopted by

Learjet before becoming standard equipment on all jets. This innovation improves aircraft safety. Howard was born in Los Angeles but grew up in San Antonio. He dropped out of school in the seventh grade, after his father passed away at age 50. He became an automotive mechanic and later an airplane mechanic while working for Western Airlines in California. During World War II, he returned to Texas, where he worked as an airplane mechanic for Braniff. In 1948 he was employed as an airplane mechanic for the newly formed Slick Airways, one of the first postwar cargo carriers. In 1947 Howard established Howard Aero Inc. in San Antonio. His first employee was Ed Swearingen (1925–), a farm boy from Lockhart and self-taught engineer who would go on to make his own mark in aviation—developing the Merlin and Metro commuter planes and the SJ30 business personal jet. Howard became an aircraft designer in the early 1950s and built over one hundred high-performance executive aircraft, such as the Howard 250, 350, and 500 models. These designs were primarily conversion designs of the Lockheed Lodestar, which he overhauled. He built the mockup of the first Learjet in 1962. In 1964 he founds the Dee Howard Company, which he would later sell off to an Italian firm. He would also sell the jet thrust reverser business to the Norden Company (D. Freeze, "Dee Howard: What's Stopping You," *Airport Journal*, March 2003, www.airportjournals .com). Howard was also known for retrofitting high-end jets, including a 90 million dollar customization of a Boeing 747 for Saudi Arabia's King Fahd in the 1980s.

July 31   Alvin H. Parker sets the thousand-kilometer world distance record in a sailplane by flying his Sisu 647 miles from Odessa, Texas, to Kimball, Nebraska on the Nebraska, Wyoming and Colorado border in ten and a half hours. For his straight-line distance flight of 647.17 miles (1,014 km), he establishes a new world record and surpasses the previous world record by more than one hundred miles. Parker was born in Irion County, Texas, in 1919. He graduated from high school in Odessa in 1937 and from Texas A&M with a degree in animal husbandry in 1941. For his achievement, he would receive the Lilienthal Medal from the Fédération Aéronautique Internationale in honor of the great gliding pioneer and pilot Otto Lilienthal. Aeronautical engineer Leonard Niemi began developing the Sisu 1 in 1952. The Arlington Aircraft Company built its first sailplanes in 1960, but production costs would overrun profits.

1965

- Braniff becomes the first airline to hire a couturier, Emilio Pucci, to design flight attendant uniforms.

June   Gemini IV becomes the first space mission managed by flight controllers at the Manned Space Flight Center in Houston. All previous missions had been controlled from Cape Canaveral in Florida. On this notable flight, Edward H. White II conducts the first American spacewalk. This mission permanently establishes the Mission Control Center at Houston as the home for all future spaceflight programs for the United States. The Gemini IV mission ends after four days and sixty-two orbits around Earth.

1966

September 8   The popular science fiction television series *Star Trek* first premieres on NBC. The show and future spinoffs would inspire many to imagine space travel. Its creator, Eugene Wesley "Gene" Roddenberry (1921–1991), was born in El Paso and raised in Los Angeles. Roddenberry draws on an ethnically and culturally diverse cast for his main characters. His stories envision a future in which mankind has put aside its many differences as well as eliminating poverty and disease. Roddenberry developed an interest in aeronautical engineering and earned a pilot's license before volunteering to fly for the U.S. Army Air Corps in 1941. He piloted a B-17 Flying Fortress in the South Pacific, where he flew some eighty-nine missions during World War II. He earned a Distinguished Flying Cross and the Air Medal. After the war, he flew for Pan American Airways as a commercial pilot before beginning his screenwriting career.

1967

- Initial founding of Air Southwest, which would become Southwest Airlines, by aviator Rollin W. King and lawyer Herb Kelleher. Braniff, Texas International, and Continental would all fight for years to keep Southwest from operating through litigation and by applying financial pressure.

January 27   A flash fire at the launch pad takes the lives of the Apollo 1 astronauts Virgil I. Grissom, Edward H. White II, and Roger B.

Chaffee during a ground test. This is a major turning point in the Apollo program that sets it back two years.

1968

- The cities of Dallas and Fort Worth agree to build a regional airport.

May 2   Staff Sergeant Roy Benavidez, a Green Beret from San Antonio, hears a call to "get us out of here" over his unit's radio while based in Loc Ninh, South Vietnam. Although Benavidez is not an aviator, he risks his life to save others, despite being wounded himself. His actions demonstrate the utility of a helicopter in battle.

December   In the view of Walter Cronkite (a former journalism student at the University of Texas at Austin), the Earthrise photograph taken from Apollo 8 raises the important question of whether humankind had an obligation to protect the beauty of Earth. This stunning photograph leads to a deeper appreciation of the Earth and its environment.

1969

July 20   The date of the first lunar landing by the crew of the Apollo 11 is one of the most important events in the history of the twentieth century, if not the history of mankind.

November 14   Launch of Apollo 12. Texas astronaut Alan Bean, born in Wheeler in 1932, a 1955 graduate in aerospace engineering from the University of Texas at Austin, is its lunar module pilot. Bean walks on the moon after flying 250,000 miles and landing on the moon's Ocean of Storms.

December 18   The Federal Aviation Administration certifies the Windecker Eagle, the world's first composite aircraft, developed by Dr. Leo Windecker and his associates.

1970

July 26   Wallace Scott (1924–2003) and Ben Greene fly a sailplane 719.95 miles (1,153.821 kilometers) from Odessa, Texas, to Columbus, Nebraska, setting an official FAI world record.

December 7   The Texas Supreme Court upholds the right to fly in Texas of the company that would become Southwest Airlines. The case is litigated by Herb Kelleher.

1971

June 18   Captain Emilio Salazar makes the inaugural flight of Southwest Airlines from Love Field. Initially, Southwest serves Dallas, Houston, and San Antonio.

1972

• Charlie R. Hillard (1938–1996), skydiver and precision aerobatic pilot, becomes the first American to win the individual World Aerobatic Championship held at Salon de Provence, France. He is the first to perform the torque roll maneuver in his two-hundred-horsepower Pitts S-15. In this maneuver, his plane seems to hang by its propellers while rolling continuously. Hillard was born on March 22, 1938, in Fort Worth. He soloed at sixteen. As a freshman at Georgia Tech, Hillard bought his first airplane, a Piper Cub. At eighteen he mastered skydiving, earning a place on the U.S. skydiving team two years later. He then placed second in the World Cup in Paris. He was the first American to pass a baton in free fall while skydiving. Hillard then began to concentrate solely on precision aerobatic flying. In 1958 Hillard began flying in air shows. In 1971 Hillard would team up with Gene Soucy and Tom Poberezny to form the Red Devils Aerobatic Team. They flew Pitt Specials. Through the years, the team performed more than one thousand exhibit flights. The three men performed together for more than twenty-five years.

June 29   Captain Steven L. Bennett, U.S. Air Force, 20th Tactical Air Support Squadron, Pacific Air Forces, loses his life in the Gulf of Tonkin while saving that of his observer when trying to recover from a surface-to-air missile attack. Captain Bennett was born in Palestine, Texas, on April 22, 1946. Bennett would receive the Congressional Medal of Honor.

1973

- Braniff becomes the first airline to introduce "flying art," when it commissions world-renowned artist Alexander Calder to design the color scheme for its DC-8 *Flying Colors*.
- F-111 aircraft are built at Fort Worth Division of General Dynamics.
- Southwest ends the year with its first annual profit, a net income of $175,000.

February 12   *Operation Homecoming* for the return of 591 prisoners of war held in North Vietnam begins at Kelly Air Force Base. Lackland Air Force Base and Fort Sam Houston are designated as reception areas in San Antonio because each has medical facilities to care for those men in need of hospitalization.

May 21   The Zachry-South Prairie Joint Venture achieves an unofficial world record for paving 6,012 linear feet of 50-foot-wide, 17-inch-thick taxiway with 16,031 cubic yards of concrete in a single day at the Dallas/Fort Worth International Airport.

July 29–September 25   Alan Bean, commander of Skylab Mission II (SL-3), along with scientist Dr. Owen K. Garriott and Marine Corps Lieutenant Colonel Jack L. Lousma, set a world record for their flight of approximately sixty days, more than double the previous record.

August 27   NASA formally dedicates the Manned Space Flight Center in Houston in honor of President Lyndon B. Johnson, on what would have been his sixty-fifth birthday.

1974

January 14   American Airlines flies the first commercial flight to carry passengers to the new Dallas/Fort Worth International Airport.

February 22   Barbara Ann Allen (Rainey) becomes the first American female naval aviator in ceremonies at the Naval Air Station in Corpus Christi.

1976

- The Lockheed F-16 Fighting Falcon, a supersonic, multi-role combat fighter, is built in the Fort Worth Division of General Dynamics.

June 17   Katherine Bessette Carl becomes the first female U.S. Air Force Aircraft Maintenance Specialist in the School of Applied Aerospace Services, Sheppard Air Force Base, Wichita Falls.

1977

- Southwest Airlines expands its routes to include new destinations in Texas to its route system: March 1, Corpus Christi; May 20, Lubbock and Midland/Odessa; June 30, El Paso.
- Hollywood stunt pilot Tom Danaher (1924–) of Wichita Falls sets an unofficial world aviation altitude record by flying an Air Tractor, a large crop duster, some thirty-two thousand feet high. He conducts production test flights and ferry flights for Air Tractor for his friend, aeronautical engineer Leland Snow.

1978

- Federal deregulation of the airlines results in intense competition among the carriers, leading to economic strain for airlines and lower prices for air travelers.
- While at first American Airlines chairman Robert L. Crandall fights the deregulation of the airlines, he then masters it through various ways that help to define the era. He comes up with the notion of supersaver fares and a computer reservation system that fills seats and maximizes revenue.

1979

January 12 Two Concordes (Air France and British Airways) fly in from the east and line up to land on parallel runways at Dallas Fort Worth International (DFW). The event marks the initiation of supersonic service between DFW and Europe by Braniff. Under an agreement with British Airways and Air France, Braniff crews fly the Concorde from DFW to Dulles Airport near Washington, DC, where European crews fly the Concorde to London or Paris and back.

January 25 Southwest begins service from Houston Hobby to New Orleans, as a result of deregulation, with one round-trip flight on weekdays. This marks Southwest's first scheduled interstate flight.

December 12   The U.S. Congress decides in favor of Southwest and allows interstate service from Love Field, but Congressman Jim Wright of Fort Worth imposes an amendment to the International Air Transportation Act, which restricts passenger service from Love Field to Texas and four neighboring states. Southwest flight attendants also receive a new uniform, which features a red blazer, vest, and skirt or tailored hot pants with a blazer. Southwest begins its "Home for the Holidays" campaign to enable more than thirteen thousand senior citizens with a demonstrated economic need to be reunited with loved ones during the holidays.

1980

- Southwest Airlines christens the first Boeing 737 completely owned by the airlines *The Rollin W. King.*
- Under the innovative management of chairman Robert L. Crandall, American Airlines creates the first frequent flier program, American Advantage.
- John F. Blaha, born in San Antonio in 1942, becomes an astronaut and will eventually fly on five shuttle missions, logging 161 days in space.

May   Braniff cancels its Concorde service due to high cost and the airline's declining revenues.

1981

April 12   The maiden launch of the Space Transportation System (STS) sends the orbiter *Columbia* into space for the first time.

November 12   The space shuttle *Columbia* becomes the first reusable space vehicle upon its successful second mission.

1982

- Southwest Airlines commences service from Las Vegas, Phoenix, San Diego, Los Angeles, and San Francisco.

September 1–30   The first around-the-world helicopter flight is made in the *Spirit of Texas*, a Bell 206L-1 Long Ranger II.

1984

- Southwest Airlines christens its first Boeing 737-300 *Kitty Hawk* in celebration of the historic first flight of the Wright brothers on December 17, 1903. The flight from Love Field to Houston Hobby to San Antonio and back to Dallas represents the original triangle route flown by Southwest in 1971.

1985

- Southwest Airlines and Muse Air merge, whereby Muse Air, founded by the son of M. Lamar Muse, becomes a subsidiary of Southwest Airlines in exchange for approximately $40.5 million in cash and approximately $20 million in stock.
- Southwest Airlines celebrates Texas's 150th year by christening one of its Boeing 737-300s *The Texas Sesquicentennial* at Houston Hobby Airport.

1986

January 28   The space shuttle *Columbia* explodes after liftoff, killing its crew of seven.

December   Dick Rutan and Jeana Yeager complete the *Voyager* flight, designer Burt Rutan's first around-the-world, nonstop, nonrefueling flight. The physical and psychological capabilities of the pilots are tested during this 24,986-mile journey. Rutan and Yeager establish eight absolute and world-class records. *Voyager* earns the Collier Trophy.

1988

July 9   Ground is broken for construction of the industrial airport at Fort Worth. Alliance Airport would be built for $55 million by the Federal Aviation Administration north of downtown Fort Worth.

1989

December 14   Alliance Airport opens for business. The runways at Alliance are now bordered by American Airlines' massive maintenance base for its 777s, a state-of-the-art FedEx hub, the internationally recognized Alliance Fixed Base Operation, Bell Helicopter's BA 609 training center, world headquarters for Galaxy Aerospace, a state-of-the-art J. C. Penney warehouse, and the southwest headquarters of the Drug Enforcement Administration, among other businesses and operations. With its vast runways (planned for extension to over eleven thousand feet), railroad tracks, depot, and highway connections, Alliance is truly an inland port.

1990

- The Bell Boeing team wins the Collier Trophy for developing the V-22 Osprey, the world's first large-scale tilt-rotor aircraft.

April 24   The Hubble Space Telescope is launched by the space shuttle *Discovery*, as "our window on the Universe." Its primary mirror deviates from the proper curvature by two microns, about one-fiftieth of a human hair—enough to blur the images. Subsequent service missions would correct the problem (Robin Kerrod and Carole Stott, *Hubble: Mirror on the Universe*, 186).

November 7 To commemorate its twentieth anniversary, Southwest unveils *Lone Star One*, a Boeing 737 painted in Texas colors to thank the people of Texas for their strong loyalty and support.

1991

- Dr. Bernard Harris, born in Temple in 1956, becomes an astronaut in July 1991. Harris's bachelor of science degree in biology (1978) is from University of Houston and his doctorate in medicine (1982) from Texas Tech University School of Medicine. He serves as the crew representative for shuttle software in the Astronaut Office Operations Development Branch. A veteran of two space flights, Dr. Harris would log more than 438 hours and would walk in space.

1992

- The "Malice in Dallas" publicity campaign features Southwest CEO Herb Kelleher and Kurt Herwald, chairman of Stevens Aviation. The two engage in an arm wrestling bout for the right to use the advertising slogan "Just Plane Smart." Herb Kelleher loses the bout, but Stevens Aviation grants Southwest the right to use the slogan. The event raises $15,000 for charity.

1993

- Southwest Airlines wins the Triple Crown a second year in a row for all three categories tracked by the Department of Transportation. Southwest begins service to Baltimore, revitalizing the airport and becoming a coast-to-coast carrier.
- Lockheed Corporation completes acquisition of General Dynamics's Fort Worth Division. The $1.5 billion purchase gives Lockheed control of the F-16 fighter line and increases the corporation's share of the F-11 program to 67.5 percent.
- Kenneth D. Cockrell, born in Austin in 1950, completes his first space shuttle flight, STS-56, on April 8–17, 1993. He would go on to fly on four more shuttle missions, logging over 1,560 hours in space. He serves as a mission specialist on STS-56 (April 8–17, 1993), pilots STS-69 (September 7–18, 1995), and is the mission commander on STS-80 (November 19 to December 7, 1996), STS-98 (February 7–20, 2001), and STS-111 (June 5–19, 2002). His bachelor of science degree (1972) is in mechanical engineering from the University of Texas at Austin.

1994

October 25   The U.S. Navy's first female F-14 Tomcat combat pilot, twenty-nine-year-old Lieutenant Kara Hultgreen, a 1987 graduate of the University of Texas at Austin in aeronautical engineering, crashes and dies in an F-14 Tomcat when her left engine stalls on approach to landing aboard the USS *Abraham Lincoln* in the Pacific Ocean about fifty miles off the coast of San Diego. Experiencing some mechanical problems, she turns away from the ship, rolls, and tries to punch out in time, but it is too late; she flies directly into the water.

1995

- *Fortune* magazine names Southwest Airlines one of America's Most Admired Corporations. Southwest wins the Triple Crown for the fourth consecutive year, having the best on-time performance, best baggage handling, and fewest customer complaints of all major airlines.

- The ten thousandth Mooney aircraft comes off the production line.

March 15   Lockheed Corporation and Martin Marietta complete their merger. The newly created Lockheed Martin Corporation has $23 billion in sales, becoming the largest aerospace and defense contractor in the world. The F-22 Raptor would be built by Lockheed Martin.

1996

- Southwest Airlines wins the Triple Crown for the fifth consecutive year.

1997

- The T-6A Texan II is unveiled. It will replace the U.S. Air Force's T-37 and the Navy's T-34 as joint primary trainer for both services.

1998

June   The first T-6A Texan II, manufactured by Raytheon, lands at Randolph Air Force Base near San Antonio for validation testing. Its name honors the North American T-6 Texan, which served as an advanced trainer from 1938 to 1956. The Texan II replaces the T-37 at Randolph Air Force Base in 2007. The Twelfth Flying Squadron would receive its first Texan II in May 1999.

1999

July 23   *Columbia* STS-93 launches successfully. With this flight, Eileen Collins becomes NASA's first female shuttle mission commander.

2000

- The first production-model T-6A Texan II aircraft arrives at Randolph Air Force Base.
- The City of Lubbock becomes the owner of the Silent Wings Museum, which is dedicated to preserving the history of U.S. glider pilots during World War II.

February 21 *Fortune* magazine names Southwest America's most admired airline and the sixth most admired U.S. company overall.

2001

- General John P. Jumper becomes the first native Texan to serve as chief of staff of the U.S. Air Force, a position he would hold until September 2, 2005. Born in Paris, Texas, in 1945, Jumper serves as the senior uniformed Air Force officer responsible for the organization, training, and equipage of more than seven hundred thousand active-duty, guard, reserve, and civilian forces. A member of the Joint Chiefs of Staff, Jumper and other service chiefs function as military advisors to the Secretary of Defense, the National Security Council, and the President. Jumper earned a bachelor of science degree in electrical engineering from Virginia Military Institute in 1966.
- Colleen Barrett becomes president of Southwest Airlines, making her the first woman to head a major airline. She would serve in this capacity until 2008, having worked her way up through the ranks.

April American Airlines completes acquisition of TWA's assets.

2002

- NASA astronaut Paul S. Lockhart is a veteran of two space shuttle flights, STS-111 (June 2002) and STS-113 (November 2002). Lockhart has logged twenty-six days, forty minutes, and twenty-two seconds in space. Born in 1956 in Amarillo, he received a bachelor of arts degree in mathematics from Texas Tech University in 1978 and a master of science degree in aerospace engineering from the University of Texas in 1981. Selected by NASA in April 1996, Lockhart reported to the Johnson Space Center in August 1996.

2003

February 1   Loss of space shuttle *Columbia* and crew on reentry, after a chunk of foam insulation from *Columbia*'s fuel tank damaged the underside of its left wing during launch on January 16.

2004

- Maybelle Montgomery Fletcher, a native Texan, receives the FAA's Master Pilot Award. This award is given to individuals who have been flying safely for fifty years. She began taking flying lessons in 1941 and earned her pilot license in 1943. She and her husband ran a fixed base operation and flight school in Virginia before relocating to Houston in 1956, where the couple promoted the Southwest Flying Club at what is now Sugarland Regional Airport. She took over and managed a flight school, which formally became Fletcher Aviation in 1968. In 1972 she relocated the business to Houston Hobby Airport. There she drew up the plans accepted by the FAA for designating Class B Airspace for Hobby. She has accumulated more than thirty thousand flying hours in more than 175 different types of single- and multiengine airplanes and has a seaplane rating. She has given more than ten thousand check rides. Many of her flight students have become airline pilots, military pilots, and astronauts.

2005

- General T. Michael Moseley becomes the second native Texan to serve as chief of staff of the U.S. Air Force. General Moseley was born in Grand Prairie in 1949. He graduated from Texas A&M University in 1971 with a bachelor of arts degree in political science. He earned a master of arts degree from Texas A&M University in 1972, also in political science. He would retire on July 1, 2008.

July 21   The American Legend Cub comes under FAA certification under the new light-sport aircraft rules. It is manufactured in Sulphur Springs, Texas, as a two-seat, single-engine piston aircraft and is also sold as a kit.

October | American begins operating from the new 2.1-million-square-foot International Terminal D at Dallas/Fort Worth International Airport.

2006

October 13 | President George W. Bush signs a bill into law repealing the Wright Amendment of 1979. Southwest, American, Dallas/Fort Worth International, and the cities of Dallas and Fort Worth all agree to the repeal with several conditions. These include keeping the Wright zone restrictions intact until 2014, lowering Love Field's maximum number of gates from 32 to 20, and limiting Love Field to domestic flights.

2007

June 8–22 | NASA astronaut Patrick Forrester flies on the STS-117 *Atlantis*. This is the 118th shuttle mission and the twenty-first mission to visit the International Space Station. Forrester accumulates thirteen hours and thirty-seven minutes of extravehicular activity time in two spacewalks. Forrester was born in El Paso in 1957. He received a bachelor of science degree in applied sciences and engineering from the U.S. Military Academy, West Point, in 1979, and a master of science degree in mechanical and aerospace engineering from the University of Virginia in 1989. A master army aviator, he has logged over forty-eight hundred hours in over fifty different aircraft. Forrester was assigned to NASA at the Johnson Space Center as an aerospace engineer in July 1993. He would also fly on STS-105 in 2001 and STS-128 in 2009.

2008

• NASA astronaut Robert S. Kimbrough completes his first space flight in 2008, logging a total of fifteen days, twenty hours, twenty-nine minutes, and thirty-seven seconds in space, and twelve hours and fifty-two minutes of extravehicular activity in two space walks. He was born in 1967 in Killeen. He received a bachelor of science degree in aerospace engineering from the

U.S. Military Academy, West Point, in 1989 and a master of science degree in operations research from the Georgia Institute of Technology in 1998.

April   Astronaut Peggy Whitson completes a six-month tour of duty aboard the International Space Station as the ISS Commander for Expedition 16. She is the first woman commander for the International Space Station. Whitson logs 377 days in space over her two long-duration spaceflights, setting the record for total cumulative time in space for any American astronaut. She was a member of the Expedition 5 crew that launched on June 5, 2002, aboard STS-111 and docked with the International Space Station on June 7, 2002.

May 31–June 14   Astronaut Karen Nyberg (University of Texas, MS 1996 and PhD 1998 in mechanical engineering) flew on STS-111.

October   Richard Garriott of Austin becomes the sixth private astronaut to travel into space.

2009

- NASA astronaut Tim Kopra, born in Austin in 1963, serves with the Expedition 20 crew as a flight engineer aboard the International Space Station. He launches with the STS-127 crew aboard the space shuttle *Endeavour* on July 15, 2009 and returns to Earth with the STS-128 crew aboard the space shuttle *Discovery* on September 11, 2009. Over the course of two shuttle missions and tours of duty aboard the station, Kopra performs one spacewalk totaling five hours and two minutes, executes assembly tasks with the space station and Japanese robotic arms, and conducts numerous science experiments. Kopra is a retired Army helicopter pilot who served in Operations Desert Shield and Desert Storm. He attended U.S. Naval Test Pilot School and was selected to join NASA's astronaut corps in 2000.

- Mooney Ovation2 GX receives certification from the European Aviation Safety Agency. This long-range single-engine piston aircraft cruises at a top speed of 190 knots at its service ceiling of twenty thousand feet. It has a range of 1,860 miles at the lower cruising speed of 173 knots.

January 15   U.S. Airways Captain Chesley "Sully" Sullenberger successfully ditches his Airbus 320 on the Hudson River after a bird strike following takeoff from LaGuardia Airport. Texas native Sullenberger, then fifty-seven, is a 1973 graduate of the Air Force

Academy. He served almost seven years as an Air Force fighter pilot before reaching the rank of captain.

May 19   The NASA space shuttle *Atlantis* crew of seven repairs the Hubble Space Telescope by overhauling its components inside the *Atlantis*'s main cargo bay using a robotic arm. It is then released and drifts away. The Hubble Space Telescope goes on to dazzle sky watchers with spectacular views of the universe.

2010

- Astronaut Shannon Walker serves as flight engineer (copilot) on a Russian Soyuz spacecraft, TMA-19, which launches on June 15, 2010. After 161 days at the International Space Station, she again serves as flight engineer on her return to Earth on November 25, 2010.

October 1 United and Continental Airlines close their merger to create United Continental Holdings, which operates more than thirty-eight hundred flights a day in the Americas, Europe, and Asia.

Appendix II

Tuskegee Airmen from Texas Who Earned Their U.S. Military Wings, 1942–1946

Class	Name	Birthplace/ hometown
42J	Terry Charleton*	Beaumont
42K	Robert B. Tresville, Jr.*	Bay City
42K	Romeo M. Williams*	Marshall
43A	George McCrory*	Fort Worth
43C	Walter L. McCreary*	San Antonio
43D	Leonard M. Jackson*	Fort Worth
43D	Ulysses S. Taylor*	Kaufman
43H	Samuel Jefferson*	Galveston
43I	Norman W. Scales*	Austin
43J	Henry F. Fletcher	San Antonio
43J	Turner Payne	Wichita Falls
44E	Henry J. Davenport	Beaumont
44I	Voris S. James	San Antonio
44I	Vernon Hopson	San Antonio
44I	Charlie A. Johnson	Marshall
44I	Louis W. Johnson	San Antonio
44J	Leroy Bryant, Jr.	Houston
44J	Frederick J. Pendleton	Texarkana
44J	Howard A. Wooten	Lovelady
44K	Lowell H. Cleaver	Prairie View

(continued)

Class	Name	Birthplace/ hometown
45A	Bertrand J. Holbert	Dallas
45B	Clyde C. Long	Itasca
45D	James E. Harrison	Texarkana
45E	Herman A. Barnett	Lockhart
45E	Mitchel N. Toney	Austin
45E	Albert Whiteside	San Antonio
45G	Alfred E. Garrett, Jr.	Fort Worth
45G	Alfonso L. Harris	Dallas
45H	Joshua J. Lankford	San Antonio
46A	Jewel B. Butler	Denison
46A	Jacob W. Greenwell	Fort Worth
46A	Abe Benjamin Moore	Austin

*"Red Tails," those individuals whose names are marked with an asterisk, saw military action overseas.

Source: List compiled by Harry Stewart for the HASRC, TAI, 2011, courtesy of retired Lieutenant Colonel Leo Gray and Dianne Bays.

Appendix III

Women Airforce Service Pilots from Texas Who Earned Their Wings While Serving as Civilians for the U.S. Army Air Corps, 1943–1944

Class	Last Name	Maiden	First Name	Birthplace or hometown
44-10	Atkeison	(Atkeison)	Ann	Mundy
44-10	Badger	(Phillips)	Jerrie	Spade
44-4	Bain	(Winston)	Susie	Bay City
44-4	Bailey	(Huffhines)	Eloise	Richardson
43-6	Beard	(Thompson)	Louesa F.	Sweetwater
43-4	Berkstresser	(Heinrich)	Betty	Houston
43-3	Berner	(Poole)	Esther D.	Houston
43-4	Brennan	(Brennan)	Ann C.	El Paso
44-6	Bretherick	(Lovvorn)	Frankie	Dallas
43-7	Bright	(Stevenson)	Nell S.	Canyon
43-6	Brooks	(Pierce)	Hazel M.	Houston
43-2	Buehner	(Bachman)	Betty J.	Dallas
43-5	Campbell	(Thomas)	Jane	Dallas
44-7	Carder	(Eckert)	Mildred E.	Mason
44-4	Carmichael	(Carmichael)	Mickie M.	Tyler
44-3	Chapman-Foster	(Crane)	Mary Helen	Kerrville
44-6	Chappell	(Gosnell)	Mary H.	Wichita Falls
44-9	Chatham	(Parker)	Catherine	Bryan
43-4	Clair	(Clair)	Virginia	Wichita Falls
43-4	Collins	(Miller)	Bertha M.	Dallas

(*continued*)

Class	Last Name	Maiden	First Name	Birthplace or hometown
43-3	Conner Risden	(Roberts)	Lillian	Fort Worth
43-4	Crout	(Lowe)	Nancye Ruth	Fort Worth
44-4	Dalrymple	(Davidson)	Mildred T.	Austin
44-4	D'Arezzo	(D'Arezzo)	Catherine	Austin
44-4	DeBehnke	(Cavette)	Mary L.	Austin
43-4	Dickerson	(Fullwood)	Rosa L. Meek	McAllen
44-4	Dula	(Tucker)	Ann Gift	Fort Worth
44-7	Edwards	(Quist)	Mary Catherine	Austin
43-8	Evernham	(Moore)	Jocelyn	Fort Worth
43-4	Fender	(Clark)	Grace C.	Wichita Falls
44-9	Ferree	(House)	Mildred H.	Houston
43-4	Florey	(Underwood)	Ruth T.	Brownwood
43-4	Ford	(L'Hommedieu)	Maryalice	Houston
44-1	Gee	(Gee)	Doris C.	Houston
44-2	Goot	(Hawkins)	Dorothy C.	Amarillo
44-3	Grona	(Grona)	Starley M.	San Antonio
43-4	Hagerstrom	(Jowell)	Virginia	Frankston
44-6	Hanks	(Hanks)	Nancy	Wichita Falls
43-7	Harding	(Loudder)	Lela	Canyon
43-4	Harris	(Tate)	Janice R.	Dallas
43-2	Helm	(Dailey)	Ruth	Grapeland
44-7	Henry	(Henry)	Annie J.	Texarkana
43-7	Holaday	(Holaday)	Ann R.	San Antonio
43-4	Houser	(Houser)	Catherine M.	Dallas
43-7	Isbill	(Isbill)	Marian	McGregor
44-4	Johannessen	(Gilbert)	Frances	San Antonio
43-3	Jones	(Jones)	Elaine	Houston
44-7	Jones	(Jones)	Winnie Lee	Ballinger
43-6	Jones	(Putman)	Grace R.	Smithville
44-8	Judd	(Brummett)	Pearl	Claude
43-5	Kari	(Green)	Frances	Galveston
43-8	Kinne	(Englund)	Irene	El Paso
44-9	Kleinecke	(Kleinecke)	Kathryn J.	Fort Worth
43-6	Lechow	(Moore)	Bernice	San Marcos
43-8	Long	(Moffat)	Doris M.	El Paso
44-3	Lore	(Lore)	Elizabeth Ann	Fort Worth
44-5	Martin	(Kiester)	Muriel V.	La Feria
44-10	McAdams	(Gimble)	Frances	Tyler
44-8	McCann	(Stuart)	Mary L.	Houston

Class	Last Name	Maiden	First Name	Birthplace or hometown
44-3	McDonald	(McDonald)	Lea Ola	Seagraves
44-5	Miles	(Boyd)	Kathryn L.	Dallas
43-1	Miller	(Miller)	Sidney	Mineral Wells
44-4	Moore	(Leon)	Madge	Dallas
44-5	Morgan	(Twitchell)	Jacqueline	Dallas
44-10	Morrison	(Morrison)	Nina K.	Beaumont
44-5	Nirmaier	(Burch)	Mary L.	Valley Mills
44-8	O'Bannon	(Braun)	Patricia	Eagle Lake
44-6	Palmer	(Palmer)	Rose A.	Fort Worth
44-3	Paschich	(Owens)	Beryl O.	Abilene
44-10	Phillips	(Rees)	Ruth	San Antonio
44-2	Potter	(Puett)	Rose L.	Dallas
44-1	Rawlings	(Bartholf)	Anne B.	Austin
44-3	Rees	(Parker)	Jimmie P.	Kosse
44-2	Reese	(Reese)	Rose D.	Fort Worth
44-6	Richardson	(Hamm)	Ava	Fort Worth
44-3	Richter	(Richter)	Hazel Sue	Austin
43-2	Roberson	(Lawler)	Florence L.	Fort Worth
44-9	Rumler	(Stahr)	Esther L.	San Antonio
43-6	Saunders	(Saunders)	Velma Morrison	Brownsville
44-3	Schwager	(DeVore)	Gloria D.	Amarillo
44-5	Shirley	(Brownfield)	Leta	Brownfield
44-10	Sproat	(Speckels)	Henrietta P.	San Antonio
44-4	Tanner	(Brinker)	Doris	Dallas
43-7	Teerling	(Teerling)	Wilhelmina M.	Alpine
43-4	Tilton	(Farley)	Mary Jo	Aransas Pass
44-7	Vandeventer	(Putnam)	Mary Alice	Lueders
44-10	Wagner	(Ceyanes)	Mary J.	Austin
44-3	Wallace	(Gilmore)	Mary T.	San Antonio
WAFS	Watson	(Miller)	Florene	San Angelo
43-5	Wheeler	(Hagemann)	Ruth	Dallas
43-5	Wheelis	(Myers)	Macie Jo	Dallas
44-2	Woods	(Woods)	W. Ruth	Dallas
44-9	Wray	(Glezen)	Lillian G.	Gilmer

Other WASPs Who "Adopted" Texas

44-10	Lucas	(Smith)	Dorothy A.	San Antonio
44-5	McKeown	(Dougherty)	Dora	Fort Worth

(*continued*)

Class	Last Name	Maiden	First Name	Birthplace or hometown
43-3	McNaul	(Gregg)	Janis M.	Georgetown
44-7	Parrish	(Bishop)	Marie B.	Waco
44-4	Reed	(Streff)	Betty Jo	N. Richland Hills
44-7	Roundtree	(Harmon)	Martha G.	Fort Worth
44-3	Smith	(Ahlstrom)	Mary Belle	Austin
44-10	White	(Hopkins)	Anna L.	Houston
43-3	Whiting	(Phillips)	Elizabeth L.	Austin
43-3	Wischmeyer	(Murphy)	Rita M.	Dallas

Source: Women Airforce Service Pilots (WASP) Collection, Texas Woman's University, courtesy of Nancy Parrish and Dawn Letson; Celeste Graves, *A View from the Doghouse of the 319th AAFWFTD* (Bloomington: Author House, 2004).

Appendix IV
Ernest L. Clark (1908–2013),
Flight Instructor in the Fifties

Ernest L. Clark (for a brief biography, see chapter 6) reflects in his own words on what it was like to train cadets in Texas:

> An instructor of Air Force cadets, or student officers, deserves far more credit than he sometimes receives. The instructor's classroom is an airplane. His blackboard consists of an instrument panel and his crayon is the manually operated controls. As every flight instructor knows, each student reacts differently while undergoing the beginning phase of his flying career. Many beginning pilots view their airborne classroom with fear and doubts during the initial phases of their flight training. The challenge of needing to know everything from day one of their flight training is often upsetting to student pilots.
>
> The flight instructor is aware of the concerns a student has during the beginning phase of his flight training. Experience has motivated them to develop unique ways of helping trainees overcome their initial fears and gain self-confidence. Some students do exceptionally well from their very first flight experience. Others progress normally and graduate on schedule. There are always one or more individuals among the trainees that are capable of solo flights but in the absence of the instructor they lack the self-confidence to do it. The moment of truth arrives when the instructor steps away from the airplane for the first time and gives the student pilot the thumbs up signal. An occasional student pilot may hesitate at this moment and request additional instruction.
>
> Flight instructors are usually wise and patient with students who are ready to solo but want a little more instruction before they

fly alone. Most flight instructors have ways of inspiring student pilots to solo when they are fully trained and ready for this exciting event. One Texas instructor had a sure-fire method for dealing with student pilots who hesitated at the last minute. It worked every time. He had his students gather around a table in a flight shack. "All right you guys, you are some of the best student pilots I ever trained. You are hot and ready. I'd risk having my loving wife fly with you on your first solo flight. That is what I think of your ability as a pilot."

Instructors boost self-confidence on the part of their students by giving them a final lecture on the safety features designed into the airplane. A familiar final lecture went something like this: "If you ever find yourself in a mental red zone and you just do not know what to do, turn the controls over to the airplane. It will fly itself better than we human beings can. Just remember that. But there is something else you might want to think about. There is a girl or wife somewhere who will consider you her hero when you tell her you flew an airplane today all by yourself."

Most student pilots can scarcely wait their turn to solo. Once in a great while a student may hesitate at the last minute and request additional instruction before taking the plane up alone. The particular instructor previously mentioned never complained. He would show up for the requested training with a false control stick stuck down in his flight togs. After he and the student went through the usual flight training procedures he would say to the student, "Hey Fly-Boy, you are hot today. I am going to show you what I think of you as a pilot. Now hold on up there while I pull up my stick."

The instructor would get down and wring the stick around in erratic circles. He gave the stick a final jerk and then held up the false control stick he had hidden in his flight togs. With a crazy grin spreading across his face he would say, "Hey Fly-Boy, do you know what this is? This is my stick. I am going to show you what I think of you as a pilot. I am just going to throw this thing overboard." He then would say to the student pilot, "Go ahead and give me one of those special touchdowns on the runway down there, or act a fool and kill us both." It worked every time.

It worked every time according to plan at least except on one particular occasion. Students had heard about the extra control stick. When it came time for the students of a certain class to solo one of them hesitated. "Sir, I need one more ride before I try to take this plane up alone." "Okay fly-boy, let's go."

The instructor was prepared for just such a request. He had his false control stick stuck down in his togs. In fact, two false control sticks went up on that particular flight. The student pilot also had one. It wasn't long before the instructor got down and started wringing his control stick. He held it up for the student to see, kissed it, and threw it overboard.

The student flew in silence for a bit and said to his instructor, "Sir, didn't you say this airplane would fly itself?" "Yep, sure did." "Well, sir, we are going to see if it will do it." The student got down and started wringing his stick around. The instructor became alarmed and shouted at the student, "What the hell are you doing?" The student held up his false control stick, kissed it, and threw it overboard. The instructor took one look and hit the panic button. He went over the side of the plane while yelling for the student to follow him.

The false stick technique worked every time. The last day it was used was also the day the student, ready or not, flew solo. The instructor said all he could think of when he made his leap was that neither he nor the student had a control stick. The C.O. had a notice posted in each of the flight shacks that there would be no more false control sticks thrown overboard. The instructor's final comment was: "Nobody can ever say the false stick didn't work, especially the last time it was used."

Source: Ernest L. Clark, "Flight Instructor," n.d.; interview with author, C. R. Smith American Airlines Museum, Fort Worth, Texas, July 2009, followed up with a series of e-mail correspondence, 2010–2012.

Notes

Chapter One

1. This first demonstrated flight was also part of a land development promotion sponsored by the Western Land Corporation and the *Houston Post*. Texas Historical Marker No. 10660, First Aeroplane Flight over Texas.

2. A few aviators might have flown in Texas before Paulhan, but no such flights have been confirmed or photographed.

3. "Farman Type Is Supreme," *Los Angeles Times*, January 13, 1910.

4. "Wright Law Suit Laid on Table," *Los Angeles Times*, January 15, 1910; "Final Cheers for Aviators," *Los Angeles Times*, January 21, 1910.

5. "Work of Paulhan Pleased Spectators," *Houston Chronicle*, February 19, 1910.

6. Texas Historical Marker No. 10660.

7. "Obituary of Louis Paulhan," *London Times*, February 12, 1963.

8. http://earlyaviators.com. Information provided by a distant relative of Leslie L. Walker, 2003.

9. *Ground effect* is a phenomenon that usually improves aircraft performance while flying close to the ground by decreasing drag, a force that limits forward thrust.

10. "Short Flight Made in an Aeroplane," *Dallas Morning News*, March 4, 1910; see also Florence Hester Wood, "Early Commercial Aviation in Texas, 1904–1934" (Master of Arts thesis: University of Texas at Austin, 1957), 8.

11. Brodie image of the Herring-Curtiss biplane he flew at the fairgrounds on March 4 and 5, 1910, Dallas Public Library, Hays Collection 1919, neg. 19-59-175.

12. Kenneth B. Ragsdale, *Austin, Cleared for Takeoff: Aviators, Business-*

men, and the Growth of an American City (Austin: University of Texas Press, 2004), 7–9.

13. For an account of the entire flight, see Eileen Lebow, *Cal Rodgers and the* Vin Fiz: *The First Transcontinental Flight* (Washington and London: Smithsonian Institution, 1989), 147–189.

14. "Some Leaders of Sports," *New York Times*, December 17, 1911, C7. On the website of the Air and Space Museum, it states that Rodgers flew some 4,321 miles at a speed of 51.5 miles per hour.

15. See Doris L. Rich, *The Magnificent Moisants: Champions of Early Flight* (Washington, DC: Smithsonian Institution Press, 1998), 136.

16. Rich, *The Magnificent Moisants*, 182.

17. "Matilde Moisant—Early Bird Aviator, Perils of Pauline," www.collect air.com.

18. David T. Courtwright, *Sky as Frontier: Adventure, Aviation and Empire* (College Station: Texas A&M Press, 2005), 31; Giacinta Bradley Koontz, *The Harriet Quimby Scrapbook: The Life of America's First Birdwoman, 1875–1912* (Flagstaff, AZ: Running Iron Publications, 2003), 170–171.

19. www.collegeparkairmuseum.com.

20. Major General Benjamin Foulois, "Early Flying Experiences," *The Air Power Historian* (April and July, 1955) in Foulois Collection, College Park Aviation Museum.

21. Jacqueline Davis, "Centennial of Military Flight: The Ground Crew that Kept Foulois in the Air," *Centennial of Military Aviation Newsletter*, March 2, 2010: AB, 6.

22. Benjamin Foulois Collection, "Flight Logbook for Aeroplane No. 1, ca. 1910," Manuscript Division, Library of Congress, 4–5.

23. Ibid.

24. Ibid.

25. Ibid.

26. Photographs and documents from the Punitive Expedition, 1916," CN 120028. CN 11248, CN10371, Explanatory Data, Camp El Valle, Mexico, September 14, 1916; "Table of Events," U.S. National Archives, College Park, Maryland.

27. Benjamin D. Foulois with Colonel C. V. Glines, *From the Wright Brothers to the Astronauts: The Memoirs of Major General Benjamin D. Foulois* (New York: McGraw-Hill Book Company, 1968), 135.

28. Ibid., 136.

29. Ibid.

30. "Letter of Mason M. Patrick, Major-General, Chief of Air Service," General Benjamin Foulois Collection, "Personnel Medals and Decorations," box 10, folder 14, Manuscript Division, Library of Congress.

31. Foulois, *From the Wright Brothers to the Astronauts*, 149.

32. U.S. Centennial of Flight Commission, "Airmail and the Growth of the Airlines," www.centennialofflight.gov.

33. "Army Pilots as Postmen: How the Air Corps is Placed to Carry Air Mail," *New York Times*, February 18, 1934.

34. See Donald B. Holmes, *Air Mail: An Illustrated History, 1793–1981* (New York: Clarkson N. Potter Inc., 1981). Amelia Earhart noted that between 1918 and 1927, thirty-two airmail pilots lost their lives. Earhart, *20 Hrs., 40 Min.: Our Flight in the Friendship* (Washington: National Geographic Society, 2003), 148.

35. Letter signed by Foulois responding to U.S. Senator Kenneth McKellar, "Army Air Mail Operation Accidents and Fatalities," February 26, 1934, General Benjamin Foulois Collection, box 12, folder 2, Manuscript Division, Library of Congress.

36. "Army to Relieve Young Fliers Taken from Airmail Duty at Kelly Field, Texas," *Washington Star*, April 6, 1934.

37. "Army Air Mail Operations, Final Report," General Benjamin Foulois Collection, box 12, folder 6, p. 31, Manuscript Division, Library of Congress.

38. "General Benjamin Foulois, 87, Dies: Was Nation's First Combat Pilot," *New York Times*, April 28, 1967.

Chapter Two

1. "Oral Interview with Katherine Stinson," Columbia University, taped July 1960, typed transcript, Katherine Stinson Otero Collection. Center for Southwest Research, the University of New Mexico, Albuquerque. Her flying certificate lists 1893, not 1891, as her birthdate.

2. "Marjorie Stinson's resume," April 2, 1963; "Marjorie Stinson to the Contest Committee of the National Aeronautic Association, Washington, D.C., January 26, 1929," Marjorie Stinson Collection, Archives of the Institute of Aerospace Sciences (IAS), box 37, Manuscript Division, Library of Congress.

3. Debra Winegarten, *Katherine Stinson*, 15. Rinehart Niekamp, *The Annotated Bibliography of Women in Aviation*, 83.

4. Marjorie Stinson, "The Diary of a Country Girl at Flying School," *Aero Digest* (February 1928).

5. "Youngest Flyer in America: A San Antonio Girl," *Aerial Age Weekly*, April 17, 1916.

6. "A Woman Who Helped Pioneer Aviation," *Southern Aviation* (December 1930), 28. The article describes Marjorie and Katherine Stinson as "among the vanguard of these women," as having fought "against almost insurmountable obstacles, but these obstacles were only temporary, for their

grit and determination would not be denied." Women aviators were not many in numerical strength, but they were staunch pioneers in aviation. They were "active, daring and fearless women—who did much to rear their aeronautical prodigy to its present growth."

7. "Marjorie Stinson Letter to John Underwood," February 20, 1962. Marjorie Stinson Collection, IAS, box 37, Manuscript Division, Library of Congress.

8. "San Antonio Girl Inspires the Texas Escadrille," *San Antonio Light*, August 19, 1917. In Marjorie Stinson Collection, IAS, box 60 oversize, Manuscript Division, Library of Congress.

9. "Marjorie Stinson to the Contest Committee of the National Aeronautic Association, Washington, D.C., January 26, 1929," in Marjorie Stinson Collection, IAS, box 37, Manuscript Division, Library of Congress.

10. Office of History, San Antonio Air Logistics Center, *A Pictorial History of Kelly Air Force Base* (San Antonio: Air Force Logistics Command, n.d.), 16.

11. "Endurance Record George Haldeman and Detroit Manufacturer Stinson," *Florida Times Union*, March 31, 1928. In Marjorie Stinson Collection, IAS, box 60 oversize, Manuscript Division, Library of Congress.

12. See *Aircraft Handbook* for 1919.

13. James Norman Hall and Charles Bernard Nordhoff, eds., *The Lafayette Flying Corps* (Boston and New York: Houghton Mifflin Company, 1920), 107.

14. Herbert Molloy Mason, Jr., *The Lafayette Escadrille* (New York: Random House, 1964; reprinted in 1995 by Smithmark Publishers), 78–83.

15. Stephen Longstreet, *The Canvas Falcons: The Men and Planes of World War I* (New York: Barnes and Noble, 1970), 245. Longstreet asserts that "the American war effort, from the manufacturing end, was a national disgrace." Four million were in the Army; two million went to France.

16. Office of Chief of Air Service, General Benjamin Foulois Collection, box 10, folder 12, Manuscript Division, Library of Congress.

17. Timothy Moy, "Transforming Technology in the Army Air Corps, 1920–1940: Technology, Politics, and Culture for Strategic Bombing," in *The Airplane in American Culture*, Dominick Pisano, ed. (Ann Arbor: University of Michigan Press, 2003), 302–303.

18. Hall and Nordhoff, eds., *The Lafayette Flying Corps*, 109. Numbers of casualties and those killed in battle vary considerably. According to one report put out by the U.S. War Department on August 12, 1919, 49,498 Americans were killed, 205,690 were wounded, 4,480 were prisoners, and 127 were missing. See *History of Texas World War Heroes* (Dallas: Army and Navy History Company, 1919), 19. The evidence is unclear whether Balsley was the first American "shot down" in combat. He was definitely wounded in the air but he managed to survive the landing.

19. "Milestones," *Time*, August 3, 1942; "The Lafayette Escadrille: Flying and Fighting for France, April–September 1916," Valiant, 2008.

20. Office of History, *A Pictorial History of Kelly Air Force Base*, 1–9.

21. Office of History, San Antonio Air Logistics Center, *A Pictorial History of Kelly Air Force Base, 1917–1980* (1980), 12–16.

22. Ibid., 11–25; World War I exhibit, Imperial War Museum, London.

23. Debbie Maulden Cottrell, "Mabelle Agnes Umland," *Handbook of Texas Online*.

24. W. David Lewis, *Eddie Rickenbacker: An American Hero in the Twentieth Century* (Baltimore: Johns Hopkins University Press, 2005), 102. See Courtwright, *Sky as Frontier*, 50.

25. Frank E. Vandiver, *Black Jack: The Life and Times of John J. Pershing* (College Station and London: Texas A&M Press, 1977), 2:646.

26. Office of History, San Antonio Air Logistics Center, *A Pictorial History of Kelly Air Force Base* (Washington, DC: U.S. Government Printing Office, 1964), 28.

27. Paul Freeman, "Abandoned and Little Known Airfields," www.airfields-freeman.com.

28. *Aircraft Year Book*, 1919 (New York: Manufacturers D. Association, 1919); "Exhibit of Texas Aces," Texas Air Museum, Stinson Field, San Antonio; www.theaerodrome.com/aces. Another ace was Henry R. Clay; see Marvin L. Skelton, *Lieutenant R. Clay: Sopwith Camel Ace.*

29. Norman Franks, *American Aces of World War I* (Botley, Oxford: Osprey Publishing, 2001), 46.

30. Personnel Medals and Decorations, Office of Chief of Air Service, General Benjamin Foulois Collection, box 10, folder 14, Manuscript Division, Library of Congress; *Tentative List of Decorations Awarded U.S. Army Air Service*, A.M.E.F. (February 27, 1920) vol. I, no. 6 (Washington, DC: Government Printing Office).

31. "William Easterwood, Jr., Posts $25,000 for Distance Flight," *Dallas Morning News*, May 27, 1927. Easterwood lost his younger brother in an airplane accident while he was flying in the marine service in the Caribbean. He is probably related to the Easterwood for whom the airport at Texas A&M at College Station is named.

32. "Out of One Tail Spin, into Another," *Dallas Morning News*, August 20, 1927.

33. "Easterwood will give $5,000 check to Mrs. W. P. Erwin," *Dallas Morning News*, August 21, 1927.

34. "Edgar Tobin," *Handbook of Texas Online*, has his birthdate as 1897 rather than 1896.

35. Texas Air Museum, Stinson Field, San Antonio, Texas, Dallas Public Library; theaerodrome.com/aces; Texas State Historical Association, The Handbook of Texas online, Edgar Tobin, www.tshaonline.org. Eleven other

prominent businessmen died in that crash, including Thomas Elmer Braniff of Braniff Airlines. The *Aircraft Year Book* for 1919 lists nine victories for William Erwin.

36. According to a secondary account, the Allied forces claimed 11,760 victories: 7,054 for the British, 3,950 for the French, and 756 for the Americans. But the Germans calculated they only lost three thousand airplanes. There are discrepancies in the number of war losses, as could be expected. Courtwright, *Sky as Frontier*, 43.

Chapter Three

1. Courtwright, *Sky as Frontier*, 40–41.

2. Although Rodgers's own memoir states that he was from Mississippi, the Texas State Historical Association lists his birth as in Tunnel Hill, Georgia, on March 7, 1889.

3. Hart Stilwell and Slats Rodgers, *Old Soggy No I: The Uninhibited Story of Slats Rodgers* (New York: Julian Messner Inc., 1954), 62.

4. Joseph Corn writes about how U.S. women pilots were used by manufacturers and designers to promote their aircraft following Lindbergh's solo flight from 1927. See Joseph J. Corn, *The Winged Gospel: America's Romance with Aviation, 1900–1950* (Baltimore, MD: Johns Hopkins University Press, 2002), 71–90. He also discusses this issue in an article, "Making Flying 'Thinkable': Women Pilots and the Selling of Aviation, 1927–1940." *American Quarterly* (Autumn 1979), vol. 31, no. 4, 556–571.

5. Stilwell and Rodgers, 31, 43–45. Wiley Post, who began his aviation career as a parachutist, also displayed criminal behavior; he was arrested in his youth for highway robbery and given a prison sentence of ten years. He later received a pardon, once he became famous, after having served part of his sentence.

6. Paul O'Neil, *Barnstormers and Speed Kings* (Alexandria, Va.: Time-Life Books, 1981), 16.

7. Ibid., 48.

8. Joe Earle, "Barnstorming Pilots Always Drew a Crowd," *The Wichita Eagle* (December 3, 1984) Wichita State University Special Collections, MS 97-02, box 14, FF3; speech by Olive Beech to the Soroptimist Club, December 10, 1941, Wichita State University Special Collections, MS 97-02, box 6, FF3.

9. Carroll V. Glines, *Roscoe Turner: Aviation's Master Showman* (Washington and London: Smithsonian Institution Press, 1995), 18.

10. Charles Lindbergh, *We* (New York: G. P. Putnam's Sons, 1927), 78–79; Jessie Woods, video interview, Ninety-Nines Museum of Women Pilots, Oklahoma City.

11. Ormer Locklear's mother wrote his biography, *The Life of Ormer Locklear Who Won the Name of the "King of the Air"*: Ormer Locklear Collection, University of Texas at Dallas, McDermott Library, Aviation History Collection.

12. *Fort Worth Telegram*, August 3, 1920.

13. Art Ronnie, *Locklear: The Man Who Walked on Wings* (South Brunswick, New Jersey: A. S. Barnes, 1973), 38–39.

14. *History of Texas War Heroes* (Dallas: Army and Navy History Company, 1919), 55.

15. Ronnie, *Locklear*, 13, 28, 213, 220; "Wing Walking," www.centennial offlight.gov/essay/Explorers_Record_Setters_and_Daredevils/wingwalkers /EX13.htm.

16. "Letter of Ormer Locklear to his mother and father," April 24, 1920, Ormer Locklear Collection, University of Texas at Dallas, McDermott Library, Aviation History Collection.

17. Doris L. Rich, *Queen Bess: Daredevil Aviator* (Washington and London: Smithsonian Institution Press, 1993), 3.

18. Since we do not have any of her own writings we cannot assess how she actually viewed herself in terms of her mixed ethnic background or dealt with problems of mixed racial identity at the turn of the century coming from a shared heritage of Native American and African American cultures. Neither the Choctaws nor the Cherokees have embraced her as one of their members, unlike black Americans who in recent decades have made her an icon and a role model. There is no need, however, to ignore Coleman's mixed racial and cultural heritage in highlighting her contribution to aviation.

19. Rich, *Queen Bess*, 4.

20. Sheila Turnage, "Bessie Coleman: Trailblazer in the Sky," *American Legacy* 6 (Spring 2000): 18–26. Eloise Coleman Patterson, *Memoirs of the Late Bessie Coleman, Aviatrix, Pioneer of the Negro People in Aviation* (n.p., 1969).

21. According to her sister, Coleman had that reputation.

22. "To any person legally authorized to solemnize marriage," 1917, David D. Orr, County Clerk, NASM, Bessie Coleman Biographical File, CC 426000-01.

23. Rich, *Queen Bess*, 23.

24. "Aviatrix Must Sign Away Life to Learn Trade," *Chicago Defender*, October 8, 1921.

25. "Passport application of Bessie Coleman, United States of America, 1920," NASM, Bessie Coleman Biographical File, CC 428000-01. Amelia Earhart started to use 1898 as the year she was born even though it is known that Earhart was born in 1897. Earhart used the 1898 date for the new passport she received in London after she traveled there as a passenger in 1928, according to Sally Putnam Chapman with Stephanie Mansfield, *Whistled*

Like a Bird: The Untold Story of Dorothy Putnam, George Putnam, and Amelia Earhart (New York: Warner Books, 1997), 189.

26. French flier Raymonde de Laroche became the first woman to earn a pilot license on March 8, 1910. See Eileen Lebow, *Before Amelia: Women Pilots in the Early Days of Aviation* (Washington, DC: Brassey's, 2002), 14.

27. Turnage, "Bessie Coleman," 18–26.

28. There are unknown numbers of descendants of native Choctaw in the United States who intermarried with blacks in the late nineteenth and early twentieth centuries. Choctaw leaders have failed to recognize people of mixed racial background, like Coleman, as tribal members. In a more pronounced statement, the Cherokee Nation in March 2007 voted overwhelmingly to exclude twenty-eight hundred members of their community who are also of African descent. Interestingly, these groups have not chosen to eliminate white members who intermarried with them. This measure clearly demonstrates that certain Native American groups are denying "black Indians" their birthrights.

29. Rich, *Queen Bess: Daredevil Aviator*, 37. Rich notes that Coleman was prone to embellishment, like other pilots of the golden age.

30. "Negro Aviatrix Arrives," *New York Times*, August 14, 1922.

31. Ibid.

32. "Colored Girl Becomes Licensed Flyer," *Savannah Tribune*, July 13, 1922; Paterson, *Memoirs*.

33. "Chicago Colored Girl Learns to Fly," *Aerial Age Weekly* (October 17, 1921), 125.

34. Amelia Earhart, *The Fun of It* (New York: Junior Literary Guild, 1932), 136–137.

35. Jean LaRene Foote Papers, Pioneer Flight Museum, Kingsbury, Texas.

36. Earhart, *The Fun of It*, 136–137.

37. "Flying Circuses a Novelty of Early Airplane Days," *Wichita Eagle*, December 3, 1984, Wright State University Special Collections, MS 97-02, box 14, FF3.

Chapter Four

1. Tom D. Friedman, "Pioneer Passenger," *Air Classics* (October 1998): 45–47. Clara Adams was the only female passenger on Germany's flying boat, the Dornier DO-X, a twelve-engine airplane that landed first in Miami and then flew from Rio de Janeiro to New York City in 1931. On May 6, 1936 she was a passenger on the first flight of the *Hindenburg* across the North Atlantic to New Jersey, a trip that lasted sixty-one and a half hours. Rick Archbold, *Hindenburg: An Illustrated History* (New York: Madison Press Books, 1994), 166. In 1939 she set an unofficial passenger record for around-the-world flight

by regular commercial airlines of sixteen days, nineteen hours. She covered 24,609 miles by air. Clara Adams Collection, History of Aviation Collection, McDermott Library, University of Texas at Dallas, box 1.

2. See "Charles A. Lindbergh," *Dallas Morning News*, August 28, 1927.

3. Stanley R. Mohler and Bobby H. Johnson, *Wiley Post, His Winnie Mae, and the World's First Pressure Suit* (Washington, DC: Smithsonian Institution Press, 1971), 3.

4. Bryan B. Sterling and Frances N. Sterling, *Forgotten Eagle: Wiley Post, America's Heroic Aviation Pioneer* (New York: Carroll & Graf Publishers, 2001).

5. "The Dallas Visit of the Question Mark," *Southern Aviation* (Oct. 1930), 41; "Aeronautics: Uphill Route," *Time* (Sept. 15, 1930).

6. Edna Gardner Whyte, *Rising Above It* (New York: Orion Books, 1991), 117.

7. "Edna Gardner Wins Feature of Air Races," *Cleveland Plain Dealer*, August 6, 1934: 10.

8. Mandrake, *National Air Races, 1932: A Pictorial Review*, "album," n.p.

9. Gardner Whyte, *Rising Above It*, 208; Ann Kieffer and Laura Smith, "ISA+21 Celebrates 30th Anniversary," *99 News* (July/August 2008), 8. Claudia M. Oakes states that Gardner applied for Chicago and Southern Airlines in 1935 but was told she did not meet the height requirements. Claudia M. Oakes, *United States Women in Aviation, 1930–1939* (Washington and London: Smithsonian Institution Press, 1991), 32.

10. Ibid.

11. Ibid.

12. Doris Lockness (1910–), who took the controls of a helicopter at age ninety-nine, as quoted in *Women and Flight* by Carolyn Russo (Boston, New York: Little Brown and Company, 1997), 174.

13. Charles Planck, *Women With Wings* (New York and London: Harper & Brothers, 1942), 187.

14. Gardner Whyte, *Rising Above It*, 212.

15. Ibid., 232.

16. Richard McLaughlin, "Girl With Wings," *Cleveland in Full Face* (1954); Ernest Clark—military aviator, flight instructor, and a friend of Edna Gardner Whyte and her husband—interview with author, June 30, 2009, followed up with correspondence.

17. An article published at the time of the Women's Air Derby in 1929 stated that Vera Dawn Walker was born in 1904 in Plainview, Texas, where she attended high school. "Many of Women Fliers in Race . . ." Ninety-Nines Museum of Women Pilots.

18. "Vera Dawn Walker, Interview with Melba Beard, February 7, 1978," in Virginia Thomas Collection, International Women's Air and Space Museum; Glen Buffington, "Vera Dawn Walker," *99 News* (September 1976), 8.

19. Gene Nora Jessen, *The Powder Puff Derby of 1929* (Naperville, Illinois: Sourcebook Inc., 2002), 155.

20. A Curtiss Robin had a 165-horsepower Challenger engine, an air-cooled radial engine, a maximum speed of 118 miles per hour, a cruising speed of 102, a range of approximately five hundred miles, and a factory price of $2,500. Juptner, *U.S. Civil Aircraft Series*, vol. 1 "Curtiss Challenger Robin."

21. "Pilot's License Notes," NASM, Ninety-Nines Collection, XXXX0470, box 1, folder 2; Melba Beard, interviews with Vera Dawn Walker, *99 News*, Virginia Thomas Collection, IWASM, "Vera Dawn Walker," Glenn Buffington, "Vera Dawn Walker," *99 News* (September 1976): 8.

22. Interview with Melba Beard, 1978, International Women's Air and Space Museum, Cleveland.

23. Clara Studer, "The Ninety-Nines's Niche in Aviation," Virginia Thomas Collection, February 1934, International Women's Air and Space Museum.

24. "Frances Harrell Joins Curtiss-Wright Exhibition Team," *Tradewind: Women in Aviation* (May 1930), 24.

25. "Airplane Demonstrator and Salesperson," *The Ninety-Nines* 12 (September 15, 1933).

26. Louise McPhetridge Thaden, *High, Wide, and Frightened* (New York: Stackpole Sons, 1938), 159.

27. "Noted Flyers at Rites in Hangar for Mrs. Marsalis," Frances Marsalis Biographical File, International Women's Air and Space Museum.

28. Thaden, *High, Wide, and Frightened*, 159.

29. Ibid.

30. Ibid.

31. George J. Marrett, *Howard Hughes: Aviator* (Annapolis: Naval Institute Press, 2004), 11.

32. "Schneck Sells to Hughes," *New York Times*, October 26, 1930; Joseph Corn, *The Winged Gospel: America's Romance with Aviation, 1900–1950* (New York: Oxford University Press, 1983), 12.

33. "Film Director Cuts Air Time from Coast," *New York Times*, January 14, 1936.

34. "Houston, Home Town, Gives Hughes Rousing Welcome," *Los Angeles Times*, July 31, 1938.

35. "Howard Hughes World Flight Archive," Florida Air Museum.

36. "Prepared Statements for Mr. Hughes on his arrival in Paris," 1938, Howard Hughes Aviation Collection, Florida Air Museum.

37. Marrett, *Howard Hughes*, 22. O'Neil, *Barnstormers and Speed Kings*, 61, 138–139, 166; Robert Sterling, *Howard Hughes' Airline: An Informal History of TWA* (New York, St. Martin's Press, 1983); Thomas Wildenberg and R. E. G. Davies, *Howard Hughes: An Airman, His Aircraft, and His Great Flights* (McLean, Va.: Paladwr Press, 2006); "Howard Hughes, Working Air-

man," from *The Official Journal of the Air Force Association*, July 1947, Biographical File, Howard Hughes, University of Nevada, Las Vegas. http://www.centennialofflight.gov/essay/Aerospace/Hughes/Aero44.htm.

38. "Millionaire Flyer Defies Fate in Skies," *Los Angeles Times* (April 6, 1948); "Howard Hughes Re-Flies the Test that Almost Killed Him," *New York Herald* (April 6, 1948); "Hughes Suit Calls Propeller Defective," *Aviation Week* (August 2, 1948), Howard Hughes Collection, Florida Air Museum.

Chapter Five

1. "Airline in the Black," *Fortune*, February 1939, from the Carl T. Solberg Papers, box 12, American Heritage Center, University of Wyoming, American Airlines. See also Chris Pieper, "Smith, Cyrus Rowlett," *Handbook of Texas Online*.

2. "Southwest Airlines Fact Sheet," www.southwest.com; Herb Kelleher interview with author, Southwest Headquarters, Dallas, 2009.

3. www.delta.com, courtesy Delta Airlines Museum, Atlanta.

4. "Landing Fields for Aircraft in United States, December 31, 1921," *Aircraft Handbook*, "1922; Airway Map of the United States, 1928," *Aircraft Handbook*, 1928.

5. S. Paul Johnson, "Thunderbird's Nest: Observations at Pan American Airways' Brownsville Base," reprinted from *Aviation* (February 1933), Pan American Airlines Collection, box 166, University of Miami.

6. The late E. J. Snyder, chief pilot for the Compañia Mexicana de Aviación (the Mexican division of Pan American) mentions that since the inauguration of the Brownsville–Mexico City mail line (that would be Lindbergh's flight) a definite system of training for blind flying (instrument training) had been gradually organized. E. J. Snyder, "Blind Flight Instruction: An Account of the Methods Developed on Pan American Airways," *Pan American Airways* (July 3, 1930), 46–47. Also see S. Paul Johnson, "Thunder Bird's Nest: Observations at Pan American Airway's Brownsville Base," *Pan American Airways*, eighth of a series on maintenance (February 1933), Pan American Airlines Collection, box 166, University of Miami.

7. Roger Bilstein and Jay Miller, *Aviation in Texas* (San Antonio: Texas Monthly Press Inc., and the University of Texas Institute of Texan Cultures, 1985), 45.

8. "Southern Transcontinental Line is Inaugurated," *Southern Aviation*, November 1930.

9. Oliver E. Allen, *The Airline Builders* (Alexandria, Virginia: Time-Life Books, 1981), 96.

10. Ibid., 96–97.

11. Ibid., 113, 133–134.

12. Robert J. Sterling, *Eagle: The Story of American Airlines* (New York: St. Martin's/Marek, 1985), 89–91.

13. "Airline in the Black," *Fortune.*

14. "Nine girls and teach parade away from American Airlines 'class-room,'" *Chicago Daily Tribune*, August 4, 1938, Carl T. Solberg Papers, box 29.

15. "With Wings of Silver and Gold," manuscript forthcoming by Linda Hieger, retired American Airlines flight attendant, information courtesy of Linda Hieger and the C. R. Smith American Airlines Museum.

16. Bonnie Tiburzi, *Takeoff!: The Story of America's First Woman Pilot for a Major Airline* (New York: Crown, 1984); Bonnie Tiburzi Caputo, interview with author, 2012.

17. Herb Kelleher, interview with author, 2010; Brian Lusk, *Airways Classics*, April 2006.

18. Herb Kelleher, interview with author, September 21, 2012.

19. Subrata N. Chakravarty. "Hit 'em Hardest with the Mostest," *Forbes* 148 (1991): 48–54.

20. Chakravarty, "Hit 'em Hardest with the Mostest"; Mark H. Rose, Bruce E. Seely, and Paul F. Barrett, *The Best Transportation System in the World* (Columbus: Ohio State University Press, 2006), 228–229; "Parting Thoughts of Chairman Crandall, American's Retiring Chief, on Deregulation, the Future of Airlines and Himself," *Washington Post*, May 17, 1998; "Southwest Airlines Flourishes in Era of Deregulation," *PR Newswire*, April 18, 2001.

21. Herb Kelleher, interview with author, September 21, 2012.

22. On December 8, 2005, Southwest Flight 1248 from Baltimore to Chicago Midway did have an accident due to pilot error and weather (a snowstorm), which led to one fatality on the ground and some injuries to others. "Pilot Error a Factor . . . ," insurancejournal.com, December 16, 2005.

23. Thomas B. Haines, "On Brand-New Wings: An Airliner's First Day on the Job," *AOPA Pilot* (February 2012): 66.

24. United Airlines notes that a groundbreaking ceremony took place in January 2012 for the building of the first phase of a three-part redevelopment project at George Bush Intercontinental Airport, dedicated to improving a terminal for its regional jet operations. See January 23, 2012, united.com.

25. A. J. High, interview with author, Houston Air Terminal, 2009; A. J. High with the assistance of Kathryn Black Morrow, *Meant to Fly: The Career of Captain A. J. High, Pilot for Trans-Texas Airways* (Houston: Morrow House Publishing, 2008).

26. "Extension of the Braniff Airlines," *Southern Aviation* September 15, 1929, 32.

27. "It's a Girl's Dream World: Braniff's New Hostess College," Dallas; Bob Skinner, "Jet-Age School for Girls: Braniff's new hostess training center com-

bines functional concepts with feminine living," Braniff Collection, Aviation Collection, McDermott Library, University of Texas at Dallas.

28. R. G. Grant, *Flight: One Hundred Years of Aviation* (New York: DK Publishing, 2002), 386.

Chapter Six

1. Charles A. Lindbergh, *We* (New York: Grosset & Dunlap, 1927), 108–109.

2. Ibid., 125.

3. Ibid., 125–150.

4. *Aero Digest* (October 1930); Rudy Purificato, "Ocker, Pioneer of 'Blind Flying,'" earlyaviators.com.

5. William P. Mitchell, *From the Pilot Factory, 1942* (College Station: Texas A&M Press, 2005), 66; Mel Brown, *Wings Over San Antonio* (Charleston, SC: Arcadia Publishing, 2001), 84.

6. "Air Force Moving Medicine School," *New York Times*, July 13, 1959.

7. Rudy Purificato, "Joint Flight Nurse Course Benefits Military Medicine," March 29, 2006, www.defense.gov; "Brooks Air Force Unit Completes Inactivation Ceremony," September 7, 2011; "Proposed Base Closings and Realignments," *New York Times*, March 1, 1995. Brooks's Human Systems Center was placed under the Aeronautical System Center at Wright-Patterson Air Force Base in Dayton, Ohio.

8. "The World's Largest Airport," *Southern Aviation* (January 15, 1930): 31–32; "Flight Training Started at the South's "West Point of the Air," *Southern Aviation* (February 1932): 13–14.

9. Victoria G. Clow et al., *The Architecture of Randolph Field, 1928–1931* (Plano, Texas: Geo-Marine Inc., 1998), 15. The Grand Central Air Terminal at Glendale, California, was also built using Spanish colonial revival architecture. John Underwood, *Images of Aviation: Grand Central Air Terminal* (Charleston, SC: Arcadia, 2006), 55.

10. "Flight Training Started . . ." *Southern Aviation*, 13–14.

11. Mitchell, *From the Pilot Factory, 1942*, 66.

12. Ibid.

13. Ibid., 88. See Donald L. Miller, *Masters of the Air: America's Bomber Boys Who Fought the Air War Against Nazi Germany* (New York: Simon & Schuster, 2006).

14. Timothy Moy, "Transforming Technology in the Army Air Corps, 1920–1940," in *The Airplane in American Culture*, ed. Dominick A. Pisano; Rebecca Hancock Cameron, Air Force History and Museums Program, *Training to Fly: Military Flight Training, 1907–1945*, (Washington, DC: U.S. Government Printing Office, 1999), 428.

15. Ernest L. Clark, "Flight Instructor," n.d.; interview with author, C. R. Smith American Airlines Museum, Fort Worth, Texas, July 2009, followed up with a series of e-mail correspondence, 2010–2012.

16. Kenneth B. Ragsdale, *Austin, Cleared for Takeoff.*

17. "History of the Department of Aerospace Engineering," University of Texas at Austin, www.ae.utexas.edu.

18. Dominick A. Pisano, *To Fill the Skies with Pilots: The Civilian Pilot Training Program 1939–46* (Urbana and Chicago: University of Illinois Press, 1993), 3.

19. Ragsdale, *Austin, Cleared for Takeoff,* 88.

20. From July 1, 1939 to June 30, 1942, 125,762 aviators earned their licenses through the CPTP, including 13,094 flight instructors and 3,565 commercial licensed pilots, according to Pisano, *Fill the Skies,* 127. "Civilian Pilot Training Program," http://www.centennialofflight.gov/essay/GENERAL_AVIATION/civilian_pilot_training/GA20.htm.

21. Sutton earned his law degree from Brooklyn Law School after 1945. He vividly describes the shabby treatment he and his new wife received while riding on a train after the war, despite having served his country, in the PBS Home Video *The Tuskegee Airmen—They Fought Two Wars, One Against the Nazis Abroad and One Against Racism at Home* (DVD, 2004). Sutton became a trailblazing civil rights attorney in New York State, where he represented Malcolm X, before launching his own political career in the New York State Assembly. He served as president of the Manhattan Borough from 1966 to 1977, then the highest-ranking elected black politician in the State of New York. Walter McCreary, interview with author, December 2009; "Percy E. Sutton, Political Trailblazer, Dies at 89," *New York Times,* December 27, 2009. See also "Percy Sutton," oral history archive, National Visionary Leadership Project at www.visionaryproject.org.

22. Author interview with retired Lieutenant Colonel Leo Gray.

23. Thomas E. Alexander, *The Stars Were Big and Bright: The United States Army Air Forces and Texas during World War II* (Abilene: State House Press, 2000, 2007), 92–95; For a detailed account of their actions in the Philippines, see the informative study, Dan Hagedorn, *Conquistadors of the Sky* (Gainesville: University Press of Florida, 2008), 402–405.

24. Alexander, *The Stars Were Big and Bright,* 36–37.

25. Author interview with Henry Madgwick, 2009; "Henry Madgwick Obituary," *Terrell Tribune,* March 14, 2012. For a fine book see Tom Killebrew, *Royal Air Force in Texas: Training British Pilots in Terrell during World War II* (Denton: University of North Texas Press, 2003); No. 1 British Flying Training School Museum in Terrell.

26. "Girl Pilots: Air Force Trains Them at Avenger Field, Texas," *Life* (July 19, 1943), 73.

27. Doris Rich's book, *Jackie Cochran: Pilot in the Fastest Lane* (Gainesville: University Press of Florida, 2007) presents a nuanced look at one of America's most accomplished pilots who became caught up in the search for speed and setting aviation records. For the latest biography of Cochran, see Rhonda Smith-Daugherty, *Jacqueline Cochran: Biography of a Pioneer Aviator* (Jefferson, NC; and London: McFarland, 2012).

28. Sarah Byrn Rickman, *The Originals: The Women's Auxiliary Ferrying Squadron of World War II* (Sarasota, FL: Disc-US Books Inc., 2001).

29. Sally VanWagenen Keil, *Those Wonderful Women in Their Flying Machines: The Unknown Heroines of World War II* (New York: Rawson, Wade, 1979), 137.

30. "More Women Join in War Aviation," *New York Times*, November 18, 1942.

31. Dora Dougherty S. McKeown, "Birth of the W.A.S.P. Program," *Friends Journal* 22 (Summer 1999), 2–5.

32. Molly Merryman, *Clipped Wings: The Rise and Fall of the Women Airforce Service Pilots (WASPs) of World War II* (New York and London: New York University Press, 1998), 39.

33. Army Air Forces Training Command, *Instructors' Manual: Basic Flying* (Randolph Field, San Antonio: Army Air Forces Training Command, n.d.), 65–67.

34. Marianne Verges, *On Silver Wings: The Women Airforce Service Pilots of World War II, 1942–1945* (New York: Ballantine Books, 1991), 191.

35. Ruth Shafer Fleisher, interview with author, June 21, 2009.

36. VanWagenen Keil, *Those Wonderful Women in Their Flying Machines*, 156.

37. David A. Stallman, *Women in the Wild Blue: Target-Towing WASP at Camp David* (Sugarcreek, OH: Echoes Press, 2006), xvii; Ruth Shafer Fleisher, author interview, December 25, 2008.

38. Ruth Shafer Fleisher, author interview, December 24, 2008.

39. Ruth Shafer Fleisher, author interview, telephone call, February 12, 2012; "Class Rosters and Graduation Data," NASM, WASP Graduations, Pictures of Life and Training, 1942–1944, ACC. Q-Z 76, 1887-0077, 1989-0123, 1990-0025.

40. Laurie Householder, "Ruth Shafer Fleisher," Florida Goldcoast Chapter, Ninety-Nines, 2004.

41. Thomas A. Manning et al., *History of Air Education and Training Command, 1942–2000* (Randolph Air Force Base: Office of History and Research, 2005), 61. Seven months later, Air Transport Command's Officer Candidate School included its first WAF students. Ruth Shafer Fleisher later joined the Air Force Reserves, where she was an air traffic controller and flight facilities officer at several Air Force bases in the United States and En-

gland. On June 14, 1948, Congress passed the Women's Armed Services Integration Act, which established women in the Air Force as permanent members. She retired with the rank of major in September 1973.

42. Lieutenant Colonel Yvonne C. Pateman, *Women Who Dared: American Female Test Pilots, Flight-test Engineers, and Astronauts, 1912–1996* (n.p.: Northstar Publishing, 1997), 47.

43. VanWagenen Keil, *Those Wonderful Women in Their Flying Machines*, 143.

44. Ruth Shafer Fleisher, interview with author, March 24, 2009.

45. Rich, *Jackie Cochran*, 110–113.

Chapter Seven

1. Michael D. Montgomery, "Lance Wade: World War II RAF Ace Fighter Pilot," *Aviation History* (November 2004); published online in 2006, www.historynet.com.

2. "Lance Wade," Index, Archival Collections, Imperial War Museum, London.

3. At the Texas Air Museum in San Antonio, there is a list of Texas aces in an exhibit. Texas Air Museum, Stinson Municipal Airport, San Antonio.

4. James Parton, *"Air Force Spoken Here": General Ira Eaker and the Command of the Air* (Bethesda, MD: Alder & Alder, 1986), 50.

5. Ira Clarence Eaker, www.arlingtoncemetery.net/iraeaker.htm.; "Ira C. Eaker, 91, Is Dead: Helped Create Air Force," *New York Times*, August 8, 1987.

6. Parton, *"Air Force Spoken Here"*, 38.

7. Captain Eaker's *San Francisco*, a Loening OA-1A, is on display at the National Air and Space Museum's new Udvar-Hazy center at Dulles Airport.

8. Ibid., 99; "Blind Flying, Record Setter," using Sperry Instruments, Ira C. Eaker Papers, box I:42, folder 7, Manuscript Division, Library of Congress; U.S. Department of Commerce, Civil Aeronautics Administration, *Civil Pilot Training Manual* (Washington, DC: Civil Aeronautics Bulletin No. 23, September 1941), 84–89.

9. Donald L. Miller, *Masters of the Air: America's Bomber Boys Who Fought the Air War Against Nazi Germany* (New York: Simon & Schuster, 2006), 49, 113.

10. Ibid., 441–442.

11. Parton, *"Air Force Spoken Here"*, 461.

12. Testimony of General Ira Eaker, February 7, 1978, Texas 139, 362, Ira C. Eaker Papers, box II:135, folder 5, Manuscript Division, Library of Congress.

13. "More Women, A Better Army," by Ira C. Eaker, Ira C. Eaker Papers,

Library of Congress, Manuscript Division, "Women in the Military," August 27, 1977, II, 149, folder 7.

14. "General Chennault is Optimistic on China's Prospects of Victory," *New York Times*, December 11, 1942.

15. Charles R. Bond, Jr., Major General USAF (retired) and Terry H. Anderson, *A Flying Tiger's Diary* (College Station: Texas A&M Press, 1984). See the official homepage of the Flying Tigers, http://www.flyingtigersavg.com/. General Bond's printed biography is available at the University Archives of Texas A&M.

16. Bond, *A Flying Tiger's Diary*, 105–106.

17. Ibid., 166.

18. "Bios for Aviation," Courtesy Katherine Best, Bob Bullock Texas State History Museum, Austin; John Toland, *The Flying Tigers* (New York: Random House, 1963), 150–151; David Lee "Tex" Hill, 1915–2007 in *Air Power History* 54 (Winter 2007), 61.

19. Photograph of black cooks at Brooks Field, San Antonio, 1924, Edward White II Memorial Museum archive, Brooks Air Force Base, San Antonio. For a brief history of the Tuskegee airmen, see Manning et al., *History of Air Education*, 34–35.

20. Walter McCreary, interview with author, December 2009, Burke, Virginia.

21. John "Mule" Miles, interview with author, 2009; Documented Original Tuskegee Airman, courtesy Office of the Historian, Randolph Air Force Base, San Antonio.

22. For a discussion of the reasons for the deactivation of the WASP program, see Merryman, *Clipped Wings*.

23. The Woman's Collection, Texas Woman's University, WASP Oral History Project; Celeste Graves, *A View from the Doghouse of the 319th AAFWFTD* (Bloomington, IN: AuthorHouse, 2004), 77–79.

24. Dawn Letson Interview with Paul Tibbets, Women Airforce Service Pilots, Oral History Project, February 24, 1997, The Woman's Collection, Texas Woman's University, 2002.

25. "Dawn Letson Interview with Dora Dougherty Strother, August 28, 1992," 48. An Oral History, Women Airforce Service Pilots, Class 43-W-3, The Woman's Collection, Texas Woman's University.

26. "Dora Jean Dougherty Strother, Fort Worth, Texas," The Woman's Collection, Texas Woman's University.

27. David A. Brown, *The Bell Helicopter Textron Story: Changing the Way the World Flies* (Arlington, Texas: Aerofax, 1995), 167; Strother, "Birth of the W.A.S.P.," 2–7.

28. Entry prepared by Edith Foltz for "The International Cyclopedia of Aviation Biography," April 30, 1930. Wright State University Archives, ICAB box 19, file 19.

29. Foltz may well have been the first female commercial airline pilot in the United States. Unlike Ruth Nichols—who has current claim to that record, having flown in an inaugural commercial flight in 1932—Foltz never made that claim, but the little evidence we have points toward that direction. As a historian, I still would like to examine Foltz's logbooks and business records for the airlines she flew for in Seattle, as well as photographs.

30. Recorded interview, ATA Operations Officer, Alison Elsie King, Production date 1986-03, No. 9240, three reels. Imperial War Museum, London.

31. "Letter of Jacqueline Cochran to Miss Helen Richey," New York City, January 28, 1942, c.o. Royal Air Force Ferry Command, Montreal, Canada, courtesy International Women's Air and Space Museum; "Edith Magalis Foltz," International Cyclopedia of Aviation Biography, May 17, 1930, Wright State University Archives.

32. "Corpus Christi Naval Station," www.cnic.navy.mil.

33. Jack and Wilma Bradley, "Tom Danaher: Not an Average Pilot," Airport Journals, www.airportjournals.com.

34. Tom Danaher, telephone interview with author, 2010.

Chapter Eight

1. Roger Bilstein and Jay Miller. *Aviation in Texas* (Austin: Texas Monthly Press, 1985), 43–45.

2. General Dynamics asserts that 3,034 B-24-type aircraft were manufactured. There are some slight discrepancies in the figures on aircraft production in newspaper articles and files at the University of Texas at Dallas's aviation collection.

3. *Continuing the Tradition: 50 Years of Building the Best, 1942–1992* (Fort Worth: General Dynamics, 1992).

4. Museum Exhibit, American Flea, the Vintage Flying Museum, Meacham Municipal Airport, Fort Worth, Texas.

5. Anne Millbrooke, *Aviation History* (Englewood, CO: Jeppesen, 2006), 6:24.

6. Ibid.; Jim Neal, "FW Plan Began with Prayer: Came to End with Heartbreak," *Fort Worth Press* (September 16, 1962).

7. *Continuing the Tradition.*

8. According to a WASP test pilot who trained in an AT-6, there were 15,485 of these aircraft produced by North American. Ann B. Carl, *A WASP Among Eagles: A Woman Military Test Pilot in World War II* (Washington, DC, and London: Smithsonian Institution Press, 1999), 117.

9. Jim Busha, "On My Father's Wing: The Incredible Journey of the Toubul Family's Corsair," *Sport Aviation* 61 (February 2012): 17–22.

10. Al Mooney as told to Gordon Baxter, *The Al Mooney Story: They all Fly through the Same Air* (Fredericksburg, Texas: Shearer Publishing, 1985).

11. "Sales statistics for March 1964," *Mooney Marker*, Vol. XI, No. 2, March 1964.

12. Caleb Pritle III, *Engineering the World: Stories from the First 75 Years of Texas Instruments* (Dallas: Southern Methodist University Press, 2005), 49–51.

13. "Reminiscences: Bartram Kelley, Chief Engineer," in David A. Brown, *The Bell Helicopter Textron Story: Changing the Way the World Flies* (Arlington, Texas: Aerofax, Inc., 1995), 28–29.

14. Jeremiah Gertler, Specialist in Military Aviation, "V-22 Osprey Tiltrotor Aircraft: Background and Issues for Congress," Congressional Research Service, March 10, 2011.

15. Theodore Windecker, "The Eagle: On the Wings of a Dream, The Story of Dr. Leo Windecker and the Windecker Eagle, the World's First All-Composite Airplane," 2005–2010, unpublished.

16. Leland Snow, interview with author, Olney, Texas, 2009; Leland Snow, as told to Al Cleave, *Putting Dreams to Flight* (Wichita Falls, Texas: Midwestern State University Press, 2008).

Chapter Nine

1. Lyndon B. Johnson, Vice President, Memorandum for the President, "Evaluation of Space Program," April 28, 1961, NASA Historical Reference Collection, NASA Headquarters, Washington, DC.

2. Heather Brand, "Fly Me to the Moon: An Exclusive Tour of NASA's Johnson Space Center," *Texas Highways* (August 2009), 49–54.

3. J. Robert Ford, interview with author, Georgetown, 2010.

4. Ibid.; "Nightmare at Midnight," *Star-Telegram*, February 16, 1997.

5. R. G. Grant, *Flight: One Hundred Years of Aviation* (New York: DK Publishing, 2002), 346; "When We Left Earth: The NASA Missions," Discovery Channel, Episode 1, Ordinary Supermen, 2008.

6. Grant, *Flight*, 346.

7. Alan Bean with Andrew Chaikin, *Apollo: An Eyewitness Account by Astronaut, Explorer Artist, Moonwalker Alan Bean* (Shelton, CT: Greenwich Workshop, 1998); "Alan Bean, Smithsonian Institution Exhibit," National Air and Space Museum, Washington, DC, July 16, 2009–January 13, 2010.

8. Ibid., 361; NASA, "Celebrating A Century of Flight," (Washington, DC: Office of Aerospace Technology, 2002).

9. VIP tour of Johnson Space Center in 2009, courtesy of NASA and the Bob Bullock Texas State History Museum, Austin; Brand, "Fly Me to the Moon."

10. *My Fox Austin* television interview with Dr. Hans Mark, January 28, 2011. Mark was deputy director a year and a half prior to the *Challenger* disaster.

11. John W. Young with James R. Hansen, *Forever Young: A Life of Adventure in Air and Space* (Gainesville: University Press of Florida, 2012), 222.

12. "Rick Douglas Husband," NASA Astronaut Biographical Data, http://www.jsc.nasa.gov/Bios/htmlbios/husband.html.

13. Liz Moscrop and Sanjay Rampal, *The 100 Greatest Women in Aviation* (Grays, Essex: Aerocomm Limited, 2008), 186–187.

Epilogue

1. Center for Economic Development and Research (CEDR), Department of Economics, University of North Texas, "Economic Impact for General Aviation in Texas 2011." http://www.txdot.gov/business/aviation/eco_impact_aviation.htm

2. "Estimated Active Pilots and Flight Instructors by FAA Region and State, December 31, 2008," Aircraft Owners and Pilots Association, www.aopa.

3. "FAA Certificated Pilots by State and Certificate, as of December 2010," www.aopa.org.

4. CEDR, "Economic Impact for General Aviation in Texas 2011."

5. Ibid. Revenues drawn from NASA, the military, and private space tourism are far more difficult to assess by comparison to general and commercial aviation. However, figures must run extremely high with the operations at Johnson Space Center, which monitors the International Space Station, besides all the astronaut training that takes place in the state, in addition to aerospace research.

6. Alaska celebrates its century of flight in 2013.

7. Courtesy of Special Collections, the University of Texas at Arlington.

8. National Transportation Report 11-013, March 14, 2011; author interview with Guy del Giudice, September 2009, Meacham Field, Fort Worth.

9. Jeana Yeager and Dick Rutan with Phil Patton, Voyager (New York: Harper and Row, 1987); Dick Rutan, "Aviation's Last First," EAA Airventure 2011, Museum Forum, July 29, 2011.

10. See chapter on "Jeana L. Yeager" in Lisa Yount, Women Aviators (New York: Facts on File, 1995), 126; Jeana L. Yeager Collection, Texas A&M University at Commerce.

11. Test pilot A. Scott Crossfield, *"Voyager"* speech. Courtesy of Scott Crossfield.

12. "Celebrating a Century of Flight," NASA Publication (2002).

13. Professor Armand Chaput, telephone interview with author, September 17, 2012.

14. E-mail communication to author from Dr. Frank Lu, Department of Aerospace Engineering, University of Texas at Arlington, February 2013.

15. Richard Garriott, telephone interview with author, September 19, 2012; "Richard Garriott," see http://www.richardinspace.com/.

16. Garriott, telephone interview with author.

17. Phil Easton, Armadillo Aerospace, email correspondence with author, September 2012.

18. www.armadilloaerospace.com.

19. "Panel reviews NASA's future," Sun Sentinel (Fort Lauderdale), August 24, 2009.

20. NASA Biography, Johnson Space Center, Shannon Walker, http://www.jsc.nasa.gov/Bios/htmlbios/walker-s.html.

21. Garriott, telephone interview with author.

22. Dawn Stover, "Deep-Space Boot Camp," Popular Science, (November 2009), 46.

23. Ibid., 43–47.

24. Charisse Jones, "United: First public Dreamliner flight will be Nov. 4," USA Today, September 28, 2012.

Bibliography

Interviews with Author in 2009–2012

Angelone, Joseph (Vought Heritage Foundation). Hurst, Texas.

Blessing, W. "Dub." Alliance Airport, Fort Worth, Texas.

Browning, Emma Carter. Austin, Texas.

Brummet Judd, Pearl (WASP, 44-W-8). Telephone interview.

Bussey, Dr. William. Telephone interview.

Clark, Ernest (C. R. Smith American Airlines Museum). Fort Worth, Texas.

Crawford, George Wolf. Addison, Texas.

Danaher, Tom. Telephone interview.

del Giudice, Guy (chief helicopter pilot, CareFlite). Fort Worth, Texas.

Dyer, Walter (Cavanaugh Aviation Museum). Addison, Texas.

Ellis, Thomas. Randolph Air Force Base, Texas.

Feller, Stanley (Mooney Factory). Kerrville, Texas.

Ford, J. Robert. Georgetown, Texas.

Kelleher, Herb (Southwest Airlines). Love Field, Dallas, Texas.

Madwick, Henry (No. 1 British Training Flying School Museum). Terrell, Texas.

McCreary, Walter (retired lieutenant colonel, USAF). Burke, Virginia.

Miles, John "Mule." Randolph Air Force Base, Texas.

Pence, Sammy. Grand Prairie, Texas.

Shafer Fleisher, Ruth (WASP; retired major, USAF Reserves). Homestead, Florida.

Snapp, Helen Wyatt (WASP). Pembroke Pines, Florida.

Snow, Leland (Air Tractor Factory). Olney, Texas.

Stanzel, Theodore (Stanzel Model Aircraft Museum). Schulenburg, Texas.

Vajdos, Robert. Telephone interview.

Wheat, William (Mooney Factory). Kerrville, Texas.
Windecker, Ted (son of Dr. Leo Windecker). Austin, Texas, telephone interview.

Other Oral Histories

Letson, Dawn. Interviews with Dora Dougherty Strother, 1992; Florene Miller Watson, 1994, 2006; Pearl Brummet Judd, 2003; Catherine Parket Chatham, 2006; Paul Tibbets, 1997 (transcribed 2002). The Woman's Collection, Texas Woman's University, Denton.
"Oral Interview with Katherine Stinson," Columbia University, taped July 1960. Albuquerque: Katherine Stinson Otero Collection. Center for Southwest Research, the University of New Mexico, Albuquerque.

Primary Sources

Bean, Alan, with Andrew Chaikin. *Apollo: An Eyewitness Account*. Shelton, Connecticut: Greenwich Workshop, 1998.
Benavidez, Roy B. Papers, 1943–2007. Dolph Briscoe Center for American History, University of Texas at Austin.
Bond, Charles R., Jr., and Terry H. Anderson. *A Flying Tiger's Diary*. College Station: Texas A&M Press, 1984.
Braniff Airlines Collection, Chance Vought Archive, Ormer Locklear Papers, History of Aviation Collection, McDermott Library, University of Texas at Dallas.
Chambers, Mary Jane, and Dr. Randall M. Chambers. *Getting Off the Planet: Training Astronauts*. Burlington, Ontario, Canada: Collector's Guide Publishing Co., 2005.
Coleman Patterson, Elois. *Memoirs of the Late Bessie Coleman, Aviatrix: Pioneer of the Negro People in Aviation*. N.p., 1969.
Corrigan, Douglas. *That's My Story*. New York: E. P. Dutton & Company, Inc., 1938.
Eaker, Ira C., Papers. Manuscript Division, Library of Congress.
Foulois, Benjamin D. "Early Flying Experiences," *The Air Power Historian* (April and July, 1955) in Benjamin Foulois Collection, College Park Aviation Museum, Maryland.
Foulois, Benjamin D. "Flight Logbook for Military Aeroplane No. 1," and papers, Manuscript Division, Library of Congress.
Foulois, Benjamin D., with Colonel C. V. Glines. *From the Wright Brothers to the Astronauts: The Memoirs of Major General Benjamin D. Foulois*. New York: McGraw-Hill Book Company, 1968.

Fuller, William G., Collection. University of Texas at Dallas, McDermott Library, Aviation Collection.

"Girl Pilots: Air Force Trains Them at Avenger Field, Texas." *Life* (July 19, 1943): 73–81.

High, A. J. *Meant To Fly: The Career of Captain A. J. High, Pilot for Trans-Texas Airways*. Houston, Texas: Kathryn Morrow, 2008.

Hughes, Howard. Aviation Collection. Lakeland: Florida Air Museum.

Hughes, Howard. Collection. Special Collections Library, University of Nevada at Las Vegas.

Jean LaRene Foote Papers, Pioneer Flight Museum, Kingsbury, Texas.

Johnson, Lyndon B., Vice President, Memorandum for the President, "Evaluation of Space Program," April 28, 1961, NASA Historical Reference Collection, NASA Headquarters, Washington, DC.

Kranz, Gene. *Failure Is Not an Option: Mission Control from Mercury to Apollo 13 and Beyond*. New York: Berkley Books, 2000.

Lindbergh, Charles. *We*. New York: G. P. Putnam's Sons, 1927.

Locklear, Ormer. Papers. History of Aviation Collection. McDermott Library, University of Texas at Dallas.

Loeblein, John M. *Memoirs of Kelly Field, 1917–1918*. Manhattan, Kansas: Aerospace Historian Publishing, 1974.

Mooney, Al, as told to Gordon Baxter. *The Al Mooney Story: They all Fly through the Same Air*. Fredericksburg, Texas: Shearer Publishing, 1985.

Pan American World Airways, Inc. Records. Special Collections, Otto G. Richter Library, University of Miami, Florida.

"Photographs and documents from the Punitive Expedition, 1916," CN 120028, CN 11248, CN10371, Explanatory Data, Camp El Valle, Mexico, September 14, 1916. "Table of Events," U.S. National Archives, College Park, Maryland.

Purcell, Stuart M. "A World War I Diary of the 147th Aero Squadron," Stuart McLeod Purcell Collection, Dolph Briscoe Center for American History, University of Texas at Austin.

Ryan, L. L. "We Interviewed Howard Hughes." *Hughes News*, August 12, 1938.

Snow, Leland, as told to Al Cleve. *Putting Dreams to Flight*. Wichita Falls, Texas: Midwestern State University Press, 2008.

Solberg, Carl T., Papers. American Heritage Center, University of Wyoming, Laramie.

Stilwell, Hart, and Slats Rodgers. *Old Soggy No. 1: The Uninhibited Story of Slats Rodgers*. New York: Julian Messner, Inc., 1954.

Stinson, Emma. "Letter of Emma Stinson to the Wright Brothers, 1910," Katherine Stinson Otero Collection, Center for Southwest Research, University of New Mexico, Albuquerque.

Stinson, Katherine. Pictorial Collection, 1850–1969, Center for Southwest Research, the University of New Mexico, Albuquerque.

Stinson, Marjorie. Collection, Archives of the Institute of Aerospace Sciences, Manuscript Division, Library of Congress.

Stinson Otero, Katherine. Collection. Center for Southwest Research, the University of New Mexico, Albuquerque.

U.S. Department of Commerce, Civil Aeronautics Administration, *Civil Pilot Training Manual*. Washington, DC: Civil Aeronautics Bulletin No. 23, September 1941.

Whyte, Edna Gardner, as told to Ann L. Cooper. *Rising Above It*. New York: Orion Books, 1991.

Women Airforce Service Pilots Collection, Texas Woman's University, Denton.

Yeager, Jeana. Collection. Texas A&M University, Commerce.

Yeager, Jeana, and Dick Rutan. *Voyager*. New York: Harper and Row, 1987, 1989.

Secondary Sources

Aircraft Year Book. Vols. 1919–1939.

Alexander, Thomas E. *Rattlesnake Bomber Base: Pyote Army Airfield in World War II*. Abilene, Texas: State House Press, 2005.

———. *The Stars were Big and Bright: The U.S. Army Air Forces and Texas during World War II*. Abilene, Texas: McMurry University State House Press, 2000, 2007.

———. *The Wings of Change: The Army Air Force Experience in Texas during World War II*. Abilene, Texas: McWhiney Foundation Press, 2003.

Allen, Oliver E. *The Airline Builders*. Alexandria, Virginia: Time-Life Books, 1981.

Barksdale, E. C. *The Genesis of the Aviation Industry in North Texas*. Austin: University of Texas Bureau of Business Research, 1958.

Barlett, Donald L., and James B. Steele. *Howard Hughes: His Life and Madness*. New York and London: W. W. Norton & Company, 1979.

Bilstein, Roger, and Jay Miller. *Aviation in Texas*. Austin: Texas Monthly Press, 1985.

Bob Bullock Texas State History Museum. *Tango Alpha Charlie: Texas Aviation Celebration, Educator Guide*. http://thestoryoftexas.com/component /docman/doc_download/6-tango-alpha-charlie-texas-aviation-celebra tion-educator-guide?Itemid=.

Brinkley, Douglas. *Cronkite*. New York: HarperCollins Publishers, 2012.

Brooks-Pazmany, Kathleen. *United States Women in Aviation, 1919–1929*. Smithsonian Studies in Air and Space, no. 5. Washington, DC: Smithsonian Institution Press, 1983.

Brown, David A. *The Bell Helicopter Textron Story: Changing the Way the World Flies*. Arlington, Texas: Aerofax, Inc., 1995.

Brown, Mel. *Wings over San Antonio: Images of Aviation*. Charleston, South Carolina: Arcadia Publishing, 2001.

Carl, Ann B. *A WASP Among Eagles: A Woman Military Test Pilot in World War II*. Washington, DC, and London: Smithsonian Institution Press, 1999.

Center for Economic Development and Research, Department of Economics, University of North Texas, *Economic Impact for General Aviation in Texas 2011* (http://www.txdot.gov/business/aviation/eco_impact_avia tion.htm).

Clow, Virginia G., Lila Knight, Duane E. Peter, and Sharlane N. Allday. Photos by Joseph S. Murphy; Don Brown, designer. *The Architecture of Randolph Field, 1928–1931*. Plano, Texas: Geo-Marine, Inc., 1998.

Continuing the Tradition: 50 Years of Building the Best, 1942–1992 (Fort Worth: General Dynamics, 1992).

Corn, Joseph J. *The Winged Gospel: America's Romance with Aviation, 1900–1950*. New York: Oxford University Press, 1983.

———. *The Winged Gospel: America's Romance with Aviation, 1900–1950*. Baltimore, MD: Johns Hopkins University Press, 2002.

———. "Making Flying 'Thinkable': Women Pilots and the Selling of Aviation, 1927–1940." *American Quarterly* (Autumn 1979), vol. 31. no. 4, 556–571.

Courtwright, David. *Sky as Frontier: Adventure, Aviation, and Empire*. College Station: Texas A&M Press, 2005.

Franks, Norman. *American Aces of World War I*. Butley, Oxford: Osprey Publishing, 2001.

Gertler, Jeremiah. "V-22 Osprey Tilt-rotor Aircraft: Background and Issues for Congress," Congressional Research Service, March 10, 2011.

Grant, R. G. *Flight: One Hundred Years of Aviation*. New York: DK Publishing, 2002.

Hagedorn, Don. *Conquistadors of the Sky*. Gainesville: University Press of Florida, 2008.

Haisler, Walter. "A History of the Texas A&M Aerospace Engineering Department from 1941–1988," Texas A&M University, Department of Engineering, compiled on April 13, 1989.

———. "TAMU Aero History, 2003," Chapter XX Texas A&M University, Department of Engineering.

Hall, James Norman, and Charles Bernard Nordhoff, eds. *The Lafayette Flying Corps*. Boston and New York: Houghton Mifflin Company, 1920.

Hancock Cameron, Rebecca. *Training to Fly: Military Flight Training, 1907–1945*. Air Force History and Museums Program. Washington, DC: U.S. Government Printing Office, 1999.

Harris, Sherwood. *The First to Fly: Aviation's Pioneer Days*. New York: Simon and Schuster, 1970.

"History of the Commemorative Air Force," CD-ROM, 9600 Wright Drive, Midland, Texas, 79771 (432) 563-1000.

Jessen, Gene Nora. *Powder Puff Derby of 1929*. Naperville, Illinois: Sourcebooks, Inc., 2002.

Kerrod, Robin and Carole Stott. *Hubble: Mirror on the Universe* 3rd ed., London: Quintet Publishing, Ltd., 2011.

Killebrew, Tom. *Royal Air Force in Texas: Training British Pilots in Terrell during World War II*. Denton: University of North Texas Press, 2003.

Leary, William M., ed., *Aviation's Golden Age: Portraits from the 1920s and 1930s*. Iowa City: Iowa University Press, 1989.

Lebow, Eileen F. *Before Amelia: Women Pilots in the Early Days of Aviation*. Washington, DC: Brassey's, 2002.

———. *Cal Rodgers and the* Vin Fiz: *The First Transcontinental Flight*. Washington, DC: Smithsonian Institution Press, 1989.

Lewis, W. David. *Eddie Rickenbacker: An American Hero in the Twentieth Century*. Baltimore: Johns Hopkins University Press, 2005.

Longstreet, Stephen. *The Canvas Falcons: The Men and Planes of World War I*. New York: Barnes and Noble, 1970.

Mallan, Lloyd. *Suiting Up for Space: The Evolution of the Space Suit*. New York: John Day Company, 1971.

Manning, Thomas A., Bruce A. Ashcroft, Richard H. Emmons, Ann K. Hussey, and Joseph L. Mason. *History of Air Education and Training Command, 1942–2002*. Randolph Air Force Base: Office of History and Research, 2005.

Marrett, George J. *Howard Hughes, Aviator*. Annapolis, Maryland: Naval Institute Press, 2004.

Merryman, Molly. *Clipped Wings: The Rise and Fall of the Women Airforce Service Pilots (WASPs) of World War II*. New York and London: New York University Press, 1998.

Miller, Donald L. *Masters of the Air: America's Bomber Boys who Fought the Air War Against Nazi Germany*. New York: Simon & Schuster, 2006.

Mohler, Stanley R., and Bobby H. Johnson. *Wiley Post, His Winnie Mae, and the World's First Pressure Suit*. Washington, DC: Smithsonian Institution Press, 1971.

Moscrop, Liz, and Sanjay Rampal. *The 100 Greatest Women in Aviation*. Grays, Essex: Aerocomm Limited, 2008.

Oakes, Claudia M. *United States Women in Aviation, 1930–1939*. Washington and London: Smithsonian Institution Press, 1991.

Office of History, San Antonio Air Logistics Center, *A Pictorial History of Kelly Air Force Base*. San Antonio: Air Force Logistics Command, n.d.

O'Neil, Paul. *Barnstormers and Speed Kings.* Alexandria, Virginia: Time-Life Books, 1981.

Parker, A. H., as told to S. A. Aldott, "New World Goal with the Sisu," *Soaring* (December 1963), 8–9.

Parker, Al, as told to E. J. Reeves, "Pioneering the 1000 Kilometers," *Soaring* (September 1964), 7–10.

Parton, James. *"Air Force Spoken Here": General Ira Eaker & the Command of the Air.* Bethesda: Adler & Adler, 1986.

Pisano, Dominick A., ed. *The Airplane in American Culture.* Ann Arbor: University of Michigan Press, 2003.

———. *To Fill the Skies with Pilots: The Civilian Pilot Training Program, 1939–1946.* Urbana and Chicago: University of Illinois Press, 1993.

Plehinger, Russell. *Marathon Flyers.* Detroit: Harlo Press, 1989.

Ragsdale, Kenneth B. *Austin, Cleared for Takeoff: Aviators, Businessmen, and the Growth of the American City.* Austin: University of Texas Press, 2004.

———. *Wings over the Mexican Border: Pioneer Military Aviation in the Big Bend.* Austin: University of Texas Press, 1984.

Rich, Doris L. *Jackie Cochran: Pilot in the Fastest Lane.* Gainesville: University Press of Florida, 2007.

———. *The Magnificent Moisants: Champions of Early Flight.* Washington and London: Smithsonian Institution Press, 1998.

———. *Queen Bess: Daredevil Aviator.* Washington and London: Smithsonian Institution Press, 1995.

Rickman, Sarah Bryn. *Nancy Love and the WASP Ferry Pilots of World War II.* Denton: University of North Texas Press, 2008.

Ronnie, Art. *Locklear: The Man Who Walked on Wings.* South Brunswick, New Jersey: A. S. Barnes, 1973.

Rose, Mark H., Bruce E. Seely, and Paul F. Barrett. *The Best Transportation System in the World: Railroads, Airlines, and American Public Policy in the Twentieth Century.* Columbus: Ohio State University, 2006.

Scott, Wally, Jr., "A Winner's Tale: The 1976 Smirnoff Derby," *Soaring* (August 1976), 13–19.

Smith-Daugherty, Rhonda. *Jacqueline Cochran: Biography of a Pioneer Aviator.* Jefferson, North Carolina; and London: McFarland, 2012.

Stallman, David A. *Women in the Wild Blue: Target-Towing WASP at Camp Davis.* Sugar Creek, Ohio: Carlisle Publishing, 2006.

Sterling, Bryan B., and Frances N. Sterling, *Forgotten Eagle: Wiley Post, America's Heroic Aviation Pioneer.* New York: Carroll & Graf Publishers, 2001.

Sterling, Robert J. *Howard Hughes' Airline: An Informal History of TWA.* New York: St. Martin's Press, 1983.

————. *Eagle: The Story of American Airlines*. New York: St. Martin's/Marek, 1985.

Stover, Dawn. "Deep-Space Boot Camp." *Popular Science* 247 (November 2009), 43–47.

Van Der Linden, R. Robert, ed. *Best of the National Air and Space Museum*. New York: HarperCollins, 2006.

Wildenberg, Thomas, and R. E. G. Davies. *Howard Hughes: An Airman, His Aircraft, and His Great Flights*. McLean, Virginia: Paladwr Press, 2006.

Windecker, Theodore. "The Eagle: On the Wings of a Dream, the Story of Dr. Leo Windecker and the *Windecker Eagle*, the World's First All-Composite Airplane." 2005–2010. Unpublished.

Winegarten, Debra L. *Katherine Stinson: The Flying Schoolgirl*. Austin: Eakin Press, 2000.

Wings Over the Alamo. DVD. San Antonio, Texas: KLRN Learning Place, 2007.

Wood, Florence Hester, "Early Commercial Aviation in Texas, 1904–1934." Master of Arts thesis, University of Texas at Austin, 1957.

Young, John W., with James R. Hansen. *Forever Young: A Life of Adventure in Air and Space*. Gainesville: University Press of Florida, 2012.

Aeronautical Journals and Newspapers

Aerial Age Weekly
Aero Digest
Chicago Defender
Dallas Morning News
Fort Worth Star-Telegram
Houston Chronicle
New York Times
Ninety-Nines News
Pan American Airways
San Antonio Express-News
Southern Aviation

Index